❧

MARY LINCOLN FOR THE AGES

MARY LINCOLN
FOR THE AGES

JASON EMERSON

Southern Illinois University Press
Carbondale

Southern Illinois University Press
www.siupress.com

22 21 20 19   4 3 2 1

Cover illustration: Mary Todd Lincoln, three-quarter-length portrait attributed to Nicolas H. Shepherd (cropped and tinted). Library of Congress, Prints and Photographs Division, Washington, D.C.

Library of Congress Cataloging-in-Publication Data
Names: Emerson, Jason, 1975– author.
Title: Mary Lincoln for the ages / Jason Emerson.
Description: Carbondale : Southern Illinois University Press, 2019. | Includes bibliographical references and indexes.
Identifiers: LCCN 2017055045 | ISBN 9780809336753 (pbk.) | ISBN 9780809336760 (ebook)
Subjects: LCSH: Lincoln, Mary Todd, 1818–1882—Bibliography. | Presidents' spouses—United States—Bibliography. | Lincoln, Abraham, 1809–1865—Bibliography.
Classification: LCC E457.25.L55 E465 2018 | DDC 973.7092—dc23
LC record available at https://lccn.loc.gov/2017055045

Printed on recycled paper. ♻

Mrs. Lincoln was a better woman than the world gives her credit for. She was a whip and sting to Lincoln's ambition—she urged him to go upward. I admit that *at times*, in her *after life*, that she was a she devil. . . . Let us be charitable for we are all weak creatures at best, no one knowing himself till conditions push him on to ruin. Bless this woman. She was Lincoln's best and wisest adviser when at herself and in her younger days.

—William Herndon to Joseph Fowler,
November 3, 1888

She was a dreadful woman in many ways, and I have always thought had more to do with the lines in Lincoln's face than all the cares of state.

—Oswald Garrison Villard to Isaac Markens,
March 26, 1927

CONTENTS

ACKNOWLEDGMENTS

Writing is a solitary act, while research is often a collaborative one—especially in a project like the present work where I had to track down and read more than four hundred writings about Mary Lincoln. In a project such as this, there are four ways to acquire materials: go to one or more libraries, find articles or books online for free, purchase the articles and books you need to read, and contact historical libraries and museums and request photocopies of works they have.

For their assistance with my research, I would like to thank Thomas D. Mackie, Jr., former director, and Michelle Ganz, former archivist and special collections librarian, both at the Abraham Lincoln Library and Museum, Lincoln Memorial University, Harrogate, Tennessee, and James Cornelius, former Lincoln curator at the Abraham Lincoln Presidential Library and Museum, Springfield, Illinois. James Cornelius not only shared photocopies with me but also was quick to suggest sources I may have overlooked or been unaware of for my bibliography, and offered valuable comments when asked for his views on the common canon of Mary Lincoln. He also generously supplied photos of the presidential library's wax figures of Mary Lincoln, two of which are used in this book.

Also on the illustrations side, I am grateful to Tim Campbell for allowing me to print his wonderful Americana portrait of Mary Lincoln; to Mark Reinhart for sharing with me images from his collection of still photographs from Lincoln movies; to Mark Pohlad for assisting me with the Charles Turzak woodcut depicting Mary Lincoln; and to Steve Rogstad for sharing his pictures of the Mary Lincoln statue in Racine, Wisconsin.

Thanks also to the editors of the *Journal of the Illinois State Historical Society* for publishing my original Mary Lincoln annotated bibliography article in 2010, as well as the 2011 supplement. Those two articles were the basis for the present book.

PART ONE

INTRODUCTION

Mary Lincoln is arguably one of the most fascinating first ladies in American history—and she is certainly one of the most written about. While no recent comparisons of the number of biographical works on first ladies have been accomplished, there is one from 2008 that shows Mary Lincoln to be the fourth-most-written-about first lady, behind only Eleanor Roosevelt, Hillary Clinton, and Jackie Kennedy.[1] Considering the publication trends in first lady biographies, it is safe to assume Mary retains her fourth position today, unless Abigail Adams, who has had a number of books written about her in recent years, has overtaken her.

Mary has all the ingredients of a fascinating life, both as her own person and as her husband's wife: an emotional, and at times traumatic, childhood; an impressive education and high intelligence; a coquettish maidenhood spent flirting with numerous suitors (many of whom became national figures); a dramatic broken engagement and last-minute wedding to Abraham Lincoln; multiple years of domestic normalcy as wife and mother; four years as first lady during a civil war; numerous scandals and headlines as first lady; her presence at her husband's assassination; years as grieving wife and mother surrounded by family deaths; years spent as a homeless wanderer around the world; a belief in spiritualism and recorded attendance at séances; public scandals during her widowhood; commitment to a sanitarium by her oldest son and her ultimate release; years in self-imposed exile in Europe; a lifelong history of physical and mental illnesses; a vast historic legacy. All of this has contributed to her rich and textured appeal and subsequently large bibliography.

What makes Mary more compelling as a historical figure is that her life is not obvious—she has been characterized as an "enigma" and disagreements abound in interpreting her story. Was she a loving wife or a shrew? An altruistic woman or an insular egotist? A laudable first lady or an unethical opportunist who enriched herself at public expense? A mentally ill woman or a misrepresented victim of male chauvinist society? A fitting partner to the first martyred president or an embarrassment to her husband's legacy? A historical charity case or a significant historical figure? Or was Mary Lincoln a combination of all these things? As presidential secretary William O. Stoddard once wrote, "It was not easy, at first, to understand why a lady who could be one day so kindly, so considerate, so generous, so thoughtful and so hopeful, could, upon another day, appear so unreasonable, so irritable, so despondent, so even niggardly, and so prone to see the dark, the wrong side of men and women and events."[2]

Through the years since her husband's assassination, Mary Lincoln has been the subject of numerous writings—newspaper articles, songs, poems, plays, scholarly articles, juvenile literature, fiction and nonfiction books—and identifying and reading through this vast selection of literature can not only elucidate who Mary Lincoln was but also illuminate how and why historians and other writers have portrayed her through the years. It is fascinating to see how a story or "fact" that everybody may know about Mary Lincoln is repeated by modern writers who copied the story from previous writers. Those writers, in turn, repeated the story from writers before them and, as you go farther down the line of writers using the same story, ultimately you find the original source—and often there is no citation or evidentiary proof that the story or "fact" was ever true in the first place. This is one of the many benefits of scholarly bibliographies and historiographies. As with anything in life, knowing where you have been helps you understand where you are going and how to proceed forward.

To truly understand Mary Lincoln's personality and life, one must read more than the handful of overused sources about her. A detailed, descriptive, and reliable bibliography concerning Mary Lincoln, therefore, is long overdue given her historical importance. While some people may find her life uninteresting on the surface—a sentiment with which I disagree—Mary was also a major part of Abraham Lincoln's life for a quarter century, and one cannot fully understand his life, personality, and motivations without comprehending who she was and how she impacted him. In fact, a majority of the sources about Mary Lincoln also include, or are even centered around, Abraham Lincoln, and they offer up further information about his life as well.

There are a few places one can look for bibliographic material on Mary Lincoln—four articles and three websites, all of which are included herein—

but nothing that is the size and scope of the present work.[3] Similarly, the essay in this book, "The Common Canon of Mary Lincoln," opens vast furrows of new ground by showing that of the more than three hundred nonfiction historical writings about Mary, only about seven—or 2 percent—are really used by writers in their research; and some of those have serious flaws. The rest are either ignored or unknown. If nearly every writer uses basically the same group of sources year after year when writing about a historic figure, how can anyone truly understand the life of that person? The answer is: we cannot.

And so it is with Mary Lincoln—she may be a fruitful muse for writers, but her story over the past many decades has become flat and shallow, written with the same stories, from the same sources, under the same predilections and presuppositions. My historiographical examination, therefore, surveys the common works about Mary utilized by writers, how those works are typically used, and their benefits and their flaws, and provides a list of twenty additional works that I feel should be used by writers but are not, and why they have been ignored for so long. In short, I offer up a new way to research Mary Lincoln, a way that will illuminate the shadowed aspects of her life. As scholars and writers, we have a comfortable shelf of Mary Lincoln books in our studies to which we constantly turn for source material; meanwhile, upstairs in the attic, there are literally hundreds of further sources long abandoned, collecting dust, waiting to be utilized. That is the purpose of this book: to rediscover the big brass key that unlocks the attic door and reveals the hidden library.

For more than twenty years, I have been studying and writing about Mary Lincoln, initially as a part of her husband's life and then as her own person. After having interpreted her life in Springfield when I worked at the Lincoln Home National Historic Site as a park ranger in my younger days, and subsequently writing or editing five books about her, writing one book in which she is a major character, authoring nearly one dozen articles about her, reviewing numerous books and articles about her, giving lectures about her at venues across the United States and on television, and now having read more than 450 writings in all genres about who she was and creating the present analytical bibliography and historiographical essay, I can say with absolute certainty that Mary was a fascinating, complex, and often contradictory woman. I have admired and detested her, defended and accused her, sympathized with and resented her, understood and puzzled over her. I have been told it sounds like I am a little in love with her, and have been rebuked that I clearly hate her. Through it all, I have simply sought to better understand who she was as a real, flawed person. And the more I research and read, the more fascinated I become.

My interest in and journey toward Mary Lincoln's bibliography started a number of years ago while preparing for publication an edition of a previously unpublished manuscript about Mary written in 1927.[4] I wondered where my book would have fallen in the timeline and what effect it may have had on historical study had it ever been published. I began to arrange a brief bibliography to satisfy my curiosity (and possibly include in the book, which it was not), and the more I dug for resources, the more I realized that no extensive bibliography of Mary Lincoln had ever been created, and certainly none annotated. I therefore endeavored to undertake the task myself, which turned out to be far more complicated, laborious, exciting, and satisfying than I ever imagined.

My initial efforts rendered an annotated bibliography of 243 entries about Mary Lincoln, which was published as an article in the *Journal of the Illinois State Historical Society* in summer 2010. The thing about compiling a bibliography is that it is addictive—like a treasure hunt—you know if you keep looking you will find more. As historian Barbara Tuchman once said, "Research is endlessly seductive; writing is hard work."[5] So of course I kept looking for Mary Lincoln source materials, and subsequently published, in fall 2011, a supplementary annotated bibliography with thirty-four additional entries, also in the *Journal of the Illinois State Historical Society*.

It was after that when the project became really addicting. I began tracking down ever-more-obscure and hard-to-find writings on Mary; I also began adding to my list items I purposefully had omitted from my two articles for various reasons. After years of further work, I increased my 277 bibliographic entries to the current 452 entries included in this book. I also revamped, revised, and extended many of the original entries published in my two articles.

This is not an exhaustive bibliography, although it is nearly so. My particular choices for including items in this bibliography were guided by certain criteria. My overall guiding principle for the nonfiction works (books and articles) was: what items were necessary to read in order to fully understand—or even write a respectable book on—Mary Lincoln's life? Some works that are ridiculously ignorant, biased, or just plain terribly researched and written also have been included, some because their prominence necessitated it and some just to warn interested readers away from their corruptive influences.

In general, I feel conscientious scholars must read the bad with the good in order to completely understand the bibliography. The nonfiction books had to be biographies or monographs specifically about Mary Lincoln, or, if focused on another individual, so important to understanding Mary's life as to necessitate inclusion. This importance was judged by facts represented, uniqueness of materials, popularity, and endurance of the assertions and assumptions offered. For example, the biography of Abraham Lincoln written by William Herndon in 1889—as well as the other books written from Herndon's materials and with his conclusions, such as those by Ward Hill Lamon and Jesse W. Weik—must be included in any complete bibliography of Mary Lincoln because his statements about her were groundbreaking at the time and have endured to this day. Similarly, books containing Herndon's personal letters that discuss Mary—such as those by Emanuel Hertz and Douglas L. Wilson and Rodney O. Davis—have been included because Herndon was such a unique individual that to truly understand his historical writing about Mary Lincoln one must understand his thoughts and feelings about her.

I chose not to incorporate general survey books about first ladies and unpublished academic theses about Mary Lincoln: the former because all such first lady collections say the same things about Mary, all based on other secondary sources, and the latter because they are so difficult to find and read without either traveling vast distances or spending too much money on photocopies that their inclusion seemed unnecessary.

The newspaper articles were chosen based on their uniqueness, apparent reliability, importance to the historiography, and contents, usually primary sources found nowhere else. This decision-making came down to who the sources (writers and interviewees) were, what the article subject was, and when the article was written. Articles based on primary sources, such as reminiscences and interviews with Mary Lincoln herself or her family members or friends, were included, as were original reports on major events in Mary's life, such as her actions as first lady (hosting balls, visiting military hospitals, traveling the North to vacation and shop, and causing scandals), her 1863 carriage accident, the Old Clothes Scandal, her commitment to a sanitarium, and her final illness and death. While nearly all these incidents had numerous stories printed and reprinted about them in papers across the country, the original reporting is cited whenever possible. A handful of articles are cited from their reprinted sources in major newspapers (a day or two after the original publication) if that original publication was too difficult to access.

The nonfiction articles, like nonfiction books, were selected by facts represented, uniqueness of materials, popularity, and endurance of the assertions and interpretations offered. Practically every scholarly or popular article I found about Mary Lincoln has been included. The only items that have been left out purposely have been general magazine articles (mainly from online magazines) from recent years that are such vanilla offerings by general writers, regurgitating decades of other writings, that they offer nothing new in fact or interpretation, or are simply not worth reading.

The fiction, juvenile, poetry, and drama titles had to be specifically about Mary Lincoln. Because these were creative works rather than historical nonfiction, I chose not to add works focused on Abraham Lincoln even if Mary appeared as a prominent character, such as in Gore Vidal's *Lincoln* or Robert E. Sherwood's *Abe Lincoln in Illinois*. Quite simply, if I added one such work, then I would have to add them all. This would not only make the bibliography enormous but also would, I think, vitiate the purpose of this entire bibliographic endeavor, which is to focus on Mary Lincoln as a historical figure in her own right and not as a secondary character. For drama, I chose only stage productions and no television shows or movies (unless adapted from the stage).

For websites, I used both those that offered substantial information and references about Mary Lincoln and those that were prominent websites to search, even if they provided nothing worthwhile.

This book also includes three indexes—by authors and editors, by title, and by subjects—to offer easier access to users searching for a particular writing.

In undertaking this book, I have read every item included in the bibliography, many of them multiple times, and the education I received from this was invaluable. Even after upwards of fifteen years of serious research and study on Mary Lincoln, I found numerous interviews, reminiscences, stories, and historical interpretations that I never knew existed, have never read, and have never seen used by any other historian or writer, all of which further opened up Mary's story and illuminated her character. I found multiple sources, from various years and perspectives, recounting the same incidents and stories about Mary, which elucidated what the true facts of the story in question may have been. Such instances of this clarification include the reason for the Lincoln-Todd broken engagement, Mary's infamous temper tantrum at City Point, Virginia, headquarters in 1865, and the happiness or unhappiness of the Lincolns as a married couple. I also tracked down the original sources for some stories that have always and ever been referenced only from previous secondary writers, and continue to be so referenced today. Two examples of this include Mary's grief after the death of Eddie in 1850 when Abraham urged her to stop ignoring food, saying, "Mary you must eat, for we must live." This story always is quoted from a 1918 book by Octavia Roberts, but originally was recounted by Mrs. John Todd Stuart in a 1900 newspaper interview.[6] A second example is Margaret Stuart (Woodrow)'s childhood reminiscences of Mary, especially Mary's "love for poetry." These are always quoted from Katherine Helm's 1928 biography of Mary, but the full interview with Woodrow was originally published in a 1909 newspaper.[7]

Some of the surprises I experienced along the journey of this bibliography and historiography included the large number of family members, friends, acquaintances, and servants who wrote or spoke reminiscences of Mary Lincoln through the years that are rarely, if ever, referenced by historians. In addition, I was astonished by the large number of medical studies and writings about Mary that were unknown or unused by scholars, including a study on the effect of the probable concussion Mary suffered in her 1863 carriage accident and a recent look at treating her many ailments using acupuncture.[8] I was not terribly surprised to discover that the largest single category of writings in the bibliography were centered on Mary's mental health and insanity case, but it was interesting to see that the majority of all poems and dramas about her were focused on or centered around that episode as well.

Certain topics about Mary Lincoln have been repeatedly examined and reexamined through the years, but it is amazing how one does not realize the prevalence of a specific issue until reading the full bibliography and compiling it as a list. Some of the predominant themes include Mary Lincoln's insanity and insanity case (60 items), William Herndon and Mary Lincoln (42 items), medical studies of Mary Lincoln's physical and mental health (24 items), the "fatal first of January" broken engagement between Abraham Lincoln and Mary Todd (21 items), Mary's belief in spiritualism (17 items), Mary Lincoln's finances and pension battle with Congress (17 items), and discovery and publication of previously unpublished Mary Lincoln letters (12 items). Mary's life as first lady is so ubiquitous as to be unnecessary to even count the number of items on the subject, which include her role as White House hostess, accusations of her rebel sympathies, her illegal and unethical conduct, her role as wife and mother in the White House, her visits to Union soldier hospitals, and her presence at her husband's assassination.

In addition to all the exciting and fascinating sources and stories about Mary Lincoln I found while completing this book, there are an equal number of resources and topical areas of research and study I *did not* find. This "negative discovery," as Daniel J. Boorstin has called it in one of his excellent historical essays, impacts not only the bibliography but also our understanding of who Mary was.[9] Mary's childhood definitely needs more examination, as does a specific treatise on her experience with slaves and her changing opinions on blacks and slavery; also a deeper look into her financial management and mentality throughout her life can offer new insights given her known mania for shopping later in life. Mary's belief in spiritualism and her travels across the United States to visit mediums are also in need of further examination. While there have been many ridiculous books published about Mary's belief in spiritualism, there has not been anything yet written based on solid research and objective analysis. Considering Mary's strong belief in the religion, and the great solace it brought her during the final two decades of her life, a solid undertaking to thoroughly understand the role of spiritualism in Mary's life is sorely needed. The glaring hole in Mary's bibliography—and biography—is her years living in and traveling around Europe. Not only are there no specific examinations of those years, but no scholar to date has conducted a thorough search of European archives, libraries, and newspapers for correspondence, articles, and other writings about Mary. Considering that Mary spent seven years of her life in Europe, that research gap is, quite frankly, inexcusable.

So what is the point of this analytical bibliography and historiographical essay about Mary Lincoln, and why should anyone care? The contents of this book are a road map to a better understanding of the historic person that was Mary Lincoln. To see when and by whom and under what historical predilections the scholarship on her began—and from where it has progressed—not only elucidates the value of each subsequent writing but also edifies the perspective of current Mary Lincoln scholars and enthusiasts. All these writings, whether succinct or verbose, whether large or small, are additional pieces to the fascinating and incomplete puzzle of the historical figure of Mary Lincoln. They further illuminate what remains a largely misunderstood and misinterpreted life of one of America's most captivating first ladies.

THE COMMON CANON
OF MARY LINCOLN

Anyone with a particular interest in Mary Lincoln, and who has done significant reading on Abraham Lincoln and his family, has learned that the information in published works used to explain and interpret Mary comes from a handful of the same sources, constantly recycled by writers and journalists over many years. As historians and history lovers, we should be concerned about this narrowness, since a historical life examined and written with the same stories, from the same sources, under the same predilections and presuppositions cannot be truly understood. The only way to combat this problem is to recognize the circular room in which we have become trapped, break free, and reexamine our approach.[1]

Mary Lincoln was a fascinating woman—a woman to be admired, sympathized with, pitied, and often disliked. But has she ever really been understood? Certainly, her family and friends understood her; but now, 137 years and hundreds of published biographical/anecdotal works after her death, do we know who she was and what the motivations of her life were? A survey of the literature about her—particularly the modern writings—makes it clear that we do not. Historian Herbert Mitgang, who labeled Mary Lincoln's life as something "akin to a Greek tragedy," once declared her to be "an enigmatic daguerreotype sitting uncomfortably in the shadow of her husband."[2] And perhaps no truer words have been uttered about this famously infamous and misunderstood woman.

Even as perceptions and interpretations of Mary have changed through the years and across the generations, she will forever be the shade to Abraham Lincoln's light. In fact, for decades after the assassination, Mary Lincoln rarely was written about as anything more than Abraham Lincoln's wife. All the books and articles were about Abraham, with Mary as a minor character, if she was mentioned at all. She was the loving little woman by his side, described by her physical appearance and her wardrobe, and the fact that she bore his children and kept the clean and loving home within which a great man dwelled as he rose to prominence. The exceptions during this time were Elizabeth Keckley's memoir and William Herndon's lectures and writings about Mary all of which caused incalculable damage to Mary and to her reputation at the time, but have since become realized as invaluable historical touchstones.

Herndon, Abraham Lincoln's law partner for twenty-five years, started working on a biography of his partner immediately after the assassination. Herndon interviewed everyone he could find who had known Lincoln—including Mary Lincoln in September 1866[3]—and, regardless of what people may think of Herndon, it is because of his research that vast amounts of primary information about Abraham Lincoln, especially about his childhood, were not lost to history. While Herndon's biography did not see publication until 1889, he started lecturing about his former law partner in late 1865. But it was in late 1866 that Herndon inflicted the first major damage to Mary Lincoln's reputation. In his lecture "Abraham Lincoln. Miss Ann Rutledge. New Salem. Pioneering, and the Poem," Herndon unleashed the New Salem love story he discovered of twenty-six-year-old Abraham Lincoln and nineteen-year-old Ann Rutledge and declared that when Ann died in 1835, Lincoln's heart was buried beside her. Lincoln never, in the following thirty years, loved another woman, according to Herndon—including his wife of twenty-three years, who bore him four children.

The country was astounded and embarrassed by Herndon's revelation, Lincoln's friends were shocked, and Mary Lincoln was outraged. Robert Lincoln, age twenty-three, was "seriously annoyed" by Herndon's bad taste, but he also looked at the story as would the majority of people both at the time and ever since, namely, that even if the love story was completely true (which Robert doubted) Herndon's lecture not only was inappropriate but "would be very ludicrous if I did not feel strongly that he speaks from having known my father for so long."[4] And this lengthy relationship has been one of the keys to the staying power of Herndon's assertions regarding Mary Lincoln—Herndon was an intimate of Lincoln for a quarter century and, presumably, knew more about him than anyone outside the Lincoln family. This knowledge would entail everything about Lincoln's home and personal life, including his marriage and the character of his wife.

When Herndon's biography of his former partner, titled *Herndon's Lincoln*, finally came out, his negative and harsh portrayal of Mary Lincoln as an insufferable termagant whom Lincoln never loved became a permanent part of Mary's official biography and historical reputation. While Herndon did speak from a position of knowledge and authority, there were also many things about Mary's life and character that he falsely stated as true. To this day, many people still believe Herndon's story that Abraham Lincoln broke off his first engagement to Mary not with words but by failing to show up for his wedding and leaving his erstwhile bride standing at the altar (which is not true). After an eighteen-month hiatus, the couple then got back together not because of love or an acknowledged mistake of cold feet the first time but because Lincoln felt duty-bound to keep his original promise to Mary, and Mary wanted not only to satisfy her ambition for high position with a man of potential but also to tie Lincoln to her in order to exact a lifetime of revenge on him for the previous jilting (which is also not true).

Herndon portrayed Mary in her younger days as attractive, vivacious, educated, charming, witty, and enthralling. But underneath those positive qualities, he said, were malicious sarcasm, an indomitable pride, and an ungovernable temper. He credited Mary with teaching Lincoln how to behave in polite society and with being her husband's "best and wisest adviser" when it came to reading the measure and machinations of other men—albeit these things she did to help herself more than her husband so she could reap the benefits of his success. But above everything else, Herndon wrote, the Lincolns did not love each other, their home was a veritable hell for Abraham, and he spent up to nine months of each year riding the legal circuit and traveling for politics less out of ambition than a desire to avoid his home. In effect, Herndon started the canard that Mary was such an awful person and wife that she drove her husband out of the house and into greatness. As journalist Walter B. Stevens wrote of Herndon's influence in this area: "Following the lead of Herndon, most writers have made the [Lincoln] marriage appear unfortunate. They have represented Lincoln as unhappy in his home life. They have attributed to Mrs. Lincoln the character of a high-tempered, extravagant, ambitious, tormenting woman. They have assumed that Mr. Lincoln endured a living martyrdom."[5]

Herndon did not believe in hagiography, and felt the only way to understand Lincoln was to know his faults as well as his virtues. He once said his motivations for all his Lincoln-related work was simply to offer understanding:

"I want the world to know Lincoln," he wrote. "This is my religion."[6] And while Herndon sought to reveal the true Abraham Lincoln—of which showing Mary's shortcomings he believed was an intricate part, which will be discussed more later—Elizabeth Keckley at the same time sought to reveal the true Mary Lincoln. Keckley, a former slave who became Mary's White House dressmaker and confidant, wrote her 1868 memoir, *Behind the Scenes*, partly to tell her own life story and partly to help renovate Mary Lincoln's poor reputation. The book was published shortly after the infamous "Old Clothes Scandal" of 1867, in which Mary, believing herself practically destitute, sought to sell her old White House clothing and jewelry in New York under a pseudonym as a way to raise money. Mary's identity was discovered, however, almost nothing was purchased, and the entire episode brought censure and humiliation to Mary as newspapers throughout the country criticized her. Keckley accompanied and assisted Mary throughout the entire episode and therefore, as she later wrote, understood "the secret history of [Mary's] transactions," which those who attacked the former first lady for being an embarrassment and unladylike spectacle did not. Part of Keckley's authorial intentions, therefore, were to tell the people of America who Mary truly was and, through the sales of the book, financially help Mary as much as possible.

Keckley's book is certainly the best primary source on Mary Lincoln for the years 1861–67. The seamstress was truly Mary's confidant, was present at events she chronicled, and wrote the book before the "cult of Lincoln" really started, when people who knew nothing about Abraham Lincoln or his family tried to write themselves into his legend merely for fame or fortune. Keckley wrote her book simply to show the world Mary Lincoln's true nature, which, Keckley believed, would make everyone see that Mary was a good woman who simply had peculiarities. Like Herndon, however, Keckley believed true judgment of Mary's character could only come through knowledge of the good and the bad about her, "the praise and the scandal," and therefore wrote down everything she knew—and included transcripts of twenty-one of Mary's personal letters to her. Keckley's book portrays Mary during the White House years as a loving wife and mother and an ambitious, strong-willed, and loyal first lady, while also revealing her to be high tempered, full of fear and anxiety, self-centered, and often self-pitying. "I never in my life saw a more peculiarly constituted woman," Keckley wrote. "Search the world over, and you will not find her counterpart."[7]

While *Behind the Scenes* today is considered one of the essential book sources about Mary Lincoln and life in the White House during the Civil War (and it has been reprinted more than half a dozen times by reputable publishers), the book was not well received when it first came out in 1868. Reviewers decried it as an unconscionable invasion of privacy on Keckley's part, and an alarming example of, as one New York reviewer called it, "the back-stairs gossip of negro servant girls." As historian Jennifer Fleischner stated in her groundbreaking book *Mrs. Lincoln and Mrs. Keckly*, Keckley faced such harsh criticism over her writing because she had "violated Victorian codes not only of friendship and privacy, but of race, gender, and class."[8] Keckley tried to defend herself by arguing not only that everything in the book was true but also that her publisher tricked her into publishing her employer's letters in the book, which she never intended to do (although the book's introduction alone belies that statement). Mary Lincoln was infuriated by the book and what she saw as Keckley's betrayal. Other than one mention of Keckley as "*the colored* historian" in a letter, there is no evidence that Mary ever spoke to or saw Keckley again—although Keckley maintained that Mary knew what was in the book when it was published, never held a grudge about it, and even continued to correspond with her for years.[9]

Other than what was reported about Mary Lincoln in newspapers throughout the country—of which there was much, both of fact and of gossip—Herndon and Keckley were the two main sources of historical information about Mary found in books during her lifetime. There were occasional mentions of her here and there, but overall, Mary's reputation from the time her husband died until years after her own death was not something to be admired.[10] Mary was viewed by most everyone as arrogant, self-centered, and uncouth; vain, avaricious, and aristocratic; so coldly shrewish that she made her husband's life a living hell; and, based on Mary's own actions, mentally and emotionally unstable, if not outright insane. As Herndon later wrote of her, "This woman was once a brilliant one, but what a sad sight to see her in any year after 1862, and especially a year or so before she died."[11] Worse than all this, however, was that Mary was so exactly the opposite of her kind, noble, and martyred husband and, worse still, as he suffered under the strain of saving the Union, Mary made his job and his life incalculably more difficult by her character and actions.

It was not until nearly the turn of the twentieth century that Mary Lincoln became seen as a historical figure in her own right. The first article about

Mary as her own person was published in 1898 by her sister Emilie Todd Helm, while the first book about her was in 1928, a family-approved biography written by her niece Katherine Helm. At that time, Mary was straddling the line between being the practically anonymous side character of "Abraham Lincoln's wife" and having a greater historical identity as "Mrs. Abraham Lincoln," the president's companion and partner who also had her own life. This dualism is also evident in Elizabeth Todd Grimsley's 1926 article about her cousin Mary (although it was actually written in 1894), "Six Months in the White House." All three of these writings (by Todd family members who certainly had vested interests in improving their kinswoman's reputation) offered reminiscences, stories, interviews, and conclusions that sought to let the admirable qualities of Mary shine brighter than the scandal and rumor that had clouded her story.

Emilie Todd Helm's article, "Mary Todd Lincoln: Reminiscences and Letters of the Wife of President Lincoln," is the first time Mary's family, childhood, and upbringing were made part of her story, all of which added context to her personal character. Seeing Mary as a studious, excitable, impulsive child raised in wealth and refinement made Mary seem more understandable than perhaps her critics had considered her. "She was singularly sensitive . . . her face was an index to every passing emotion," Helm wrote. "Without desiring to wound, she occasionally indulged in sarcastic, witty remarks that cut like a Damascus blade; but there was no malice behind them. She was full of humor but never unrefined." Helm also refuted Herndon's theories about the Lincoln wedding and marriage, stating Mary was never left at the altar and she and her husband were certainly happy and in love. "They understood each other thoroughly, and Mr. Lincoln looked beyond the impulsive words and manner, and knew that his wife was devoted to him and to his interests," Helm wrote.[12]

Following her mother's lead, Katherine Helm sought to impart the positive character of Mary Lincoln through what was and remains the only "authorized" biography of Mary ever written—as well as the first book solely about her—*The True Story of Mary, Wife of Lincoln*, published in 1928.[13] While the book is short, general, and hagiographic in nature, it was written with the use of Emilie Helm's diaries and letters, Todd and Lincoln family lore, and the full support of Robert T. Lincoln, Mary's only surviving son, and contains family materials and reminiscences found no place else. Helm's book avoids references to any unpleasant or embarrassing events in Mary's life, such as her many scandals while first lady and all but the bare fact of her 1875 insanity trial, but really a complete understanding of Mary was not the point of the book. Like her mother before her, Katherine Helm wanted to rehabilitate her aunt's reputation and help make her a historical figure worthy of standing beside the martyred president and savior of the Union.

Grimsley's article, unlike the writings of the Helms, focused exclusively on life in the White House during the first six months of the Lincoln administration, although it also sought to show Mary Lincoln in a positive light and refute many of the incorrect rumors and newspapers articles written about Mary at the time. Grimsley focused on "the inner life of a household," as she called it, and mostly revealed Mary as a devoted wife and loving mother during this time. But she also portrayed Mary as an impressive White House hostess, social leader, and even loyal Union supporter. These inside views of the White House at the beginning of the war are invaluable, and portray Mary as more than just her husband's shadow. One particular story Grimsley relates occurred after the disastrous Union loss at Bull Run, when everyone in Washington thought the capital would be overrun and captured. Winfield Scott, the commanding general of the Union army at the start of the war, insisted that Mary, Grimsley, and the Lincoln boys should go north until the capital was safe. According to Grimsley:

> Mrs. Lincoln turned to her husband saying, "Will you go with us?" and his speedy answer came, "Most assuredly I will not leave at this juncture;" and the response was just as prompt, "Then I will not leave you at this juncture;" and the general found he had met as determined, brave, and fearless wife, as he was an officer. . . . and I cannot believe in his heart of hearts, [the president] was sorry at not being left alone, or of his wife's devotion to him thus proved, as she was a very timid woman, usually in time of trial. Nor was this the only occasion when it was thought best for her to leave the capital for a place of safety, but always with like result.[14]

It was not until 1932 that the first objective books on Mary Lincoln were published by writers who sought to give readers an unalloyed, professionally approached examination of her unique character and historical life. In quick succession, the books *Mrs. Abraham Lincoln: A Study of Her Personality and Her Influence on Lincoln,* by W. A. Evans, and *Mary Lincoln: Wife and*

Widow, by Carl Sandburg and Paul M. Angle, offered carefully researched, data-driven biographies of Mary that not only detailed the episodes and incidents of her life but also undertook to better understand her personality and character. "Very few people think of Mrs. Lincoln at all, or have any real opinion about her," Evans wrote. "This does not prevent many of them from repeating, somewhat superficially, what they have read or heard about her. ... If such expressions can be called a prevailing opinion, then one may say that it is generally accepted that Mrs. Lincoln was and is not deserving of the goodwill of her fellow countrymen."[15] But as both Evans and Sandburg (primary author of his book with Angle) made clear, Mary was far more complex, and far less reprehensible, than anyone really understood or portrayed up to that time. "So all the babblings about her are only a vain exercise of the tongues of those who misunderstand," Sandburg declared.[16]

Evans's work was the first complete history and analysis of Mary Lincoln written by a physician, and it shows. He not only approached his work through a scientific methodology—that is, his research methods included the discovery, collection, classification, and interpretation of the facts—but also applied his medical expertise to Mary (and her family members) to uncover the etiology of her personality. Evans examined Mary's family history, upbringing and childhood, marriage, children, and daily life, as well as the known symptoms of her mental and physical health. Evans was an assiduous researcher. He read all available books, journal articles, and newspaper articles about Mary Lincoln, and also consulted with numerous Lincoln scholars and collectors, Todd family members and friends, and medical experts. His work ultimately became the essential biography of Mary Lincoln for almost fifty years, although today it is largely overlooked by most writers and historians. Yet *Mrs. Abraham Lincoln* contains source materials long ago forgotten by modern historians as well as original interviews with Mary's family and friends that can be found no place else.

Carl Sandburg called Evans's book "[t]he most valuable and extensive discussion and appraisal which has thus far appeared ... fine human values flow from his work."[17] And while Evans's book has survived the test of time and still is referenced by modern writers and historians—although not as much as it should be—Sandburg's work has not. Sandburg, despite being a poet, was and is best known for his multivolume biography of Abraham Lincoln, of which part 1, *The Prairie Years* (in two volumes), was published in 1926, four years before his work on Mary Lincoln. Like that book, *Mary Lincoln: Wife and Widow* is as much narrative as it is history, filled with purple passages of prose that elevate the work beyond mere factual recitation. Yet Sandburg's writing was also fact-based and objective (with a dash of empathy clearly present) in his desire, like Evans, to show a truer picture of Mary than had yet been shown. The second half of the book, compiled by Lincoln scholar Paul M. Angle, was a collection of Mary Lincoln documents (mostly letters), some of them never before published, that were used by Sandburg in writing the biographical first half. Sandburg and Angle's book, while well done, did not have much staying power as a source on Mary's life, simply because it was eclipsed by other works.

By the 1940s and 1950s, Mary grew fully into the character of Mrs. Abraham Lincoln. True to the social mores of the time, the new interpretation of Mary was as a June Cleaver–type character of wife, mother, and housekeeper but also as a solid companion for her husband without whom he would not be complete. Some of the articles about Mary during this period had titles such as "Mrs. Lincoln Refurbishes the White House," by Harry E. Pratt and Ernest E. East; "Mary Todd Lincoln, Helpmate—Her Springfield Years" and "Mary Todd Lincoln, Helpmate—Her White House Years," both by Montgomery S. Lewis; "The Woman in Lincoln's Life, with Special Emphasis on Her Cultural Attainments," by Louis A. Warren; and "'My Tired & Weary Husband': Mary Lincoln on Life in the Executive Mansion," by William E. Baringer. The pinnacle of this point of view came with Ruth Painter Randall's 1953 book, *Mary Lincoln: Biography of a Marriage.*[18]

Randall, who had a master's degree in history from Indiana University, was the first trained historian to write a book about Mary Lincoln. Randall had a long interest in Lincoln studies and, before writing her own works, assisted her husband James G. Randall (one of the most respected Lincoln scholars of his generation) in two chapters of his 1945 book, *Lincoln the President: From Springfield to Gettysburg.* That work led Ruth Randall to the conviction that Mary Lincoln "needed a new trial before the court of historical investigation," which meant considering all the evidence of Mary's life, old and new, positive and negative, again with fresh eyes and seeking out the closest truth to her character as possible. The main work Randall does in her 1953 biography is to firmly attack and disprove Herndon's damning conclusions that Lincoln never loved his wife because of his love for Ann Rutledge and that he left Mary standing at the alter in 1841. After refuting Herndon, Randall continues her appeal that Mary Lincoln, while she had her shortcomings, was a woman to be admired and later pitied. She was a strong, intelligent, attractive woman, a devoted wife and conscientious mother, and a somewhat victimized first lady who was also temperamental, emotionally immature, self-centered, and easily manipulated. While Randall tried to show a balanced view of Mary, she could not overcome her defiant sympathy for Lincoln's wife and thus offers more advocacy than objectivity. As one contemporary reviewer said of the book, "Mrs. Randall has certainly made the best possible case for Mary Lincoln and her marriage. If she had handled the favorable materials as carefully and critically as she has the unfavorable, she would have produced a more convincing book."[19] Despite Randall's sympathetic bent, *Mary Lincoln: Biography of a Marriage* is one of the most impressively researched books on Mary Lincoln to date and, along with W. A. Evans's book, one of the best books on Mary Lincoln written.

Less than twenty years later, one of the most referenced works on Mary Lincoln, *Mary Todd Lincoln: Her Life and Letters*, was published by Justin and Linda Levitt Turner. In the ninety years between Mary's death and the publication of her compiled letters, journal and newspaper articles revealing and publishing newly discovered letters of Mary Lincoln were some of the most exciting publications in the canon. Mary being such a complex, even dichotomous, figure, every new letter had the potential for amazing new revelations about her, her husband, or her years in the White House. The Turners' work in compiling all these disparate letters into one volume added a much-needed context to Mary's voluminous outpouring of correspondence. This book, an impressively objective biography that focuses on factual presentation rather than historical interpretation, tells Mary's life story chronologically with her complete (at the time it was published) correspondence as a supplement. In the forty-six years since its publication, however, the Turners' book has become outdated, with at least two hundred Mary Lincoln letters subsequently discovered or located and yet to be added to the story they started.

By the 1980s, with the rise of women's studies and feminist revisionism, biographical work on Mary Lincoln went in a new direction, and with it, Mary as "Mrs. Abraham Lincoln" gave way to her being identified and recognized as "Mary TODD Lincoln"—her own woman, a woman ahead of her times, a woman apart from her husband with her own ideas and strengths who was battling against a patriarchal society.[20] This historical pivot was most clearly defined in Jean Baker's 1987 work *Mary Todd Lincoln: A Biography*—the book that to this day remains the most popular and most referenced work on Mary Lincoln, despite its many and serious flaws (which will be discussed in detail later). Baker's work is a revisionist psychobiography of Mary Lincoln with an overt feminist agenda that portrays her as a female pioneer in a chauvinistic society—to the historical detriment of her husband and most of the people around her.[21] Baker's work is well researched, and offers some of the best context for Mary's life in understanding the social and political mores of the time for women of Mary Lincoln's social status—a status that was ever changing, going from an aristocratic upbringing to a middle-class midlife to a stint as first lady of the country and then a fall to lonely and publicly discarded widow. As Ruth Painter Randall does in her biography of Mary Lincoln, Baker seeks to show Mary's faults as well as her virtues, but the end result is more sympathetic—often defensive and exculpatory—than objective.

Since the turn of the millennium in 2000, Mary has become a feminist icon who was actually the brains behind the bumpkin Lincoln: she wrote his speeches, advised him on policy, and really was Hillary Clinton 150 years too soon. The most recent biographies of her include those by Catherine Clinton, Stacy Pratt McDermott, and Betty Boles Ellison. Clinton's book is an unoriginal rehash of previous writers' materials and conclusions; McDermott's work is a succinct overview of Mary's life and, while excellent in research and perspective, contains nothing new or groundbreaking in its scholarship. Ellison's book, meanwhile, is an example of revisionism and presentism run amok, ascribing to Mary qualities, ideas, and characteristics she never had, could never have had at the time, and would rail against as ridiculous were she living today. While personal bias and political agendas always have been and will remain historical stumbling blocks, such an überfeminist interpretation, unsupported by facts, has become the dominant theory about who Mary was in recent years. This change may stem partially from the political rise of women in general over the past thirty years, or it may come specifically from the rise of Hillary Clinton, a former first lady who became the first female presidential candidate nominated by a major party in American history. Whatever the reason, Mary's admirers and defenders constantly seek to place her on a pedestal as high as, or higher than, her husband's. Unfortunately, such historical revisionism, or more accurately such presentism, fails to account for Mary as she was during the time in which she lived.

Much of the blame for the insubstantial writings about Mary Lincoln in recent years can be placed on writers' shallow understanding of Mary based on their constant rehashing of the same tired works about her. There are really only seven major works that have become the common canon of Mary Lincoln—approximately 2 percent of more than three hundred nonfiction writings about Mary.[22] These books are the main informers of what the general public, journalists, essayists, book reviewers, general writers, and historians, and even many Lincoln scholars, use when needing information about Mary—for better or worse. Some of them are excellent sources; some are flawed and vitiated by bias; all, it could be argued, are outdated. These seven books are Herndon and Weik, *Herndon's Lincoln*; Keckley, *Behind the Scenes*; Katherine Helm, *Mary, Wife of Lincoln*; Randall, *Mary Lincoln: Biography of a Marriage*; Turner and Turner, *Mary Todd Lincoln: Her Life and Letters*; Baker, *Mary Todd Lincoln*; and Mark Neely and R. Gerald McMurtry, *The Insanity File: The Case of Mary Todd Lincoln*. The last work has become one of the main sources for people seeking information about Mary's insanity period and trial, although it has become outdated and surpassed by more recent works.[23] In addition to these books, a few choice quotations from Mary's contemporaries (typically negative and critical remarks by presidential secretaries John Hay and William O. Stoddard) are often quoted by modern writers, but those barbs are merely punctuative points rather than anchoring source material.[24]

Within this common canon, there are two books, more than any others, that are the foundation for everything else written, spoken, and believed about Mary Lincoln: *Herndon's Lincoln*, by William Herndon, and *Mary Todd Lincoln: A Biography*, by Jean Baker. These two books are responsible for both showing Mary as she was during the time in which she lived, and completely corrupting any honest understanding of her character by the overt biases those authors brought into their works. By continuing to base our knowledge of Mary on these two sources—rather than simply incorporating their positive aspects as small pieces of a larger canon of research—the lies, false stories, misunderstandings, and misinterpretations of who Mary truly was will not only never end but will continue to be perpetuated by future writers and historians.

Herndon's contributions to Mary's story and reputation, as previously mentioned, are mainly the negative ones (even though he also offers her praise), mostly that Mary never loved Lincoln, was a cold shrew who married him for revenge and personal advancement, made his life a living hell, and drove him out of the house and into greatness. But Herndon's assertions are fascinating in that they cannot be taken at face value—one must understand who he was and how he thought to make the best use of his work. Herndon believed he knew Lincoln better than anyone else, probably even Mary, did, and that he also was the gatekeeper to the truth of who Lincoln was. But he recognized the truth in a rather peculiar way (what may also be called an egotistical, self-satisfied way). As Lincoln scholar Paul M. Angle has astutely observed, "Emotional, sentimental, steeped in New England transcendentalism, Herndon was inordinately fond of peering into the souls of his acquaintances in what would now be called psychoanalytical fashion. He was firmly convinced that truth could be got at by intuition, and he never doubted his own clairvoyant capacity."[25]

Historian David Herbert Donald, who studied the life of Herndon more deeply than anyone, agreed that Herndon sought truth through introspection. "If you wished to explain a man's actions, look to your own soul, where you would find identical motives reflected. All men operate on the same laws, and these laws can explain any human behavior," Donald wrote.[26] And yet, by comparing Lincoln's life and motivations to his own, Herndon badly misinterpreted his law partner's domestic situation. For example, Herndon loved his wife and children dearly and being away from home made him unhappy. Lincoln, on the other hand, traveled the judicial circuit for months at a time without going home. Clearly, believed Herndon, Lincoln therefore did not really love his wife and being home did not make him happy.

But this unhappiness, according to Herndon, was because Lincoln did not love his wife: it was not Mary's fault he did not love her; he was just never able to forget his New Salem love Ann Rutledge. So Herndon's public assertion in speeches and writings that Abraham Lincoln never loved his wife and lived a miserable life as Mary's husband was made, as Herndon said multiple times, because he thought he was doing Mary a favor. He repeatedly stated that he sympathized with Mary, he was her friend, and he did not blame her for her domestic unhappiness—and by having her terrible truths come from a family friend rather than strangers, he was trying to protect her reputation.[27] Understanding this motivation—that Herndon wrote from stated or apparent sympathy rather than malice—one can read Herndon's statements with a new perception, even a modicum of trust. This point of view shows us that not everything Herndon wrote or said about Mary Lincoln should be summarily discarded.[28]

One example of Herndon's thinking in this vein comes from an 1888 letter in which he wrote, "Mrs. Lincoln was a better woman than the world gives her credit for. She was a whip and a sting to Lincoln's ambition—she urged him to go upward. I admit that *at times*, in her *after life*, that she was a she devil[.] . . . Let us be charitable for we are all weak creatures at best, no one knowing himself till conditions push him on to ruin. Bless this woman. She was Lincoln's best and wisest adviser when at herself and in her younger days."[29] This strange dichotomy in Herndon's feelings about Mary Lincoln makes his writings and reminiscences about her particularly dangerous to be used by the uninitiated. No one should seek his counsel on Mary Lincoln without first reading his biography and his personal letters and understanding who he was and how and why he believed and wrote what he did. These books to be read first include his letters as published by Emanuel Hertz, and by Douglas Wilson and Rodney Davis; David Donald's biography, *Lincoln's Herndon*; and articles about the relationship between Mary and Herndon by both Donald and Wilson.

Jean Baker's contributions to modern understandings and interpretations of Mary Lincoln are also dichotomous. On the one hand, she offers up an impressive portrayal of Mary Lincoln as she fit within the social landscape of the times in which she lived, showing her to be both a woman of her time and perhaps even slightly ahead of her time (although only slightly, and no more so than many of her female contemporaries). But then on the other hand, Baker's book swerves into a one-sided feminist—often accusatory and exculpatory—diatribe in which Mary is a saint who rarely stepped a wayward foot in her life. Baker portrays her as a female pioneer in a chauvinistic society—while simultaneously stating that Mary was no different than other women of her day—misrepresents the role she played in her husband's political life as being far more important and impactful than it was, and seeks to give her credit for all the positive events in her life while simultaneously shifting blame to others for anything negative that occurred.

One example of this misrepresentation (out of many that could be used) occurs when Baker discusses how Mary refurbished the White House in 1861. Baker states that Mary reversed the usual arrangement between the first lady and the commissioner of public buildings, in that "it was she, and not he," who led the way into the stores, chose the furnishings, and impatiently carried her purchases back to the hotel rather than waiting for delivery. It was Mary, according to Baker, who single-handedly, wisely, and appropriately brought the White House back to being a symbol of power and a vision of prestige and style through her refurbishment project. But Mary overspent her four-year appropriation of $20,000 in less than one year, for which she was soundly criticized in the press and public—and her husband was furious. But, as Baker states, it was not Mary but the commissioner of public buildings who overspent the budget, because, after all, he was in charge of the money. But, since Mary was a woman without legal rights, "she was held liable for what neither law nor custom gave her control of." This is a case where Baker wants Mary to have her cake and eat it too. She cannot say Mary single-handedly and without heed to the opinions of the commissioner of public buildings refurbished the White House in a way that brought prestige to her husband's administration (thereby giving her credit for political acumen) and then turn around and say that these purchases, done frivolously and expensively, at taxpayer expense, was not her fault at all but the commissioner's.[30]

Baker's book takes a turn from a fairly solid historical work to an illiberal feminist tirade after the assassination, when an adult Robert Lincoln becomes head of the family under the Victorian social values of the time. Any objective reading of Baker's book cannot deny the fierce depiction of Robert as all that is evil in the world of men; he is a scoundrel, a wastrel, a selfish prig who hates his mother, and the cause of everything bad in his mother's life. This characterization goes directly to Mary's insanity episode in 1875 and Baker's portrayal of it—which has become the standard understanding of the event, even though it is outright wrong, fabricated, and even libelous. Baker's story is that a perfectly sane Mary was railroaded into the asylum by Robert out of embarrassment and a desire to steal her money, that he bribed the judge and jury to find his mother guilty, and he planted the "fake news" story that his mother tried to commit suicide the day after the insanity verdict as "a son's exculpation of filial treachery."[31] This entire interpretation is proven by the historical facts—when viewed in their entirety and not parsed to prove political agendas—to be absolutely, unequivocally false.[32]

In the end, it is clear that Baker's book, just like Herndon's, is both essential reading in the study of Mary Lincoln and also extremely dangerous reading when what it says is taken at face value. While Baker seeks to show Mary as a typical—and somehow also extraordinary—woman within the social customs of the times, she then steps beyond the desire to understand Mary and defensively lashes out at anyone who accused or accuses her of any impropriety as being nothing but insular sexists. Again, it is essential to realize that both Herndon's and Baker's works cannot and should not be the basis for any understanding of Mary Lincoln (as no single book should be), but rather should be nothing more than contributing pieces to the much larger whole. This modern reliance on these two works specifically, and all seven of the works within the common canon of Mary Lincoln generally, has prevented any deeper analysis; it is a historical hamster wheel in which Mary's story is always the same, time and again. Writers and readers seeking to find the more complicated and interesting Mary Lincoln need to expand their source material.

Every generation requires a new interpretation of history. But to do this, that generation must not only revisit all the source material previously used but also strike out and find new, updated sources. As historian Leopold von Ranke once declared, "In order for us to put together a work which does not bear the imprint of the past, our research must proceed to a stage at which the whole truth in its full extent can be safely determined."[33] While the seven works listed above have become the common canon of Mary Lincoln, this list falls far short of the sources that should be used—and must be used—in order to gain a more complete understanding of Mary's life and personality.

As stated previously, W. A. Evans's 1932 biography is sometimes consulted by writers, but it is a far more essential source on Mary Lincoln than has been generally accepted. It is, in fact, fair to say that it is still the best biography of Mary yet written, based on its objectivity, its impressive research, its medical diagnoses and methodologies, its goal to not just explain the facts of Mary's life but to seek to understand who she was, and the fact that Evans's interviews of numerous family members and friends of Mary offer much first-hand information found no place else.[34] As a work of history, the book is written differently than most anything one will read today. It is compelling and colloquial, but also contains outlines of major incidents in Mary's life at the beginning of each chapter, lists of quotations about Mary from personal writings or from newspaper reporting, and topical divisions within a larger chronological approach. This last aspect makes it easier for interested readers to delve into specific topics about Mary, such as her physical appearance, her medical health during the final years of her life, and her financial worries throughout her life, which formed a major part of her mentality.[35]

Likewise mentioned above, to understand much of what William Herndon said and wrote about Mary Lincoln—and to understand his unvarnished personal opinions of her—interested students should read through books of Herndon's writings and recollections by Hertz and by Wilson and Davis, Donald's biography of Herndon, and articles considering the relationship between Mary and Herndon written by Donald and Wilson. By better understanding Herndon's mentality one can get a clearer picture of his portrayals of Mary through the years in his public writings and statements. No distinct understanding of Mary Lincoln and her influence on her husband can be had without dealing with Herndon and his writing about her.

The White House secretaries, so often mentioned in the Lincoln story but rarely consulted, wrote far more about Mary Lincoln than just the few quotations from them constantly cited by writers. John Nicolay, John Hay, and William O. Stoddard were all inveterate writers who published books and articles about Abraham Lincoln, or had their wartime letters and journals published in books, for the remainder of their lives. And much of what they wrote mentioned the first lady. While Nicolay and Hay are best known as President Lincoln's secretaries, and their writings illuminate broad swaths of life inside the Lincoln White House, including many of the problems they had with the president's wife (with whom they had a mutual dislike), it was Stoddard, the "third secretary," who also came to be known as "Mrs. Lincoln's secretary," whose writings offer the most historical information on Mary. Stoddard, a journalist turned civil servant during the war, was a prolific writer who authored numerous articles and books about Abraham Lincoln, the Civil War, and his time as a White House secretary during the war. Stoddard became known as Mary's secretary because he genuinely liked her, and she him, and he could work with and get along with her—something Nicolay and Hay both could not do, and did not care to do. "I understood her thoroughly and formed a much higher opinion of her real character than a lot of foul-mouthed slanderers permitted to go out to the country," as Stoddard later wrote in his autobiography.[36]

Among Stoddard's multiple Lincoln-related writings, such as *Abraham Lincoln: The True Story of a Great Life* (N.Y.: Fords, Howard, and Hulbert, 1884), *The Table Talk of Abraham Lincoln* (N.Y.: Frederick A. Stokes, 1894), and *Lincoln at Work: Sketches from Life* (Boston: United Society of Christian Endeavor, 1900), it is his 1890 book *Inside the White House in War Times* (particularly the 2000 reprint supplemented by thirteen "White House sketches") that sheds the most light on Mary Lincoln from Stoddard's perspective. Ruth Painter Randall called *Inside the White House in War Times* "[o]ne of the best defenses of Mrs. Lincoln," although it is more an attempt at understanding her through Stoddard's personal experiences and observations than an outright defense of her.[37] Stoddard discusses Mary's virtues as well as her faults, and even, in his determination to figure out the first lady and her sometimes bizarre behaviors, consulted a doctor for further insight. He shows Mary both as a sensible, caring woman and as a petulant, emotional virago—both sides of which he witnessed constantly. But he makes clear that he feels whatever Mary's foibles, her treatment by the press and the Washington rumor mill was unfair and unjust. "People in great need of something spicy to talk or write about are picking up all sorts of stray gossip relating to asserted occurrences under this roof, and they are making strange work out of some of it. It is a work which they will not cease from," Stoddard wrote. "They will do it, to the very end, so effectively that a host of excellent people will one day close their eyes to the wife's robe dabbled with her husband's blood."[38]

One of the aspects of Mary's life that is vital in understanding her is her belief in spiritualism, the solace it gave her in her immense grief, and the years she spent visiting spiritualist mediums and attending séances; yet what little has been written on the topic is rarely read. Newspapers contemporary to Mary Lincoln are filled with stories of her visits to mediums both while she was first lady and during the years of her widowhood. Only two published writings, however, reliably explain anything about the topic. Nettie Colburn Maynard's 1891 memoir, *Was Abraham Lincoln a Spiritualist? or, Curious Revelations from the Life of a Trance Medium*, is the best source on the topic. Maynard was a young spiritualist who held numerous séances with Mary Lincoln both in and out of the White House during the Civil War, and who impressed Mary so much with her ability that the first lady got the young medium a government job in order to keep her in Washington. This book details many of the now-famous spiritualist stories from the Lincoln presidency, and shows glimpses of Mary's traits of excitability, devotion to her husband, emotional fragility, and matronly kindness. Of all the supposed spiritualists in Mary Lincoln's life who wrote memoirs, this one not only rings most authentic but is generally accepted by scholars as the most reliable. The other writing worth reading is Jay Monaghan's excellent 1941 article "Was Abraham Lincoln Really a Spiritualist?," which examines and judges the eleven writings (at the time) about Abraham Lincoln as a believer in spiritualism. Monaghan eliminates all but two of the writings as unreliable (one of the two reliable works being Maynard's book). While focused on Abraham Lincoln's belief in spiritualism, this article is an essential source for understanding Mary's belief in spiritualism and her experiences consulting with spirit mediums during her time in the White House.

Both during and after her life, Mary's belief in spiritualism was considered by many to be an illness she bore, either as a symptom of a physical brain disease or of insanity. And while her spiritualist tendencies need to be better understood as to how they affected Mary specifically, both her physical and mental health in general are not just major but essential aspects of her life that also must be studied to a much greater degree than is currently done. Strangely, for all the talk about Mary's myriad physical ailments during her life, and especially the argument over whether or not she suffered some form of mental illness, the multiple works on the subject, nearly all written by trained physicians, are rarely consulted.

In addition to W. A. Evans's 1932 book that examines Mary's physical and mental health through her life, there have been other excellent works published on both topics. Dr. James A. Brussel published a professional psychiatric case study of Mary Lincoln in 1941 that declared that while Mary apparently suffered numerous psychiatric symptoms such as hallucinations, terror, depression, suicidal intentions and attempts, and feelings of persecution, his diagnosis was that she was a victim of migraines and possibly epilepsy. In 1966 Dr. John M. Suarez also published a professional psychiatric case study, although his diagnosis was that Mary suffered from a violent temper, emotional instability, depression, auditory and visual hallucinations, and delusions of poverty and grandeur. In 1999 physiologists Norbert Hirschhorn and Robert G. Feldman published a medical study of Mary Lincoln's physical health during her final years that declared she probably suffered from post-traumatic stress syndrome, diabetes, and the spinal disease tabes dorsalis, and that many of her physical ailments were "misinterpreted as madness" during her commitment in 1875.[39]

Recent years have seen some exciting new medical examinations of Mary Lincoln. In 2012 historian Glenna R. Schroeder-Lein published *Lincoln and Medicine*, an excellent medical history of the Lincoln family that looks into Mary's frequent migraines, her mood swings, her carriage accident injury, the possibility that she suffered mental illness, and her multiple physical ailments during her final years. In 2014 Mary Lee Esty and C. M. Shifflett, in their book *Conquering Concussion*, offered an utterly fascinating theory that Mary's 1863 carriage accident resulted in a traumatic brain injury that forever altered her personality, abilities, health, and behavior. They cite her worsened migraines, hallucinations, delusions, spending and hoarding, and photophobia all as results of her head injury. In 2016 the newest medical theory about Mary was published—that all her physical and mental illnesses were the result of pernicious anemia, a syndrome of vitamin B_{12} deficiency. The article "'What an Affliction': Mary Todd Lincoln's Fatal Pernicious Anemia," by Dr. John G. Sotos, was written about in newspapers and periodicals around the United States and caused quite a stir, although he admitted that the disease is now extinct, unknown to modern doctors and, therefore, impossible to prove.

When considering Mary Lincoln's insanity period and historians' writings about it, books by Baker (1987) and by Neely and McMurtry (1986) are typically the first sources consulted, even though both are incomplete in their study of the subject, as mentioned previously. Both of these books have been augmented and supplanted by multiple later works, and it is these more recent works that should become the standard reference materials on the subject. Baker's biased failure to accurately or objectively portray the insanity period has already been examined, and, while Neely and McMurtry's book is a well-done work, more updated information, based on never-before-published sources in two recent books, offers a greater understanding of Mary's mental health and her insanity period. My books *The Madness of Mary Lincoln* and *Mary Lincoln's Insanity Case: A Documentary History* use previously unknown and unpublished primary materials and offer a new thesis on what exactly happened to Mary Lincoln during this period, and why. The latter book is especially important because it is a compilation of every primary source available on the topic and shows exactly what happened, and what was understood to be happening at the time, by all the people involved. To understand Mary's insanity case, it is also essential to comprehend the character and motivations of her oldest son, Robert T. Lincoln, who was also the man who had her committed to the sanitarium in 1875. My biography *Giant in the Shadows: The Life of Robert T. Lincoln* not only offers a greater depth of understanding of both Mary and Robert and their specific relationship than any previous books, but it also examines Robert's motivations as to why he committed his mother.

In addition to my books, two articles are also essential reading to the insanity case. Rodney A. Ross's 1970 article "Mary Todd Lincoln: Patient at Bellevue Place, Batavia" examines Mary's four-month stay in Bellevue Place sanitarium after being declared insane in 1875 and the facts behind her ultimate release, and describes the Bellevue Place grounds and accommodations, its doctors, and Mary's medical treatment while a patient. Most important, the article contains transcriptions of the sanitarium's daily patient progress reports during the time of Mary's commitment from May to September 1875, so readers can see how Mary was behaving during this seminal period in her life. The other excellent source is Norbert Hirschhorn's 2003 article "Mary Lincoln's 'Suicide Attempt': A Physician Reconsiders the Evidence," which proves definitely that Mary Lincoln did attempt suicide on May 20, 1875, the day after she was declared insane by a Chicago jury, and it was not an instance of "fake news" generated by Robert Lincoln to make his mother look bad and himself look better, as has been alleged.

To understand Mary Lincoln's character and personality, one must also appreciate her family members and the household dynamic in which she grew up. Historian Stephen Berry has written two works that shed valuable light on this topic: his book *House of Abraham: Lincoln and the Todds, a Family Divided by War*, and an article that distills the essential points of the book, "There's Something about Mary: Mary Lincoln and Her Siblings," printed in the 2012 book *The Mary Lincoln Enigma*. In both of these works, Berry examines the Todd family history, personalities, and dynamics, and shows that Mary, far from being some strange anomaly, some person impervious to analysis, was, in fact, more than anything else, a Todd. "In tracing Mary back to the childhood she shared with her siblings, one gains a better vantage not only on her unique attributes and faults, but also on those traits common to her family, her region, and her times," Berry writes. "The Todds were the matrix in which Mary was formed and lived her life."[40]

As one of fourteen children from her father's two families, Mary grew up in a loud, bustling, frenetic household filled with siblings, visiting family, slaves, and numerous guests. The Todd clan, as Berry shows, were proud, intelligent, opinionated people who also had sharp tongues and quick tempers, and who could be affectionate and emotional while also cruel and selfish. As Mary's sister Elodie wrote to her fiancé at the start of the Civil War, "I am a *Todd*, and some of these days you may be unfortunate enough to find out what they are."[41] They were simply a big family, as Berry states, "teeming and tempestuous." And while Berry's works are not examinations of the Lincoln marriage in any way, by seeing Mary's beginnings and childhood influences, one can also gain some insight into the Lincoln marriage and see that Abraham Lincoln, who spent more time with various Todd relatives than he did with Lincoln relatives, knew full well who Mary was when he married her and exactly what he was getting into on his wedding day. He was not tricked into marrying some two-faced harpy, but rather he had fallen in love with a strong, proud, intelligent woman who knew her mind and kept him on his toes and looking toward an ambitious future.

In the world of Lincoln scholarship, few, if any, scholars are as meticulous and exhaustive in their research as Michael Burlingame—and few have such a disdain for Mary Lincoln. Burlingame believes that while there is much to "deplore" in Mary's behavior, she is "more to be pitied than censured," although he certainly has never been shy in his censure of her.[42] And while many admirers and defenders of Mary actively avoid Burlingame's writing about her, to do so deprives them of some of the most essential research on Mary ever accomplished. Mary Lincoln was human, having both positive and negative traits to her character, and while she has been reviled for decades, much of her bad reputation came from rumor, innuendo, and supposition. Burlingame, on the other hand, uses his indefatigable research skills to bore to the heart of some extremely unsavory aspects of Mary's character and actions, and presents his description and interpretation of Mary supported by voluminous facts. While readers may not like what Burlingame has to say, it is extremely difficult to refute what he has uncovered in his research and exposed like a raw nerve.

Two of Burlingame's essays are absolutely critical to a holistic understanding of Mary Lincoln: "The Lincolns' Marriage: 'A Fountain of Misery, of a Quality Absolutely Infernal'" and "Mary Todd Lincoln's Unethical Conduct as First Lady."[43] The first of these offers an interpretation of the Lincoln marriage similar to that of Herndon, in that, for Lincoln, it was a hell on earth. Burlingame paints the Lincoln marriage as an unhappy match between two irreconcilably different people and portrays Mary as an emotional and physical abuser of her husband, a jealous woman with an uncontrollable temper, and possibly even an unfaithful lover.

The reminiscences and interviews on which Burlingame bases his writing include family, friends, and neighbors of the Lincolns offering evidence that Mary would hit her husband in the face with firewood, chase him around the house and even the neighborhood with a broom or a kitchen knife, and verbally abuse him and lock him out of the house, among other behaviors. But, like Herndon, Burlingame sees Lincoln's marital suffering as an ultimate good for the country in that the unpleasantness of his home kept him out riding the judicial circuit and practicing politics, thus preparing him for the presidency. Similarly, dealing with such a tempestuous wife prepared

Lincoln for "handling difficult people he encountered as president," and helped foster within him the attributes of patience, tolerance, forbearance, and forgiveness.[44]

While much of the evidence on which Burlingame bases his conclusions about the state of the Lincoln marriage is primary materials, some of it is second- and even thirdhand hearsay, which has led some scholars to doubt his findings and interpretations. But even if one concedes that not everything in the essay may be accurate (whether by clouded memories decades old or people seeking to write themselves into the Lincoln legacy with false stories), the overwhelming magnitude of the evidence that the Lincoln marriage was often tempestuous cannot be ignored, and Burlingame's conclusions cannot be dismissed as simple bias or misogyny. The foundations of his conclusions are just too solid. But, as Burlingame also notes, Abraham Lincoln was not a perfect husband, and many of Mary's outbursts of temper were caused by Abraham's own conduct. Similarly, a justifiable question can be asked about how much some of Mary's temper tantrums and petulance really affected her husband. As Lincoln is known to have said when asked by friends why he would let his wife rant at him or boss him around, "If you knew how little harm it does me and how much good it does her, you wouldn't wonder that I am meek."[45] No marriage is perfect and every couple has their ups and downs, and this indispensable essay proves the Lincolns were no different. Their marriage was not some fairy-tale love story (although they certainly loved each other), and Mary was no angel wife or mother, as many of her defenders would have readers believe.

During her eighteen years of marriage in Springfield, Mary was a wife and mother; but when she got to Washington in 1861, she became the first lady, and her life was utterly changed. Mary became the social leader of Washington society, the arbiter of fashion in the North, and the consort to the president of the United States. As a vain woman extremely susceptible to flattery, and one who felt entitled and more important than common people, Mary Lincoln was perfectly unsuited to be first lady, especially during a time of war, as Burlingame concludes in his groundbreaking study of Mary's "unethical conduct" in the White House. According to Burlingame, this conduct included influence peddling, bribe taking, account padding, document leaking, theft of government property, and possibly even sexual affairs. Burlingame's work, while seemingly unsavory, is, like his essay on the Lincoln marriage, based on exhaustive research and bolstered by myriad citations.

It is an essential contribution to the Mary Lincoln bibliography and while it can be disagreed with, it cannot be ignored.

One of the more recent books that should be added to the list of essential works about Mary Lincoln is *The Mary Lincoln Enigma: Historians on America's Most Controversial First Lady*, edited by Frank J. Williams and Michael Burkhimer. This unique collection of essays offers glimpses into vast aspects of Mary's life—some well-known and some not—such as her childhood and upbringing, her years in Springfield, her thoughts on race and slavery, her relationships with people such as William Herndon and her son Robert, her love of fashion and of traveling, her political acumen and mental health, and her portrayals in both art and fiction. This is the most wide-ranging book about Mary, and one that delves deeper into certain aspects of her life than a straight biography typically allows. Within the vast Mary Lincoln bibliography, *The Mary Lincoln Enigma* is gaining traction as one of the more popular and referenced works about her life.

Finally, when discussing published sources about Mary Lincoln, the importance of newspaper articles—both contemporary to her life and after her death—cannot be overstated. And while as recently as a decade or so ago to look for historical facts in old newspapers meant hours of dizzying, torturous skimming through microfilm reels in libraries and museums, online databases—easily accessible and many of them free—now make looking for information in historic newspapers just as easy as, if not easier than, reading through books and articles.

As is shown in the analytical bibliography in part 2 of the present book, some of the most important source materials on Mary's life are found in contemporary newspaper coverage. To get the facts straight from the reporters when things happened is crucial. In Mary's case, events such as her actions as first lady during the Civil War, her 1875 insanity trial and time in Bellevue Place sanitarium, and her general travels around the United States and Europe during her widowhood all are chronicled in great detail in newspapers. Much of Mary's negative historical reputation, in fact, started with the newspaper criticism aimed at her during her years as first lady and ultimately informed and influenced many of the first people who wrote about her. She was pilloried in the press for her penchant for traveling, shopping, and holding official parties in the midst of war; she was harangued for the company she kept and her lack of ministering to the war wounded; and she was generally attacked as unsuited for the position she held (which was another way to attack the

president himself). The newspaper attacks, whether founded in fact or politically motivated—and there were plenty of both by the overtly political
newspapers of the day—left a bad taste in the mouths of many people in the
United States as to Mary's character.

Some of the most interesting contemporary newspaper articles about Mary
were written in 1881 and 1882, the last two years of her life. The newspapers
at that time were rife with stories about her physical and mental health, her
relationship with Robert and his children, and how she generally spent her
days. Most important, in summer 1881, when Mary applied for an increase
to her government pension, she was examined by three physicians and their
complete report of her physical health based on their personal examinations
was printed in the press. And of course, after Mary's death, the obituaries and
reminiscences by people who knew her also are invaluable historical fodder.

In general, most historians and writers do not make enough use of contemporary historical journalism, often called "the first draft of history." Not
only do newspapers hold the original reporting of important incidents, often
with interviews of historic characters, later newspaper articles also contain
interviews and reminiscences of people who knew or worked with the historical subject being studied—and only in those newspapers can many of those
primary stories be found. There is no excuse to ignore historical reporting,
especially in today's computer age where so many articles can be accessed
and searched by keywords in online databases. Similarly, the vast writings
from the late nineteenth and early twentieth centuries about Mary seem to
have been forgotten through the years and disappointingly overlooked in
recent scholarship on Mary's life. Many of these sources hold vast amounts
of primary information found nowhere else, and most of these also can be
easily searched through online databases.

While there certainly has been much written about Mary Lincoln (more
than many people would probably expect) and modern scholars know many
facts about her, she remains a misunderstood woman. It can be argued she
is seen one-dimensionally by most people, either as the nagging shrew who
made her husband's life hell and ended up in a lunatic asylum, or the feminist
heroine, suppressed and unappreciated in her own time, suffocated and destroyed by a chauvinist, patriarchal society that did not allow her to flourish
to her full potential. As is so often the case with such diametrically opposed
interpretations, the truth lies somewhere in the middle. It does Mary Lincoln's reputation and historical character no service when modern people

seek to mold her into a person they want her to be, rather than to simply discover and explain her for who she truly was, as she existed within the context of the times in which she lived.

Mary Lincoln was an intelligent, opinionated woman who enjoyed politics and surely discussed political issues with her husband. She supported her husband's work and sought to be the best companion and helpmate that she could be, a role in which she both succeeded and failed at various times. That is an admirable, logical, understandable, and *human* character trait for her to have, and in no way demeans her as a historical figure. True to the culture of the mid-nineteenth century, Mary was not a politician, did not want to be a politician, and did not think of herself as a politician, and never acted, overtly or surreptitiously, as some sort of a White House consigliere. So why do modern writers and historians continue to try to portray her as one? To do so may further their own contemporary political objectives, but this does nothing to enhance the understanding of Mary Lincoln and why she is a fascinating woman in her own right, worthy of study for her own life as she chose to live it. History does not need to be enhanced or changed to be interesting or relevant today. People in the nineteenth century were different from us in the twenty-first century in many ways, and yet many of their struggles and achievements are also incredibly similar to what we strive for today—and that is where we can continue to learn from them by reading and writing about them in a historically fair and accurate way.

Mary Lincoln constantly felt that history was unfair, especially to her and her family. She wrote more than once that many of the writings about her husband in the years after his death by people who did not know him startled her in their pretentions to intimacy and in their inaccuracies. She once considered assisting with, or perhaps even writing, some sort of biography of her husband at the request of one publisher, but ultimately decided not to do so. "The temptation to me is sometimes very great that many incidents that occurred in so momentous a time, under my immediate notice connected with my beloved husband . . . should be truthfully placed before the public," Mary wrote in 1868 to publisher A. D. Worthington. "It will be impossible for me, under *present circumstances*, to subject myself to the annoyance of public clamor. You understand the American people quite as well as myself and will appreciate my feelings for preferring silence."[46]

Mary never did write any sort of memoir or reminiscence for public consumption, and so we will never know what she might have told posterity about her husband and the war he presided over that only she knew. And while we have over seven hundred of her letters published in some way, and hundreds more known but unpublished, Mary never wrote publicly about herself either, and so much of what has been written about her has been imperfect. Is she doomed to remain "an enigma to be pitied but never completely understood," as one writer has lamented?[47] Biographer Ruth Painter Randall once declared the prevailing impression of Mary Lincoln was a caricature. "Conspicuous defects of her personality have been used as lines to draw a picture which is more cartoon than a rounded portrait," she wrote. "One hears much of the 'Lincoln Myth.' There is also a Mary Lincoln myth."[48] And the entrenched vitality of myth is something nearly impossible to overcome. Right or wrong, people have certain notions about who Mary Lincoln was, and changing their minds is a difficult task for even the most persuasive of historians. Maybe, by expanding the Mary Lincoln canon beyond the comfortable, worn-out sources upon which her reputation has rested for so long, her life and character can be cleansed of decades of misinformation and myth and illuminated for the complicated, intricate, and overall imperfectly *human* person that she was.

PART TWO
ANALYTICAL BIBLIOGRAPHY

✐
Nonfiction
(Books and pamphlets)

1.

Keckley, Elizabeth. *Behind the Scenes; or, Thirty Years a Slave, and Four Years in the White House.* N.Y.: G. W. Carleton, 1868. 371 pp., index.

This memoir by Mary Lincoln's black White House seamstress and confidant details the first lady's experiences as wife and mother in the White House during the Civil War, and chronicles Mary's first years after her husband's assassination, especially concerning her finances and the Old Clothes Scandal of 1867. The book, which also contains twenty-one of Mary Lincoln's letters to Keckley, was intended as "an attempt to defend Mrs. Lincoln and to place her in a better light before the world," but was seen more as an embarrassing exposé about a pathetic former first lady. Someone even wrote a racist parody called *Behind the Seams: By a Nigger Woman Who Took in Work from Mrs. Lincoln and Mrs. Davis,* which is now considered one of the rarest Lincoln-related titles. Keckley's book is a reliable and necessary primary resource for the period of Mary Lincoln's life it covers. The book has been reprinted numerous times since its original publication, including Buffalo, N.Y.: Stansil and Lee, 1931; Salem, N.H.: Ayer Co., 1985; N.Y.: Oxford University Press, 1988; Chicago: R. R. Donnelley and Sons, 1998; Champaign: University of Illinois Press, 2001; N.Y.: Penguin Books, 2005; Chapel Hill: University of North Carolina Press, 2011.

2.

Smith, Matthew Hale. *Sunshine and Shadow in New York,* Hartford, Conn.: J. B. Burr and Co., 1868. 718 pp., illus.

Smith, a minister, journalist, and author, includes in this book of sketches about New York City an anecdote concerning Mary Lincoln and a "notorious" New Yorker who was a frequent visitor to the White House (pp. 285–289). This New Yorker—not named but generally accepted to be the "Chevalier" Henry Wikoff—was constantly at the White House through the flattered patronage of the first lady, and was believed to have been feeding the press stories about information and events inside the executive mansion. According to Smith, a group of the president's friends sent the author to see Lincoln, during which he told the president of the plot and showed him proof of Wikoff's purported doings. Following the revelation, Lincoln immediately went downstairs and personally removed Wikoff from the premises, after which the chevalier never returned. This is an interesting anecdote, and coincides with the fact that Wikoff, after being jailed for twenty-four hours by Congress for his refusal to tell who gave him the president's annual message to Congress before it was delivered, was believed to be protecting Mary Lincoln as his source.

3.

Lamon, Ward H. *The Life of Abraham Lincoln: From His Birth to His Inauguration as President.* Boston: James R. Osgood, 1872. 547 pp., illus.

This biography of Lincoln by his friend and legal colleague Lamon uses William Herndon's research materials and was ghostwritten by Chauncey F. Black, an anti-Lincoln Democrat. It characterizes Mary Lincoln as a termagant who made her husband's life intolerable, thereby driving him out of the house and into legal and political success.

4.

Ames, Mary Clemmer. *Ten Years in Washington: Life and Scenes in the National Capital, as a Woman Sees Them.* Hartford, Conn.: A. D. Worthington & Co., 1873. 587 pp., illus.

A contemporary woman's account, simultaneously critical and sympathetic of Mary Lincoln's character and actions as first lady (pp. 235–242). Mary is portrayed as an ambitious and self-centered woman who spent her time shopping and having parties while the rest of the country sacrificed to support the war effort; yet she also is commiserated with as the only first lady ever to be so personally assailed by the press and the public due mostly to political and sectional prejudices.

5.

Mumler, William H. *The Personal Experiences of William H. Mumler in Spirit-Photography.* Boston: Colby and Rich, 1875. 68 pp.

Mumler's memoir contains his recollection of Mary Lincoln visiting his Boston studio in 1872 to have her spirit photograph taken. The resulting image—now infamous—contained the "spirits" of Abraham and Tad Lincoln hovering over Mary's shoulders. This recollection is a retelling by Mumler of the event as he previously described and published it in the *Spiritual Magazine* in 1872 (entry 218). Unlike that article, which simply related the visit, Mumler's memoir embellishes the event to include his wife "almost instantly" going into a spiritualist trance, being "taken over" by Tad—mistakenly identified as "Thaddeus" by the spirit—who then had a "long conversation" with his mother. Reprinted in Louis Kaplan, *The Strange Case of William Mumler, Spirit Photographer* (Minneapolis: University of Minnesota Press, 2008), 92–93.

6.

Swisshelm, Jane Grey. *Half a Century*. Chicago: Jansen, McClurg & Company, 1880. 363 pp.

This autobiography of Swisshelm, a noted abolitionist during the Civil War, recalls her first meeting with President and Mrs. Lincoln at a White House reception. Swisshelm entered the party in disdain of the Lincolns, particularly Mary's supposed Southern sympathy, but left in awe of both husband and wife, the latter whom she believed to be a true abolitionist, and in whom she found a friend for many years afterward.

7.

Holloway, Laura C. *The Ladies of the White House*. Philadelphia: Bradley & Company, 1882. 736 pp., illus.

This book on the lives of the first ladies was written to rectify their forgotten contributions to history. It contains a brief survey of Mary Lincoln's life (pp. 526–545), especially her years in the White House; it also declares Mary and her husband were incompatible and unhappy, and briefly mentions her insanity. Mary's chapter is vague and full of common facts and more focused on Abraham Lincoln.

8.

Boyden, Anna L. *War Reminiscences; or, Echoes from Hospital and White House*. Boston: D. Lothrop and Company, 1887. 250 pp.

Based on the letters and diaries of Civil War nurse Rebecca Pomroy, who became close with the Lincoln family from 1862 to 1865, *War Reminiscences* is full of vignettes and recollections of Mary Lincoln as first lady: her reaction to her son Willie's death in 1862, her belief in spiritualism, and her general mental and physical health. While simply offering observations of Mary Lincoln (and President Lincoln), Pomroy's work also illuminates certain aspects of Mary's personality, such as her devotion to her family, her emotional fragility, her incredible selfishness, and her impressive kindness. This is an important yet largely overlooked book pertaining to Mary Lincoln.

9.

Badeau, Adam. *Grant in Peace from Appomattox to Mount McGregor: A Personal Memoir*. Hartford, Conn.: S. S. Scranton & Co., 1887. 591 pp., illus.

A memoir by one of Ulysses S. Grant's headquarters staff members who had numerous interactions with Mary Lincoln, Badeau's work contains infamous stories of Mary's embarrassing temper while at Union army headquarters in City

Point, Virginia, in 1865, and her jealousy regarding her husband. Badeau also blames Mary for the absence of the Grants and the Stantons at Ford's Theatre on the night of April 14, and declares Mary's insanity understandable once her actions are known. Badeau's characterizations of Mary seem to be true, yet full of hyperbole, and at the time were both verified and refuted by other witnesses. The Mary Lincoln section (chapter 41) was excerpted as "Adam Badeau's Letter: A History of the Insanity of Mrs. President Lincoln," *Chicago Tribune*, Jan. 17, 1887, 10 (entry 180).

10.
Herndon, William H., and Jesse W. Weik. *Herndon's Lincoln: The True Story of a Great Life*. 3 vols. N.Y.: Belford, Clarke & Company, 1889. Vol. 1: pp. vii–199, vol. 2: pp. 205–418, vol. 3: pp. 423–638; illus.

This work is the most influential—and damning—book ever published concerning Mary Lincoln. After first stating that Abraham Lincoln never loved another woman after the death of his sweetheart Ann Rutledge, Herndon portrays Mary as a relentless, ambitious, vicious shrew who tormented her husband and thereby drove him away from home and into political greatness. Herndon intensely disliked Mary (although he repeatedly denied it and even claimed that he respected her so much that he was telling the painful truth about her before other, less-friendly people could) and so anything he stated about her should never be blindly accepted as fact—which is not to say that everything he wrote about her was incorrect, just suspect without verification. As the foundation of nearly all subsequent interpretations about Mary, this book is an essential read for any study of her life. An excellent updated edition of *Herndon's Lincoln* with annotations and other additions, edited by Douglas L. Wilson and Rodney O. Davis, was published in 2006 by University of Illinois Press. To understand Herndon's perceptions of Mary, it is also necessary to read his comments and letters about her, which can be found in *The Real Lincoln: A Portrait*, by Jesse W. Weik (entry 23); *The Hidden Lincoln: From the Letters and Papers of William H. Herndon*, by Emanuel Hertz (entry 37); and *Herndon on Lincoln: Letters*, edited by Douglas L. Wilson and Rodney O. Davis (entry 118).

11.
Stoddard, William O. *Inside the White House in War Times*. N.Y.: Charles L. Webster & Co., 1890. 244 pp. illus.

A memoir by Abraham Lincoln's "third" White House secretary, whose job was often to deal with the needs and desires of Mary Lincoln. Stoddard's previously unpublished reminiscences reveal aspects of Mary's life as first lady such as her role as White House hostess, the relentless public criticisms she endured, the accusations of her traitorous or unethical conduct as first lady, her visits to soldiers in Union hospitals, and even considerations about her mental health. Stoddard portrays Mary as a mercurial woman with a vicious temper but also as a kind and well-intentioned woman easily led astray by others and unfairly maligned by the press. Stoddard was a keen observer of events and people around him, and his years of close proximity to Mary, along with his fearless descriptions of both her virtues and her faults, make this book essential reading for better understanding Mary's White House years. Reprinted in 2000 by the University of Nebraska Press, edited by Michael Burlingame and supplemented by thirteen of Stoddard's "White House Sketches," which were previously published in 1866.

12.
Maynard, Nettie Colburn. *Was Abraham Lincoln a Spiritualist? or, Curious Revelations from the Life of a Trance Medium.* Philadelphia: Rufus C. Hartranft, 1891. 264 pp., illus.

Memoir of a young female spiritualist who held numerous séances with Mary Lincoln both in and out of the White House. This book tells firsthand many of the now-famous spiritualist stories from the Lincoln presidency, such as the floating piano tale at the Laurie house in Georgetown, but Maynard also imbues her text with the personalities of both of the Lincolns, and she shows glimpses of Mary's traits of excitability, devotion to her husband, emotional fragility and matronly kindness. An interesting book that offers glimpses and anecdotes— generally verified by other contemporary sources—of Mary Lincoln in private and as a believer in the spiritualist religion. Of all the supposed spiritualists in Mary's life who wrote memoirs, this one not only rings most authentic but is generally accepted by scholars as the most authentic as well. See for example Jay Monaghan's excellent 1941 article, "Was Abraham Lincoln Really a Spiritualist?" (entry 250).

13.
Whitney, Henry C. *Life on the Circuit with Lincoln.* Boston: Estes and Lauriat, 1892. 601 pp., illus.

This memoir by a friend and colleague of Abraham Lincoln treats Mary Lincoln as a wrongly maligned martyr in her own right (pp. 90–102). She is portrayed as a highly ambitious yet deeply devoted wife who certainly had her faults but also had many virtues. Whitney states that the Lincolns had a thoroughly loving marriage, that Mary was a great encouragement and was "the emery, corundum and polishing wheels" that fashioned her husband into a great statesman, and that she went insane after the assassination. Reprinted with annotations and index added by Paul M. Angle in 1940 by the Caxton Press.

14.

Porter, Gen. Horace. *Campaigning with Grant.* N.Y.: The Century Co., 1897. 546 pp., illus., index.

Porter's memoir of his service in the Civil War under Gen. Ulysses S. Grant contains multiple anecdotes of seeing and meeting Mary Lincoln, including her infamous trip to City Point, Va., in 1865. Contrary to Adam Badeau's account of Mary's temper tantrum, however, Porter eschews the incident and says only that Mary was in a bad mood and did not enjoy the day.

15.

Tarbell, Ida M. *The Life of Abraham Lincoln.* 2 vols. N.Y.: Lincoln Memorial Association, 1900. Vol. 1: 429 pp., vol. 2: 475 pp., app., index.

A biography of Abraham Lincoln that contains an excellent examination of the Lincoln-Todd engagement, broken engagement, and marriage (1:170–191). Tarbell specifically makes the case against William Herndon's story of Lincoln leaving Mary standing at the altar in 1841 and of a subsequently unhappy marriage as false, and instead asserts the engagement was broken by Lincoln's fear of inadequacy as a husband. Excerpted in Tarbell, "The Loves of Lincoln," *New York Times,* Nov. 29, 1908, 1 (entry 196).

16.

Logan, Mrs. John A. *Thirty Years in Washington.* Hartford, Conn.: A. D. Worthington & Co., 1901. 752 pp., illus.

This fascinating book, published by subscription only, offers itself as a guide to the buildings, departments, people, and workings of the federal government from its inception to the beginning of the twentieth century, as well as providing biographical portraits of the presidents and first ladies from Washington to McKinley. The author, the wife of a U.S. senator, Civil War general, and vice presidential candidate, lived in Washington from 1858 to 1888 and personally knew and experienced much of what she wrote, and her book is a common reference for historians writing about presidential and governmental history in the Gilded Age. The thirteen pages (pp. 643–655) devoted to Mary Lincoln—whom Mrs. Logan knew personally—paint a wholly unflattering picture, portraying Mary as vain, highly temperamental, selfish, and, ultimately, "semi-insane." "It will ever be to the regret of all loyal women that Mrs. Lincoln failed to rise to the height of her magnificent opportunities," Mrs. Logan wrote, "At the time when the need of her country was the greatest for the highest, holiest ministration of women, she [was] engrossed in trivialities."

17.

Villard, Henry. *Memoirs of Henry Villard: Journalist and Financier, 1835–1900.* Vol. 1. Boston: Houghton, Mifflin and Company, 1904. 436 pp. illus., maps, chronology.

Only the first of Villard's two-volume memoir contains references to Mary Lincoln—and they are not flattering. Unlike Villard's reporting in the *New York Herald*, which depicted Mary as a plucky, no-nonsense matron, his memoirs offer how he really felt about Abraham Lincoln's wife. Villard depicts her as a liability to her great husband: weak, gullible, self-centered, vain, and "at heart a secessionist." Villard's comments are worth noting in that he, as a reporter often in the White House and generally in the know around Washington, gives insight into Mary's social susceptibility to flattery. Villard tells how Mary "allowed herself to be persuaded" to accept presents in exchange for influence in her husband's appointments, and how her vanity and gullibility led her to surround herself with a sometimes unsavory set of characters, such as the "Chevalier" Henry Wikoff.

18.

Fuller, Frank. *A Day with the Lincoln Family.* N.Y.: Hotel Irving, 1905. 3 pp., illus.

The author, who met Robert Lincoln at Phillips Exeter Academy, describes a visit to Lincoln's Springfield, Illinois, home in July 1860. While the mention of Mary Lincoln in this pamphlet is brief, Fuller testifies to Mary's love of poetry both in Springfield and in the White House.

19.

Gerry, Margarita Spalding, ed. *Through Five Administrations: Reminiscences of Colonel William H. Crook.* N.Y.: Harper & Brothers Publishers, 1907. 280 pp., illus.

These reminiscences of one of President Abraham Lincoln's bodyguards, who served in the White House from November 1864 until after the assassination, offers observations of Mary Lincoln's appearance, her role as White House mistress and social hostess, her 1865 visit to the army headquarters in City Point, Virginia, and her character in the days and weeks after her husband's murder. Crook was a witness to Mary's infamous outburst against Mrs. General James Ord at City Point, although he does not offer details in his book. He also accompanied Mary, Robert, and Tad Lincoln to Chicago in May 1865 when they left the White House. Overall, Crook's reminiscences do not offer extensive testimony about Mary but do contain a number of interesting historical gems.

20.
Tripler, Eunice. *Eunice Tripler: Some Notes of Her Personal Recollections.* N.Y.: The Grafton Press, 1910. 184 pp., illus., index.

Tripler, the wife of Gen. Charles Stuart Tripler, the medical director of the Army of the Potomac from 1861 to 1862, offers interesting—and not terribly flattering—glimpses of Mary Lincoln during the Civil War. Some of Tripler's characterizations of the first lady include "ugly," "ridiculous," and "virago." Tripler also includes contemporary gossip about Mary stealing from the federal purse by firing employees in order to spend more money on herself, getting White House staff commissioned as army officers and keeping their pay, selling manure from the White House stables in order to spend it on official entertainments (rather than her own money, as was the custom with first families), and trying to steal White House silver when she moved out in 1865. While some of Tripler's stories sound a bit exaggerated, many reiterate known bad behaviors of Mary Lincoln as first lady.

21.
Smith, Adelaide W. *Reminiscences of an Army Nurse during the Civil War.* N.Y.: Greaves Publishing Company, 1911. 263 pp., illus.

This work recounts Mary Lincoln's visit to a Philadelphia army hospital and the first lady's care and kindness to the patients, and reprints the letter of a wounded soldier who tells of the first lady's generosity to him and his friend. It also describes Mary's appearance during a White House reception.

22.
Rankin, Henry B. *Personal Recollections of Abraham Lincoln.* N.Y.: G. P. Putnam's Sons, 1916. 412 pp., illus., index.

These recollections of Lincoln's Springfield years supposedly by a student in Lincoln's law office contain extensive stories of Mary Lincoln as a wonderful woman, wife, and mother; a woman without whom Lincoln never would have been president; and a deeply misunderstood person. Rankin's hagiographic reflections of Mary were written as a direct challenge and contradiction to her portrayal as a ruthless shrew in William Herndon's 1889 *Herndon's Lincoln* (entry 10). Historian Michael Burlingame has proven, however, that Rankin never lived in Springfield in the 1850s nor studied in the Lincoln-Herndon Law Office, that he waited to publish his book until all persons who could contradict him were dead, and that he merely wanted to write himself into the Lincoln lore. Rankin's book is considered unreliable by Lincoln scholars, yet its long history as a source, however dubious, requires its inclusion in any bibliography. See Burlingame, "'A Hard-Hearted Conscious Liar and an Oily Hypocrite': Henry B. Rankin's Reliability as a Lincoln Informant," in Jesse W. Weik, *The Real Lincoln: A Portrait*, ed. Michael Burlingame, 389–398 (1922; repr., Lincoln: University of Nebraska Press, 2003).

23.

Weik, Jesse W. *The Real Lincoln: A Portrait*. Boston: Houghton Mifflin Company, 1922. 323 pp., illus., index.

A portrait of Abraham Lincoln's Springfield years written by William Herndon's one-time collaborator, the book is founded on Herndon's research and conclusions but based on Weik's own supplemental investigations. Weik's brief portrayal of Mary Lincoln is redolent of his mentor Herndon: Mary was relentlessly ambitious, with an ungovernable temper and haughty air, who prodded Lincoln to success both by her encouragement and by her shrewish nature driving him out of the house and into political greatness. Reprinted in 2003 by University of Nebraska Press, edited and with additional materials added by Michael Burlingame.

24.

Bradford, Gamaliel. *Wives*. N.Y.: Harper & Brothers, 1925. 298 pp., illus., notes, index.

This book about the wives of famous men and how they influenced, or were influenced by, their husbands, offers an impressively shrewd analysis of Mary Lincoln's character based on the scant sources available at the time. Bradford portrays Mary not only as a good mother in a typical marriage but also as an incredibly ambitious woman whose temper and sheer bad luck made her numerous enemies as first lady. Bradford paints a decidedly realistic portrait of Mary, midway between William Herndon's castigations and Henry B. Rankin's hagiography. Chapter 2, on Mary Lincoln, was also excerpted as "The Wife of Abraham Lincoln," *Harper's Monthly* 151 (Sept. 1925): 489–498.

25.

Pease, Theodore Calvin, and James G. Randall, eds. *The Diary of Orville Hickman Browning*. 2 vols. Collections of the Illinois State Historical Library, vols. 20, 22; Lincoln Series, vols. 2–3. Springfield: Trustees of the Illinois State Historical Library, 1925. Vol. 1: 700 pp., vol. 2: 698 pp.

Browning, a longtime Lincoln family friend in Illinois and a U.S. senator during the Civil War, includes numerous mentions of Mary Lincoln in his diary. Most of the references simply state that he visited, talked with, or took a carriage ride with Mary, but a few have more substance. Browning's diary mentions Mary telling him about a spiritualist séance she attended in 1862, his observances of the Lincoln family after the death of Willie Lincoln, and Mary's state of mind after her husband's assassination. While the diary gives a useful insight into the everyday life of Mary and her family from a friend's perspective, perhaps more interesting are the parts about Mary intentionally left out of the published diary. These omissions, opened to the public in 1994 although not yet published, show Mary in a bad light. The entries accuse her of padding White House bills, charging taxpayers for personal expenses, accepting bribes to secure lucrative government appointments, and leaking the president's private papers to a reporter. The fact that these accusations were made in the private diary of a longtime family friend give them much greater credence than if they were made by opposition newspapers or politicians, and verify a darker side of Mary's character while she was first lady.

26.
Barton, William E. *The Women Lincoln Loved.* Indianapolis: Bobbs-Merrill, 1927. 377 pp., illus.

Barton provides a sketch of Abraham Lincoln's life against the background of the women who were an important part of his world: his grandmothers, mother, sister, step-mother, childhood crushes, mature relationships, and his wife. Barton devotes nearly half the book to Mary Todd Lincoln, and offers a sympathetic cradle-to-grave biography of her in 158 pages. He portrays Mary as a lively, intelligent woman, with a quick temper and a great ambition, but overall as a loving and beloved wife and mother. Barton did an impressive amount of research for all his Lincoln work during the early twentieth century, and his books, including this one, are well worth reading today.

27.
Helm, Katherine. *The True Story of Mary, Wife of Lincoln: Containing the Recollections of Mary Lincoln's Sister Emilie (Mrs. Ben Hardin Helm), Extracts from Her War-Time Diary, Numerous Letters and Other Documents Now First Published.* N.Y.: Harper & Brothers, 1928. 299 pp., illus.

Written by Mary Lincoln's niece with the aid and encouragement of Robert T. Lincoln, this is the only "authorized" biography of Mary ever written. It is short, general, and hagiographic in nature but contains family materials and reminiscences found no place else, including transcriptions of letters and diaries that no longer exist. An essential read for anyone who seeks to know Mary Lincoln.

28.
Goltz, Carlos W. *Incidents in the Life of Mary Todd Lincoln: Containing an Unpublished Letter.* Sioux City, Iowa: Deitch & Lamar Company, 1928. 58 pp.

This short work offers stories of various incidents throughout Mary Lincoln's life from her girlhood and Springfield years. The main purpose of the book, however, was to reveal a previously unpublished letter from Mary to her Springfield friend Julia Ann Sprigg (written shortly after Willie Lincoln's death in 1862) as well as an unpublished reminiscence of Mary by Julia Isabelle Sprigg who, as a child, often played at the Lincoln home with the two youngest Lincoln sons.

29.
Morrow, Honoré Willsie. *Mary Todd Lincoln: An Appreciation of the Wife of Abraham Lincoln.* N.Y.: William Morrow & Co., 1928. 248 pp., illus.

Morrow herself called the book "an irregular sort of life story"; it begins with a forty-page essay describing Morrow's primary research and raw historical findings, then tells of Mary Lincoln's life based on the author's discoveries but with fictionalized dialogue. This is an excellently researched book on Mary for its time and has value as an informational source since Morrow quotes, in full, primary source writings on Mary by people who knew her, such as William Herndon, Emilie Todd Helm, Elizabeth Todd Grimsley, William Stoddard, and many others.

30.
Townsend, William H. *Lincoln and His Wife's Home Town.* Indianapolis: Bobbs-Merrill, 1929. 402 pp., illus., notes, bib., index.

Although focused on Lincoln's personal contacts with slavery, which largely centered on his wife's family and her home town of Lexington, Kentucky, this book contains a history of the Todd family and an excellent portrait of Mary Ann Todd as a young girl, as well as much information on her years as Mrs. Abraham Lincoln. Townsend's primary sources included information from Mary's half-sister Emilie Todd Helm and her niece Katherine Helm that no longer exists (like Emilie's diary) or can no longer be found.

31.
Phillips, Catherine Coffin. *Cornelius Cole: California Pioneer and United States Senator.* San Francisco: John Henry Nash, 1929. 379 pp., illus., bib., index.

This biography of U.S. senator Cornelius Cole, who, along with his wife, Olive, was friendly with President and Mrs. Lincoln during the Civil War, is based on Cole family diaries, letters, and writings. The book contains statements, anecdotes, and opinions about Mary Lincoln as wife, mother, and first lady published no place else. It also includes a mention of Mary's 1872 spirit photograph, a copy of which she sent to Olive Cole shortly after it was taken.

32.
Bayne, Julia Taft. *Tad Lincoln's Father*. Boston: Little, Brown & Company, 1931. 206 pp., illus.

This view of the Lincoln family in the White House by a teenage girl is one of the more endearing books in the Lincoln canon. Bayne, a daily visitor to the White House at ages sixteen to seventeen whose brothers were friends with the Lincoln boys, offers reminiscences of the Lincolns as a family and as her friends, rather than as historic giants in a time of civil war. Through Bayne's eyes, Mary Lincoln is portrayed as a warm and friendly matron, a loving mother and wife, and also a strong woman who encourages the young girl to speak her mind. This wonderful book offers some of the best views of Mary's character as mother and first lady in the bibliography. Excerpted in parts in "Willie and Tad Lincoln," *St. Nicholas* 24, no. 4 (Feb. 1897): 277–282; "Tad Lincoln's Father," *Atlantic Monthly* 133, no. 5 (May 1924); and "Julia Taft Bayne Recalls Good Times in the White House," *Dearborn [Michigan] Independent*, Feb. 12, 1927, 12–13. Reprinted in 2001 by University of Nebraska Press.

33.
Stoltz, Charles. *The Tragic Career of Mary Todd Lincoln*. South Bend, Ind.: Round Table, 1931. 62 pp.

This small book, written by a physician with experience dealing with mental disorders, is an interesting survey of Mary Lincoln as partner to her husband and then as beleaguered widow. Stoltz finds Mary and Abraham to be "an intellectual match" not incongruous to their varied upbringings, and also characterizes Mary as a "born politician" without whom her husband never would have been such a political success. As a widow, Stoltz finds, Mary was beset by sorrow in the deaths of her siblings, children, and husband, stung by vituperative journalists and an apathetic Congress, and inevitably the victim of a mental collapse.

34.
Evans, W. A. *Mrs. Abraham Lincoln: A Study of Her Personality and Her Influence on Lincoln*. N.Y.: Alfred A. Knopf, 1932. 364 pp., illus., bib., index.

This is the first complete history and analysis of Mary Lincoln written by a physician. It examines her family history, upbringing and childhood, marriage, motherhood, and daily life, as well the known symptoms of her mental and physical health, to attempt an understanding of her personality and influence on her husband. The book, which includes information based on interviews with some of Mary's surviving friends, family, and acquaintances, was considered the essential biography of Mary Lincoln for decades. Today it is largely overlooked, yet it remains one of the best books written about her, particularly since it is impressively objective in its conclusions. Reprinted in 2010 by Southern Illinois University Press with a new foreword by Jason Emerson.

35.

Sandburg, Carl, and Paul M. Angle. *Mary Lincoln: Wife and Widow.* N.Y.: Harcourt, Brace, and Company, 1932. 357 pp., illus., app., index.

This biography of Mary Lincoln occurs in two parts: part 1 is a sympathetic narrative biography written by Sandburg in which he depicts the Lincoln marriage as one full of love and understanding; part 2 is Mary's life told through a selection of her letters as explained and edited by Angle. An appendix examines the Lincoln-Todd courtship and broken engagement. It is a great resource, especially the documents in part 2, but its limited scope was surpassed with the 1972 publication of *Mary Todd Lincoln: Her Life and Letters* (entry 56).

36.

Gernon, Blaine Brooks. *The Lincolns in Chicago.* Chicago: N.p., 1934. 63 pp.

The second part of this booklet focuses on "Lincoln's Widow and Children in Chicago," and surveys Mary Lincoln's life in that city from 1865 to her death in 1882. It is based on contemporary newspaper accounts and the few biographies of Mary published at the time, and discusses the Lincoln family's general life, where and how they lived, and events such as the Old Clothes Scandal, Mary's battle to receive a congressional pension, and her insanity trials in 1875 and 1876. A well-done work, especially for the period in which it was written.

37.

Hertz, Emanuel. *The Hidden Lincoln: From the Letters and Papers of William H. Herndon.* N.Y.: Viking Press, 1938. 461 pp., illus., app., index.

Hertz described his book as "Herndon's work in Herndon's own language." It is a chronological compilation of letters to and from William Herndon that expands on Abraham Lincoln's life as revealed by Herndon's interviews and research, as well as on the methods and motivations behind Herndon's vast biographical study of Lincoln. The book also includes a section of Herndon's own writings of notes and monographs. The contents elucidate and magnify Herndon's negative characterizations of Mary Lincoln as printed in his 1889 *Herndon's Lincoln* (entry 10) and his reasons for writing them.

38.
Dennett, Tyler, ed. *Lincoln and the Civil War in the Diaries and Letters of John Hay*. N.Y.: Dodd, Mead & Company, 1939. 370 pp., index of persons, index.
These selections from the diary and letters of one of Abraham Lincoln's two White House secretaries reveal interesting anecdotes and impressions of Mary Lincoln as first lady, including her relationship with her husband, her role as White House hostess, her temper, her bad personal conduct, and her many travels. Mary often did not get along with her husband's secretaries, and so the portrait of her as seen through Hay's eyes is not always flattering. Reprinted by Da Capo Press in 1988 with a new foreword by Henry Steele Commager.

39.
Villard, Harold G., and Oswald Garrison Villard, eds. *Lincoln on the Eve of '61: A Journalist's Story by Henry Villard*. N.Y.: Alfred A. Knopf, 1941. 105 pp.
This edited collection compiles the reporting of Henry Villard, correspondent for the *New York Herald*, about presidential candidate and president-elect Abraham Lincoln from late 1860 to early 1861. Villard, who reported from Springfield and as a passenger on the inaugural train journey to Washington, includes some comments about Mary Lincoln in his daily observations. Villard's stories include some now-commonly-told tales, including Mary's "pluck" at declaring she would ride the entire inaugural journey with her husband and see him installed in the White House despite rumors of attacks and assassination attempts; her shopping trip to New York and the fact that she returned home three days late, during which the president-elect waited for her arrival at the train station each evening; and Mary's preparations for leaving Springfield for Washington. Though Villard's depictions of Mary in his newspaper reports are laudatory, he has little positive to say about her in his memoirs.

40.
Larrimore, Hazel Rice. *Stories of Abraham and Mary Todd Lincoln in and about Springfield*. Chautauqua, N.Y.: Chautauqua Literary and Scientific Circle, 1942. 18 pp.
This interesting little booklet offers some facts and stories about Mary Lincoln from conversations and writings of Mary's family, friends, and neighbors.

They include a diary entry from Mrs. Benjamin F. Edwards (related to Mary through marriage) about the day and the manner in which Mary Todd and Abraham Lincoln were married, an interview with a Lincoln family neighbor discussing the "married happiness" of the Lincolns, and a reminiscence about the Lincolns' personalities by a group of church women who knew Mary and Abraham in Springfield. Whether a reader trusts these reminiscences as accurate or not, they corroborate the same statements told in numerous other sources in the Mary bibliography.

41.
Washington, John E. *They Knew Lincoln*. N.Y.: E. P. Dutton, 1942. 244 pp., illus., app.
This rare book is a look at Abraham Lincoln through interviews with African Americans who knew him, mainly the black White House servants. While the narrative focuses on Abraham, there are a number of reminiscences about Mary Lincoln by the interviewees. There is also nearly forty pages concerning Mary's seamstress Elizabeth Keckley, her relationship with Mary, and the creation of and reaction to her 1868 book, *Behind the Scenes; or, Thirty Years a Slave and Four Years in the White House* (entry 1). According to Washington, the White House servants loved Mary and said she treated them kindly and with respect. Washington also declares that Keckley always said Mary knew she was writing the book, never had any hard feelings about it, and continued friendly communication with Keckley in later years. This is an important statement, if it can be believed, because historians have always maintained Keckley's book caused an irreparable rift between her and Mary. Overall, this important historical work offers rare glimpses into Mary's role as mistress of the White House, as well as gives the story of Keckley's book and its impact on the Keckley-Lincoln relationship. Reprinted by Oxford University Press in 2018 with an introduction by Kate Masur.

42.
Pratt, Harry E. *The Personal Finances of Abraham Lincoln*. Springfield, Ill.: The Abraham Lincoln Association, 1943. 198 pp., illus., app., index.
This is the first and still most authoritative investigation of Abraham Lincoln's personal finances as a way to shed new light on his life. The book offers much insight into Mary Lincoln's life through finances as well, including drug store receipts from her everyday life in Springfield, purchases she made of books to put in the White House, an examination of the administration of Abraham Lincoln's estate after his death, as well as a brief narrative describing Mary's personal finances from 1865 to 1882.

43.
Wilson, Rufus Rockwell. *Intimate Memories of Lincoln*. Elmira, N.Y.: The Primavera Press, 1942. 629 pp., index.

Wilson's book of sixty compiled firsthand reminiscences about Abraham Lincoln, many of them unpublished at the time, covers all phases of his life. Multiple entries include mentions of Mary Lincoln on subjects such as her determination to make her husband president, her kindness, her early days after her son Robert's birth, her fits of temper and how Abraham handled them, how she disciplined Tad on one occasion, how she donated liquor to army hospitals, her love for poetry, and her ideas to simplify the help and condition of affairs in the White House when she was first lady. An excellent book of some primary source materials on Mary.

44.
Snow, Florence L. *Pictures on My Wall: A Lifetime in Kansas*. Lawrence: University of Kansas Press, 1945. 161 pp., illus.

This memoir through personal letters contains one remarkable entry in which Snow, who as a child was a friend of Mary "Mamie" Lincoln—Robert Lincoln's daughter—recalls spending the summer of 1882 at the Harlan house in Mt. Pleasant, Iowa, during which she witnessed Mary Harlan Lincoln going through her dead mother-in-law's numerous trunks of possessions. Snow also remembered asking Mamie what she thought about having Abraham and Mary Lincoln as her grandparents. Reprinted in "Some Intimate Glimpses into the Private Lives of the Members of the Robert Lincoln Family," *Lincoln Lore*, no. 1525, Mar. 1965.

45.
Donald, David. *Lincoln's Herndon*. N.Y.: Alfred A. Knopf, 1948. 378 pp., index.

This biography of William Herndon also examines his relationship with Mary Lincoln during and after Abraham Lincoln's death; Herndon's opinions and conclusions about Mary as woman, wife, and mother; his research and writing of *Herndon's Lincoln*; and his motivations for portraying Mary so negatively—which he believed would actually benefit her legacy. This is the first book to seek to understand why Herndon treated Mary so harshly as a historical subject and is necessary reading for anyone interested in the Herndon-Mary dynamic.

46.
Nicolay, Helen. *Lincoln's Secretary: A Biography of John G. Nicolay*. N.Y.: Longmans, Green, and Co., 1949. 363 pp., illus., index.

Nicolay's work is a detailed look inside Abraham Lincoln's White House, using her father's own words, her own reminiscences of facts and stories her father told her, and information she gleaned from friends and colleagues of her father, including the president's only living son, Robert T. Lincoln. Nicolay offers numerous glimpses into Mary Lincoln's character and life during the Civil War, such as how she looked and what she wore, her relationship with her husband, and her relationship with the presidential secretaries. Some of the more detailed and interesting events related include Mary's social rivalry with Kate Chase, daughter of the treasury secretary, the unrelenting criticism of the first lady during the war years, and John Nicolay's written opinions on whether Mary was a Confederate sympathizer and whether she truly acted so outrageously against Mrs. General Ord and Mrs. Grant at City Point in 1865. Overall, it is an excellent book filled with primary information directly from the mouth and pen of President Lincoln's main secretary.

47.
Randall, Ruth Painter. *Mary Lincoln: Biography of a Marriage*. Boston: Little, Brown & Company, 1953. 555 pp., illus., notes, bib., index.
This cradle-to-grave biography of Mary Lincoln, with a focus on her marriage to Abraham, was the first about Mary written by a professional historian. Considered by many the best researched biography of Mary ever written, its greatest flaw is its overtly apologetic tone—its magnification of Mary's virtues and minimization of her vices—which arguably makes the book more advocacy than objective historical examination. Randall takes special efforts to rebut and rebuke the negative interpretations of Mary by William Herndon.

48.
———. *Lincoln's Sons*. Boston: Little, Brown & Company, 1955. 373 pp., illus., bib., index.
This story of Lincoln's children contains much information on Mary Lincoln as a wife and a mother, especially her relationship with her oldest son, Robert. Randall's book was the first work at the time to cover this subject, and it remains the only resource dedicated to the lives of the Lincoln children, Mary as a mother, and Mary's relationship with Robert. It is an excellent study, but its effectiveness and trustworthiness are severely diminished—or at least open to question—by the lack of any source citations in the form of endnotes, although it does have an extensive bibliography.

49.
———. *The Courtship of Mr. Lincoln*. Boston: Little, Brown & Co., 1957. 219 pp., illus.

A detailed examination of the Abraham Lincoln–Mary Todd romance and marriage that focuses on refuting the negative stories promulgated by William Herndon. Randall portrays the Lincolns as a loving couple in a happy marriage despite the differences in their backgrounds and temperaments. She gives great attention to the stormy courtship and broken engagement, and declares Lincoln never left Mary at the altar as Herndon said. Randall wrote this book after feeling her examination of the subject in her previous work, *Mary Lincoln: Biography of a Marriage*, was too cursory. Similar to her book on the Lincoln marriage, *The Courtship of Mr. Lincoln* also can be criticized for its apologetic nature.

50.
King, Willard L. *Lincoln's Manager: David Davis*. Cambridge, Mass.: Harvard University Press, 1960. 383 pp., illus., notes, bib., index.
    This biography of Lincoln's longtime friend, legal colleague, and presidential campaign manager David Davis contains a wealth of previously unpublished primary information from Davis's family letters regarding Mary Lincoln, especially her married life and relationship with Lincoln in Springfield and her post-assassination life. The book offers a detailed look at Mary from 1865 to 1882, especially in how she dealt with her general lifestyle, her finances, her public image, her mental health, and her relationship with son Robert. As the executor of the Lincoln estate and the man Robert went to as a "second father," Davis had the best inside view of the Lincoln family during the post-assassination years from anyone outside the immediate family.

51.
Temple, Wayne C., ed. *Mrs. Frances Jane (Todd) Wallace Describes Lincoln's Wedding*. Harrogate, Tenn.: Lincoln Memorial University Press, 1960. 12 pp.
    Temple's pamphlet reprints an original 1895 newspaper interview with Frances Todd Wallace, Mary Lincoln's sister, concerning the Lincolns' courtship, wedding, and home life. Mrs. Wallace offers direct rebuttal to the then-accepted statements of William Herndon that the Lincoln marriage was unhappy and that Lincoln once left Mary standing at the altar. "They certainly did live happily together—as much as any man and woman I have ever known," Mrs. Wallace said. The pamphlet also explains the publication history of the article.

52.
———, ed. *Mrs. Mary Edwards Brown Tells Story of Lincoln's Wedding*. Harrogate, Tenn.: Lincoln Memorial University Press, 1960. 8 pp.

This pamphlet contains a transcript and brief historical explanation of a 1920 newspaper interview with Mary Lincoln's grandniece concerning the arrangements, nuptial service, and scene of the Lincoln-Todd wedding in 1842 based on Todd family tradition.

53.
Croy, Homer. *The Trial of Mrs. Abraham Lincoln.* N.Y.: Duell, Sloan, and Pearce, 1962. 148 pp., app., index.

The first book dedicated to the story of Mary Lincoln's insanity trial and institutionalization in 1875, it is supposedly based on historical research—almost exclusively from Chicago newspapers in 1875—but Croy added dialogue and events as they "must have" occurred as he "understood" the characters, which resulted in much historical inaccuracy. He posits the theory that Mary was a perfectly sane woman railroaded into the asylum by a cruel and vicious son intent on stealing her money. This book should be considered more as fiction than nonfiction and has no historical value other than as entertainment.

54.
Ostendorf, Lloyd. *The Photographs of Mary Todd Lincoln.* Springfield: Illinois State Historical Society, 1969. 64 pp., illus.

Reprinted from *Journal of the Illinois State Historical Society* 61, no. 3 (Autumn 1968): 269–332. This small book is the first attempt to enumerate and catalogue all twenty-six known photographs of Mary Lincoln, including some previously unknown to the public at the time of publication.

55.
Simmons, Dawn Langley. *A Rose for Mrs. Lincoln: A Biography of Mary Todd Lincoln.* Boston: Beacon Press, 1970. 197 pp., illus., sel. bib.

This general, sympathetic biography of Mary Lincoln from birth to death paints her as a strong, passionate woman who was an essential element to her husband's political success, and who, after his murder, suffered a tragic widowhood. It is a book intended for popular audiences based on secondary sources.

56.
Turner, Justin G., and Linda Levitt Turner. *Mary Todd Lincoln: Her Life and Letters.* N.Y.: Alfred A. Knopf, 1972. 750 pp., illus., app., bib., index.

A book on Mary Lincoln's life as chronologically told and supplemented by her complete (at the time) correspondence. The Turners' work is an impressively

objective biography that focuses on factual presentation rather than historical interpretation. This is one of the best books on Mary in print, yet, with the discovery
of numerous letters in subsequent years, a work sorely in need of updating.

57.
Ross, Ishbel. *The President's Wife: Mary Todd Lincoln; A Biography.* N.Y.: G. P.
Putnam's Sons, 1973. 378 pp., illus., notes, bib., index.
    Ross's well-researched and well-written biography of Mary Lincoln seeks a
sympathetic understanding of her life, her marriage, and her influence on her
husband.

58.
Stone, Irving. *Mary Todd Lincoln: A Final Judgement?* Springfield, Ill.: Abraham
Lincoln Association, 1973. 16 pp.
    This thoughtful and thought-provoking speech by Stone to the Abraham Lin-
coln Association examines the various stages of Mary Lincoln's life—Lexington,
Springfield, Washington, post-Washington—and concludes she was a loving
wife and mother, a large influence on her husband's political success, a "brilliant" first lady unfairly criticized by the press, and the victim of character assassination by William Herndon. Son Willie's death in 1862 is portrayed as the
beginning of Mary's mental decline; unfortunately, Stone's account of Mary's
institutionalization is full of errors.

59.
Simon, John Y., ed. *The Personal Memoirs of Julia Dent Grant (Mrs. Ulysses S.
Grant).* N.Y.: G. P. Putnam's Sons, 1975. 346 pp., illus., notes, index.
    While the book's subject is Mrs. Grant, with heavy emphasis on her mar-
ried life, the manuscript does contain a few golden nuggets of anecdote and
observation about First Lady Mary Lincoln. These include mainly Mrs. Grant's
interactions with Mary in the final months of the war at City Point, Virginia,
where Julia reveals, and in one case clearly resents, Mary's condescending at-
titude toward those she found inferior in social rank or, in Mrs. Grant's case, a
potential threat to her status as first lady. Mrs. Grant also wrote about Mary's
moments of jealousy and indignation concerning other women getting close to
her husband while traveling out to the battlefront. Adam Badeau's characterizations of the same incidents were printed in his 1887 book *Grant in Peace from
Appomattox to Mount McGregor: A Personal Memoir* (entry 9) and in the article
"Adam Badeau's Letter: A History of the Insanity of Mrs. President Lincoln,"
Chicago Tribune, Jan. 17, 1887, 10 (entry 180).

60.

Ward, Geoffrey C. *Lincoln and His Family.* Springfield, Ill.: Sangamon State University, 1978. 28 pp.

A survey of the Lincoln family's life in Springfield, from the courtship and marriage of Abraham and Mary, through the raising of their four children, until Lincoln was elected president in 1860. This is an indispensable little pamphlet that gives all the relevant details of the Lincolns in Springfield and offers insights into their personalities. For Mary, this work shows her as a woman, a wife, and a mother, and gives some understanding to her life in Springfield before the turbulent White House years. There is also a list of works for further reading on the Lincoln household in the back. This pamphlet was one in a series of six published about Abraham Lincoln for "public educational purposes," and its text was reviewed by nine historians, including four of the leading Lincoln scholars of their day: Roy P. Basler, Richard N. Current, Don E. Fehrenbacher, and Robert W. Johannsen.

61.

Strozier, Charles B. *Lincoln's Quest for Union: Public and Private Meanings.* N.Y.: Basic Books, 1982. 271 pp., illus., notes, index.

This is an excellent psychobiography of Abraham Lincoln by a trained psychiatrist and historian. Mary Lincoln's psyche also is impressively analyzed (pp. 67–108) to show her complexity and "contrariness" of personality and how it intensified as she grew older; her relationship with her husband, especially how he acted as a father figure and emotional salve for her but they grew apart because of his presidency and the war; how she and William Herndon fought for Lincoln's love and attention like rival siblings, which led to their mutual dislike; how her position as first lady underlined her faults but obscured her virtues; and how the deaths of Willie, Abraham, and Tad crushed her emotionally and mentally.

62.

Brinkley, Phyllis C. *The Lincolns: Targets for Controversy.* Waunakee, Wis.: P. Brinkley, 1985. 77 pp., bib.

This booklet, based entirely on secondary sources (Randall, Sandburg and Angle, Helm, Pratt, and the Turners), reviews the early lives of both Mary Todd and Abraham Lincoln, as well as their lives together as a couple. Mary was a "maligned" historical figure who was "grossly misunderstood" by the American public during her life, according to Brinkley. There is no real "controversy" described in this book, and nothing new at all of either fact or insight.

63.

Neely, Mark E., Jr., and R. Gerald McMurtry. *The Insanity File: The Case of Mary Todd Lincoln.* Carbondale: Southern Illinois University Press, 1986. 203 pp., illus., app., notes, index.

A study of Mary Lincoln's mental health, based on the discovery of Robert Todd Lincoln's personal "Insanity File"—a complete documentary record of his mother's institutionalization at a sanitarium in 1875—this book is well researched and dispassionately objective in its narrative. It examines not only Mary but also the social, medical, and legal context of the time during which she was committed, and how the contemporary social mores may or may not have influenced the decision to have her declared insane. It includes previously unpublished letters by Mary discovered in the insanity file as an appendix.

64.

Baker, Jean H. *Mary Todd Lincoln: A Biography.* New York: W. W. Norton & Company, 1987. 429 pp., illus., notes, index.

A revisionist psychobiography of Mary Lincoln with an overt feminist agenda, Baker's work portrays Mary as a female pioneer in a chauvinistic society. This well-researched work goes farther than nearly every other biography in putting Mary's life within the context of the social and political mores of the time for women of Mary Lincoln's social status—a status that changed during the different periods of her life. Like Ruth Painter Randall's biography, Baker's is more sympathetic than objective when it comes to addressing Mary's faults and mistakes, although not to Randall's degree. Unlike Randall, Baker's palpable hatred of son Robert Lincoln taints and corrupts every interpretation relating to his actions and interactions with his mother. Since Mary's widowhood lasted for seventeen years, during which time Robert was a major part of her life, Baker's misandry perverts a major portion of her historical work and is a critical flaw in the biography. Despite its faults, Baker's book remains the major reference work for Mary's life.

65.

Schreiner, Samuel A., Jr. *The Trials of Mrs. Lincoln.* N.Y.: Donald I. Fine, Inc., 1987. 333 pp., illus., index.

This is an unapologetic defense of Mary Lincoln against the charges of her insanity, and an indictment against Robert Lincoln as a cruel, avaricious monster of a son who wrongly imprisoned his mother. Like *The Insanity File* of Neely and McMurtry (entry 63), this book utilizes Robert Lincoln's "Insanity File" for evidence, but it lacks any sort of citations, it fictionalizes dialogue, and makes no attempt at objectivity. This is a poorly executed book better discarded in favor of Neely and McMurtry's far superior work.

66.
Van der Heuvel, Gerry. *Crowns of Thorns and Glory: Mary Todd Lincoln and Varina Howell Davis; The Two First Ladies of the Civil War.* N.Y.: E. P. Dutton, 1988. 306 pp., notes, bib., index.
This sympathetic biographical portrait of Mary Lincoln and Varina Davis, both as individual women and in comparison of the two as first ladies and the wives of Civil War political leaders, is a well-researched, well-written book.

67.
French, Benjamin Brown. *Witness to the Young Republic: A Yankee's Journal, 1828–1870.* Edited by Donald B. Cole and John J. McDonough. Hanover, N.H.: University Press of New England, 1989. 675 pp., illus., bib., index.
This diary of President Lincoln's commissioner of public buildings, who closely worked with and observed Mary Lincoln nearly day to day for more than three years, is one of the best sources of Mary's personality in public and private while she was in the White House. French's diary offers intimate glimpses of Mary as mother, wife, first lady, hostess, and employer; and gives a firsthand account of her extravagant spending in the White House and of her reactions to son Willie's death in 1862 and her husband's assassination in 1865.

68.
Hickey, James T. *The Collected Writings of James T. Hickey from Publications of the Illinois State Historical Society, 1953–1984.* Springfield: The Illinois State Historical Society, 1990. 232 pp., illus., notes.
This collection of twenty-one articles written by Hickey, former Lincoln curator of the Illinois State Historical Society, and published in the *Journal of the Illinois State Historical Society,* is a necessary addition to any Lincoln bookshelf. Four of the articles in the book contain specific references and information regarding Mary Lincoln. One is a study of the Globe Tavern in Springfield, where Abraham and Mary boarded when first married, and what their lives were like living there; one publishes two previously unpublished letters, one by Mary Lincoln and one describing Mary during the inaugural journey; one describes what Robert Lincoln did to preserve and possibly destroy family letters during his lifetime, with some specific references to his mother's papers;

and one examines the Lincoln account at a local Springfield drugstore from 1849 to 1861 and interprets what the purchases mean about the family's life during that time. These four articles are excellent sources about various times in Mary's life that too often get overlooked.

69.
Friedman, Jane M. *America's First Woman Lawyer: The Biography of Myra Bradwell*. Buffalo, N.Y.: Prometheus Books, 1993. 217 pp., illus., notes, index.
This book tells the life story of abolitionist, feminist, and legal pioneer Myra Bradwell, the first woman in America to pass a state bar exam. Bradwell was a close friend of Mary Lincoln, and one chapter of the book (pp. 47–70) examines how the two women collaborated to achieve Mary's early release from Bellevue Place sanitarium in 1875. The chapter is unique because it examines the event from Bradwell's perspective rather than from Mary's, and it also uses previously ignored contemporary newspaper articles and unpublished Bradwell family manuscripts. These new facts, while important, are, however, misunderstood, misinterpreted, and placed incorrectly within the timeline of events.

70.
Burlingame, Michael. *Honest Abe, Dishonest Mary*. Racine, Wis.: Lincoln Fellowship of Wisconsin, Historical Bulletin no. 50, 1994. 51 pp.
This story of the Lincolns' divergent ethics while living in the White House reveals Mary Lincoln's bad behavior, including influence peddling, bribe taking, account padding, and document leaking. Burlingame's research uncovered a revolutionary new interpretation of Mary as first lady. Revised and reprinted in 2000 as "Mary Todd Lincoln's Unethical Conduct as First Lady" (entry 328).

71.
Peterson, Merrill D. *Lincoln in American Memory*, N.Y.: Oxford University Press, 1994. 482 pp., illus., notes, index.
A history of Abraham Lincoln's place in American thought and imagination from the moment of his death to the present, this book looks at Lincoln through the memorials, memorabilia, historians, and mantle claimers in the years after his death. Mary Lincoln plays a large part in this book as Lincoln's widow, and Peterson delves into her public and private pronouncements on her husband's life and legacy, the books and monuments to him, and the artwork portraying him. Peterson also looks at Mary's historic reputation, how certain historians handled her life, and even how she has been portrayed in modern

films. As such, this book shows Mary Lincoln mainly as Lincoln's widow and opinionator of his life and legacy—a unique perspective in the many writings concerning Mary.

72.

Temple, Wayne C. *Abraham Lincoln: From Skeptic to Prophet.* Mahomet, Ill.: Mayhaven Publishing, 1995. 446 pp., illus., notes, index.

Temple's work is an unparalleled study of Abraham Lincoln's religious views and heritage, containing numerous facts previously unpublished. The book also contains an excellent examination of Mary Lincoln's life before, during, and after her husband's presidency, including her own religious heritage and faith, her belief in spiritualism, the impact of the deaths of her children and husband, and her life as a widow.

73.

Ostendorf, Lloyd, and Walter Olesky, eds. *Lincoln's Unknown Private Life: An Oral History by His Black Housekeeper Mariah Vance, 1850–1860.* Mamaroneck, N.Y.: Hastings House Book Publishing, 1995. 563 pp., illus.

This book, purported to be an oral history of life in the Lincoln home by one of Abraham Lincoln's black housekeepers during the years 1850 to 1860, is one of the most dangerous books in the Lincoln canon—and should never be used as a source. While Mariah Vance did work for the Lincolns, her "recollections" have been proven to be corrupted by the stenographer and the later editors and publishers of the book. Whatever truth there may be in the recollections can now never be discerned, and nothing the book says about Mary Lincoln as wife and mother can be trusted.

74.

Fehrenbacher, Don E., and Virginia Fehrenbacher, eds. *The Recollected Words of Abraham Lincoln.* Stanford, Calif.: Stanford University Press, 1996. 648 pp., notes, index.

Although this book, a comprehensive collection of remarks attributed to Abraham Lincoln by his contemporaries, is focused on Abraham, it also contains approximately two dozen reminiscences about Mary Lincoln. The Mary-centric topics include the 1860 and 1864 presidential elections, her courtship and marriage, her fashions and her furnishing of the White House, her actions at City Point, Virginia, in 1865, Robert's desire to enlist in the army, and her opinions of and interactions with specific individuals in the presidential cabinet and the government. All the Mary Lincoln items in the book are previously known and published, but it is handy to have them compiled in one volume.

75.
Burlingame, Michael, ed. *An Oral History of Abraham Lincoln: John G. Nicolay's Interviews and Essays.* Carbondale: Southern Illinois University Press, 1996. 167 pp., notes, index.

While this collection of previously unpublished interviews and essays by Lincoln's White House secretary is on Abraham Lincoln, the book contains important nuggets of firsthand information on Mary Lincoln, including her personality, her mental health, and her relationship with her husband. The most detailed, and interesting, mentions of Mary include the story of the Lincoln-Todd courtship and Mary's influence in her husband's decision not to accept a position as governor of the Oregon Territory in 1848.

76.
Temple, Wayne C. *Alexander Williamson: Friend of the Lincolns.* Racine: The Lincoln Fellowship of Wisconsin. Serial publication no. 1, 1997. 46 pp., illus., notes.

This work examines Williamson's life and interaction with the Lincoln family during the 1860s. Williamson was hired by Mary Lincoln to tutor Willie and Tad Lincoln in the White House and, after the assassination, became Mary's agent to help her repay debts acquired as first lady. Previously printed as *Alexander Williamson—Tutor to the Lincoln Boys* (Racine: The Lincoln Fellowship of Wisconsin, Historical Bulletin no. 26, 1971). The 1997 revision contains more information on Mary Lincoln.

77.
Brooks, Noah. *Lincoln Observed: Civil War Dispatches of Noah Brooks.* Edited by Michael Burlingame. Baltimore: Johns Hopkins University Press, 1998. 291 pp., notes, index.

A collection of the wartime dispatches, selected letters, and personal reminiscences of California journalist Noah Brooks, who covered the Lincoln White House from 1862 to 1865 and became personal friends with Abraham Lincoln. Through years of daily access to the Lincoln family, Brooks's writings offer firsthand insights into the life and character of First Lady Mary Lincoln on topics such as her appearance, her character and reputation, her White House receptions and role as hostess, and her reaction to her husband's assassination and its aftermath. While many readers are familiar with Brooks's book *Washington in Lincoln's Time*, that work contains only one reference to Mary, while *Lincoln Observed* is an excellent cache of primary material on the first lady.

78.

Rogstad, Steven K. *Companionship in Granite: Celebrating the Abraham and Mary Todd Lincoln Monument*. Racine, Wis.: Kenson Publishing, 1998. 45 pp., illus., notes.

This pamphlet gives a history of the only monument ever erected in honor of Mary Lincoln, which resides in Racine, Wisconsin. It includes an examination of both Mary and Abraham's visits to Wisconsin, especially Mary's 1867 visit to Racine to inspect Racine College for Tad's possible enrollment, as well as an appraisal of Mary's historical legacy. This excellent work about an overlooked monument contains much obscure information about Mary's travels to Wisconsin, as well as a photographic essay on the statue.

79.

Wilson, Douglas L. *Honor's Voice: The Transformation of Abraham Lincoln*. N.Y.: Alfred A. Knopf, 1998. 383 pp., notes, index.

An excellent study of Abraham Lincoln's transformation from small-town shopkeeper to rising politician during the years 1831 to 1842, Wilson's work declares that the "greatest and most consequential" transition for Lincoln during this period "came to focus" in his ill-starred courtship with Mary Todd, which Wilson examines more thoroughly than previously accomplished (pp. 215–292). He contends that the courtship challenged Lincoln's mental stability, his ability to function as a political leader, and his self-confidence, and that Lincoln's marriage to Mary fixed these problems and ultimately assisted him in reaching his goals.

80.

Wilson, Douglas L., and Rodney O. Davis, eds. *Herndon's Informants: Letters, Interviews, and Statements about Abraham Lincoln*. Urbana: University of Illinois Press, 1998. 827 pp., app., index.

This is the first complete publication of William Herndon's research materials and interviews about Abraham Lincoln's life, collected in the late 1860s, and used by Herndon to write his book, *Herndon's Lincoln* (entry 10) in 1889. Herndon's materials are the foundation of all subsequent Lincoln studies, and contain vast amounts of primary materials concerning Mary Todd Lincoln as well, including the Lincoln-Todd courtship and marriage, her character and intellect, her temper and bad behavior, her roles as wife and mother, and her own 1866 interview with Herndon.

81.
Burlingame, Michael, ed. *At Lincoln's Side: John Hay's Civil War Correspondence and Selected Writings.* Carbondale: Southern Illinois University Press, 2000. 294 pp., appendixes, notes, index.

An edited collection of the Civil War–era personal writings of John Hay, one of President Lincoln's private White House secretaries, and a young man with whom Mary Lincoln did not get along. Hay's comments about Mary have become as famous and as often-quoted as those of her other major antagonist, William Herndon. In this volume are some of the professional letters and missives Hay wrote for and to Mary, as well as Hay's personal observations of Mary as first lady, wife, and mother. Also included as an appendix is Burlingame's essay "Mary Todd Lincoln's Unethical Conduct as First Lady"—one of the most eye-opening accounts of Mary's bad behavior ever penned, and essential reading for anyone desiring a well-rounded understanding of Mary's character (entry 328).

82.
Winkler, H. Donald. *The Women in Lincoln's Life.* Nashville, Tenn.: Rutledge Hill Press, 2001. 274 pp., illus., notes, sel. bib., index.

This work is an attempt to explain how Abraham Lincoln was "dramatically shaped" by "a succession of remarkable women," but the book merely glorifies Ann Rutledge (to whom the author is related) and reviles Mary Lincoln. The book portrays Mary as an intolerable termagant—the same basic thesis founded by William Herndon—but contains no original or worthwhile contributions of its own. Reissued in 2004 as *Lincoln's Ladies: The Women in the Life of the Sixteenth President.*

83.
Gary, Ralph V. *Following in Lincoln's Footsteps: A Complete Annotated Reference to Hundreds of Historical Sites Visited by Abraham Lincoln (Illinois).* N.Y.: Basic Books, 2001. 468 pp., appendixes, index.

This book offers a reportedly complete listing of all the geographic sites visited by Abraham Lincoln throughout his life. Arranged by state, and by cities in each state, the book takes readers through every conceivable historic site connected to Lincoln, with brief contextual histories of Lincoln's visit to each location. The book contains extensive references in its listings to Mary Lincoln and where she was during Lincoln's life, as well as an appendix recording all the known (in

2001) geographical sites connected with Mary after April 15, 1865. The history explained in each geographic reference is only of the most basic kind, based on secondary works, but the references to Mary's whereabouts during her life offer a valuable resource to anyone interested in tracking her movements.

84.

Sellers, John R. ed. *Washington during the Civil War: The Diary of Horatio Nelson Taft, 1861–1865*, 3 vols. Washington, D.C.: Manuscript Division, Library of Congress. Published online, Feb. 12, 2002, www.memory.loc.gov/ammem /tafthtml/tafthome.html.

The detailed diary of Taft, who was an examiner for the U.S. Patent Office and whose children were friends of the Lincoln boys and frequent visitors to the White House, mentions Mary Lincoln numerous times, such as her attendance at White House social events and when Taft saw her shopping in Washington. He also comments on relations between the Taft and Lincoln families, how Mary treated his children, and her words and actions the night of her husband's assassination. The diary is scheduled for print publication by the Lincoln Studies Center at Knox College in Galesburg, Illinois.

85.

Pinsker, Matthew. *Lincoln's Sanctuary: Abraham Lincoln and the Soldiers' Home.* N.Y.: Oxford University Press, 2003. 256 pp., illus., chron., notes, bib., index.

The first and definitive study of the Lincolns' time at the "summer White House," the Soldiers' Home, and the events that transpired there during the war, Pinsker's book contains numerous overlooked facts and anecdotes about Mary Lincoln as wife, mother, and first lady, as well as items found in previously unpublished soldiers' letters.

86.

Fleischner, Jennifer. *Mrs. Lincoln and Mrs. Keckly: The Remarkable Story of the Friendship between a First Lady and a Former Slave.* N.Y.: Broadway Books, 2003. 373 pp., illus., notes, index.

The story of the unlikely friendship and personal bond between First Lady Mary Lincoln and her black seamstress Elizabeth Keckly (spelled "Keckley" elsewhere in this bibliography) during and after the White House years. While books on the relationship between Lincoln and Keckly now seem ubiquitous, Fleischner's book was the first—and remains the best. She skillfully plumbs the depths of this friendship, examining how it affected each woman—especially Mary Lincoln and the presence and influence of black women in her life as well as Keckly's role in the Old Clothes Scandal—and even how it offered an insight into race relations at the time.

87.
Hayden, Deborah. *Pox: Genius, Madness, and the Mysteries of Syphilis*. N.Y.: Basic Books, 2003. 400 pp., illus., app., notes, bib., index.
Within this book about famous historical individuals who supposedly suffered from syphilis, the chapter on Mary and Abraham Lincoln (pp. 120–132) examines the possibility that Mary contracted syphilis from her husband. Hayden relies mainly on William Herndon's statement that Lincoln contracted syphilis from a prostitute in 1835 or 1836, which cannot be proven and has been rejected by nearly all Lincoln scholars as unsubstantiated hearsay. Hayden also refers to a previous article published in the *Journal of the History of Medicine and Allied Sciences* that suggests the possibility of syphilis but refuses to make an outright diagnosis.

88.
Dershowitz, Alan M. *America on Trial: Inside the Legal Battles That Transformed Our Nation*. N.Y.: Hachette Book Group, 2004. 586 pp., index.
Renowned civil liberties attorney and legal scholar Dershowitz offers "an episodic history of America as viewed through the prism of its most dramatic and influential court proceedings," from the Salem witch trails in colonial America up through the cases of the 9/11 terrorist detainees at Guantanamo Bay. The post–Civil War period in this fascinating study includes the 1875 insanity trial of Mary Lincoln. Dershowitz offers a balanced summary of Mary's case, giving the provable facts as well as the multiple conspiracy theories. He states that while Mary clearly was "a disturbed and eccentric woman," legal cases such as hers "are rarely black and white . . . [and] make it impossible to point a finger of blame at any one target." Dershowitz declares the case was an important trial, both in the history of committing the mentally ill and of women's rights. This is an interesting look at Mary's insanity trial by one of today's most respected civil liberties attorneys, as well as a fascinating book in general.

89.
Dunn, Peggy. *"Mrs. Lady President" and the Women of Washington Society*. Springfield, Ill.: History on Fire, 2005. 119 pp., illus., bib.
A self-styled book about "Mary Lincoln and fashion," it is a brief look at Mary as first lady and White House hostess, including her experiences and tastes in shopping for clothing and new furnishings for the White House and putting on

presidential receptions. The work also contains brief biographies of Mary's main social rivals in Washington, as well as many pages of information, illustrations, and citations regarding 1860s dress and fashions. While the book includes some basic historical information about Mary Lincoln and fashion, its audience clearly is people who are interested in 1860s fashions and clothing, of which Mary was simply a part during her four years in the White House.

90.

King, C. J. *Four Marys and a Jessie: The Story of the Lincoln Women*. Manchester, Vt.: Friends of Hildene, Inc., 2005. 250 pp., illus., notes, index.

King's work chronicles the story of four generations of Lincoln women, beginning with Mary Todd Lincoln and ending with her great-granddaughter Peggy Lincoln Beckwith. The first half of the book is about Mary Todd Lincoln's life, beginning with her courtship by Abraham Lincoln; it is based on secondary sources and contains no unique or new facts or interpretations. The remainder of the narrative about Mary Harlan Lincoln (Robert Lincoln's wife), Mary Lincoln Isham and Jessie Lincoln Beckwith (Robert Lincoln's daughters), and Peggy Lincoln Beckwith (Robert Lincoln's granddaughter), can be found in no other books about the Lincolns.

91.

Bachmann, Clemens. *Briefe einer Verzweifelten: Mary Todd Lincoln im Frankfurter Exil [Letters of a Desperate Woman: Mary Todd Lincoln's Exile in Frankfurt]*. Auflage, Germany: Societäts-Verlag, 2005. 196 pp., illus., bib., notes.

This is an examination of Mary Lincoln's life in Frankfurt, Germany, from 1868 to 1870 through her letters at the time. The letters used by Bachmann are the same as those from Frankfurt printed in *Mary Todd Lincoln: Her Life and Letters* (entry 56) but there are included some German newspaper articles about Mary previously unpublished in the bibliography.

92.

Packard, Jerrold M. *The Lincolns in the White House: Four Years That Shattered a Family*. N.Y.: St. Martin's Griffin, 2006. 290 pp., illus., notes, bib., index.

This book purports to be the story of the Lincoln family as it endured a terrible and tumultuous life in the White House. The family faced not only political grief but personal tragedy and turmoil, including the death of son Willie, the estrangement of son Robert, and a growing divide between Abraham and Mary. This is a poorly done popular, rather than academic, book that relies on secondary sources and contains numerous historical errors.

93.
Holzer, Harold, ed. *Lincoln's White House Secretary: The Adventurous Life of William O. Stoddard*. Carbondale.: Southern Illinois University Press, 2007. 405 pp., illus., notes, index.

The previously unpublished autobiography of Stoddard, commonly known as President Lincoln's "third" secretary, is an interesting look at Stoddard's long and prolific life; but its major historical contribution is its firsthand look inside the Lincoln White House. Stoddard, also known as "Mrs. Lincoln's secretary" since he took care of all the issues relating to her, respected the first lady, stating, "I understood her thoroughly and formed a much higher opinion of her real character than a lot of foul-mouthed slanderers permitted to go out to the country." The book offers readers a few brief glimpses at Mary's character, her abstinence from alcohol, and her White House receptions. Stoddard's 1890 book, *Inside the White House in War Times* (entry 11), however, offers much greater detail about his experiences with and observations of Mary Lincoln.

94.
McCreary, Donna. *Fashionable First Lady: The Victorian Wardrobe of Mary Todd Lincoln*. Charlestown, Ind.: Lincoln Presentations, 2007. 182 pp., illus., notes.

This is a unique and detailed examination of Mary Lincoln's clothing and what it reveals about her personality as a woman and a first lady. While the premise (and title) of *Fashionable First Lady* may sound like something only of interest to clothing historians or reenactors, the book actually uses Mary's fashions as the gateway to examining her as a historical figure and the historical events in which she participated. It also includes information about nineteenth-century fashion and mourning attire, and White House social functions. This is a fascinating book that looks at Mary from a completely different angle than other works.

95.
Berry, Stephen. *House of Abraham: Lincoln & the Todds, a Family Divided by War*. Boston: Houghton Mifflin, 2007. 255 pp., illus., notes, index.

While this study of the Todd family and its influence on Abraham Lincoln is not specifically about Mary Lincoln, its research and conclusions offer valuable insight into who she was as a person by showing the personalities and overall dynamics of the multitudinous family into which she was born and raised. Berry shows that many of Mary's negative qualities—such as pride, vanity, selfishness, and even insanity—where not aberrant or singular to her, but were in fact Todd family traits in which she shared. Berry espouses the belief that the

Lincolns never really loved each other and, in particular, Mary's ambition loved her husband more than her heart did. But the value of this book is not so much in its direct narrative on Mary but in what can be learned about her by gaining a deeper understanding of her family. Overall, it is not only a good read but also a solidly researched and well-documented work of history.

96.
Emerson, Jason. *The Madness of Mary Lincoln*. Carbondale: Southern Illinois University Press, 2007. 255 pp., illus., notes, app., index.

An examination of Mary Lincoln's mental health from childhood to death, based on the discovery of a cache of unpublished letters she wrote while in Bellevue Place sanitarium, as well as other unpublished primary documents and consultations with psychiatric experts. This book also is the first to thoroughly examine the personality of Robert Lincoln, his relationship with his mother, and his motivations for having her committed to a sanitarium in 1875. Emerson concludes that Mary most likely suffered bipolar disorder and her son was correct in having her committed. The newly discovered letters plus other previously unpublished documents are transcribed in the appendixes.

97.
Schwartz, Thomas F. *Mary Todd Lincoln: First Lady of Controversy*. Springfield, Ill.: Abraham Lincoln Presidential Library Foundation, 2007. 96 pp., illus.

Published to supplement an exhibit of the same name at the Abraham Lincoln Presidential Library for six months in 2007, this catalogue gives a general overview of Mary Lincoln's life accompanied by images of her possessions and correspondence that were part of the exhibit. While the text of the catalog offers nothing unique or extraordinary about Mary's life, the images are what gives the booklet its interest and value. There is a certain connection to her that one feels when looking at letters in her own handwriting, her bloodstained fan from the night of the assassination, her letter opener and letter box, her clothing, dinnerware, and other personal items.

98.
Epstein, Daniel Mark. *The Lincolns: Portrait of a Marriage*. N.Y.: Ballantine Books, 2008. 559 pp., illus., notes, index.

Advertised as the story of the Lincolns' relationship and marriage, this is really a hagiography of Mary Lincoln as political partner and source of her husband's success. This unreliable book is based on predetermined conclusions and poor research.

99.

Sotos, John G. *The Physical Lincoln Sourcebook*. Vol. 2. Mt. Vernon, Va.: Mt. Vernon Book Systems, 2008. 506 pp., illus., bib.

Sotos's annotated medical history of Abraham Lincoln and his family takes the raw information from primary historical sources and organizes it like a medical record. The section on Mary (pp. 263–310) contains exhaustive analyses of both her physical and mental health issues, everything from her physical appearance to her handwriting, her diet and digestion, her nervous system, and the sound of her voice. A special section on Mary (pp. 454–460) contains a table of every expression Mary made of physical complaints in her known correspondence as published in her collected letters (entry 56). Sotos offers no particular diagnosis of Mary's mental or physical symptoms in this book but simply documents everything on the issues he has found. *The Physical Lincoln Sourcebook* is the second in a two-volume work. Volume one is titled *The Physical Lincoln*; the complete work is called *The Physical Lincoln Complete*.

100.

Burlingame, Michael. *Abraham Lincoln: A Life*. 2 vols. Baltimore: Johns Hopkins University Press, 2008. 2,008 pp., illus., notes, bibliography, index.

This book, the most definitive and extensive biography of Abraham Lincoln published in at least a century, based on indefatigable research, contains numerous materials on Mary Lincoln as a young belle, wife, mother and first lady. Staying faithful to his numerous other writings about Mary, Burlingame paints the Lincoln marriage as an unhappy match between two irreconcilably different people and portrays Mary as an emotional and physical abuser of her husband, a jealous woman with an uncontrollable temper, and possibly even an unfaithful lover. Her behavior as first lady is just as nefarious in that it, according to Burlingame, included influence peddling, bribe taking, account padding, and document leaking. While Burlingame clearly does not like or respect Mary, his conclusions about her personality and conduct cannot be ignored because they are based on reams of primary evidence.

101.

Carlson, A. Cheree. *The Crimes of Womanhood: Defining Femininity in a Court of Law*. Champaign: University of Illinois press, 2009. 189 pp., notes, references, index.

Mary Lincoln's insanity case is discussed in detail in chapter 4 (pp. 69–84). This is a feminist look at "womanhood on trial" and the unfair ways in which women were typically treated in historic court cases by the men in charge.

To Carlson, a professor of women's studies, there is no truth, only rhetoric, and which "white male lawyers" tell the best stories to "white male juries." Carlson examines six selected cases between 1864 and 1925, including the sanity trial of Mary Lincoln, which, according to Carlson, was more about "society's need to draw the line between charming feminine frailty and embarrassing incompetence" than about Mary's "obvious" mental disorder. This examination of Mary's case is so woefully ignorant of the facts of the case, so blatant in ignoring and omitting the history and context of Mary's life, as to be completely unreliable. In addition, the book is written in such a pedantic academic style as to be unreadable at worst and unable to make clear, cogent arguments at best.

102.
Clinton, Catherine. *Mrs. Lincoln: A Life*. N.Y.: HarperCollins, 2009. 415 pp., illus., notes, bib., index.

A postmodernist biography of Mary Lincoln based mainly on secondary sources, this book, similar to Jean Baker's biography, seeks to exculpate Mary Lincoln from previous historical criticism—to the point of ignoring Mary's proven faults, especially as first lady—and paint her as a monumental historical figure in spite of her presidential husband. The paucity of primary archival research and failure to delve past the obvious surface stories of Mary's life betray a lack of scholarly depth and create a book that offers nothing new in fact or interpretation to recommend it as a resource.

103.
Beidler, Anne E. *The Addiction of Mary Todd Lincoln*. Seattle: Coffeetown Press, 2009. 180 pp., app., bib.

This examination of Mary Lincoln portrays her as a woman in great physical and emotional pain who turned to opiates for relief. Beidler argues that what has been wrongly considered a mental illness in Mary was actually the symptoms and actions of a drug addict, and that her family, her doctors, and her friends all connived to suppress the truth of her condition. The book is simply a conspiracy theory based on secondary sources, factual omissions and misinterpretations, and a complete misunderstanding of Mary's life, source materials about her life, and historiography.

104.
Martinez, Susan B. *The Psychic Life of Abraham Lincoln*. Franklin Lakes, N.J.: New Page Books, 2009. 287 pp., notes, bib., index.

This laughable book should be read only for amusement, or by die-hard paranormal believers who will not find it so ridiculous as to believe it must be satire. The book, which is focused on Abraham Lincoln's "belief" in spiritualism and brings in Mary only as a secondary character, states that Abraham had "psychic" abilities and Mary was a clairvoyant. More than that, Martinez claims that Mary had no mental or emotional instability at all but rather was constantly possessed by evil spirits. The book is rife with historical errors, conspiracy theories, and naïve reliance on the most outlandish and unreliable statements and theories by previous writers.

105.
Reinhart, Mark. S. *Abraham Lincoln on Screen: Fictional and Documentary Portrayals on Film and Television.* Jefferson, N.C.: McFarland & Company, Inc., 2009. 241 pp., illus., chronol., bib., index.

Despite the hundreds of books and articles written about Mary Lincoln for more than 150 years, many people know her only as she is portrayed in television and movies—such as by Mary Tyler Moore in *Gore Vidal's Lincoln* or by Sally Field in Steven Spielberg's *Lincoln*—and, as such, Reinhart's book is an essential source. While Mary has had few large- or small-screen productions in her own right (see list of Drama entries below), she has been portrayed numerous times as a supporting character in productions about Abraham Lincoln, and *Abraham Lincoln on Screen* lists them all. But more than just listing each production, Reinhart also judges and explains how historically accurate, or inaccurate, each film and character portrayal is, giving readers not only a resource for where they can see Mary portrayed on screen but also how truly good or awful each performance is. Whether one is a film buff or not, this book is a fascinating look at the changing image of Mary in artistic and popular culture since the birth of the motion picture medium.

106.
Emerson, Jason. *"I have done my duty as I best know, and Providence must take care of the rest": Reconsidering Mary Lincoln's Sanity and Robert Lincoln's Motivations.* Bulletin of the 68th Annual Meeting of The Lincoln Fellowship of Wisconsin, Apr. 18, 2009, Historical Bulletin no. 63. 18 pp., illus., notes.

This booklet contains the text of a speech Emerson gave to the Lincoln Fellowship of Wisconsin concerning Mary Lincoln's mental health and Robert Lincoln's motivations for committing his mother to an insane asylum in 1875. The speech was based on Emerson's book *The Madness of Mary Lincoln* (entry 96).

107.
Pritchard, Myra Helmer. *The Dark Days of Abraham Lincoln's Widow, As Revealed by Her Own Letters*. Ed. and annot. Jason Emerson. Carbondale: Southern Illinois University Press, 2011. 186 pp., illus., notes, bib., index.
This previously unpublished manuscript by the granddaughter of Mary Lincoln's close friend Myra Bradwell is based on a collection of letters between the two friends. Pritchard's book tells a long-held family tale of the most extraordinary episode in Mary Lincoln's life—her commitment to an insane asylum—using many Bradwell family anecdotes and opinions that are published no place else. It also is a fervent defense of Mary as a poorly abused and perfectly sane woman. Written in 1927, *Dark Days* was suppressed by Robert Lincoln's widow but discovered by editor Jason Emerson in 2005. Emerson's introduction explains the history of the manuscript, while his edits and annotations clarify and explain Pritchard's interpretations, information, and source materials.

108.
Winkle, Kenneth J. *Abraham and Mary Lincoln*. Carbondale: Southern Illinois University Press, 2012. 147 pp., illus., essay on sources, bib., index.
This book is a succinct and objective examination of Abraham Lincoln and Mary Todd as individuals, spouses, parents, and occupants of the White House. Winkle does an excellent job investigating just who Mary was, what she did, and why she acted the way she did. He illuminates Mary's virtues as well as her flaws, does not shy away from the embarrassing or controversial aspects of her life—such as her misdeeds in the White House or her post-Washington behavior—and gives an overall balanced view of Mary such as has not been written in many years.

109.
Williams, Frank J., and Michael Burkhimer, eds. *The Mary Lincoln Enigma: Historians on America's Most Controversial First Lady*. Carbondale: Southern Illinois University Press, 2012. 376 pp., illus., index.
This volume of collected essays, written by prominent and respected scholars, seeks to explore the enigma of Mary Lincoln from multiple perspectives. The chapters examine the full gamut of Mary's life, including her childhood, marriage, family relations, social relations, mental health, political inclinations, and place and reputation in the Lincoln historiography. The book is an original and valuable addition to the Lincoln literature that illuminates many aspects of Mary's life previously overlooked or underexplored.

110.
Schroeder-Lein, Glenna R. *Lincoln and Medicine*. Carbondale: Southern Illinois University Press, 2012. 128 pp., illus., notes, bib., index.

Schroeder-Lein's medical history of the Lincoln family outlines, surveys, and examines all the possible medical diagnoses of Abraham Lincoln through the years and uses primary evidence to support or discount the major theories of Lincoln's medical life. Mary Lincoln's medical history is included in the study as well, and looks at her frequent migraines, her mood swings, her carriage accident injury, her possible mental illness (which Schroeder-Lein believes Mary "probably" did not suffer), and her multiple physical ailments toward the end of her life. An excellent and succinct look into Mary's medical health.

111.
Emerson, Jason. *Giant in the Shadows: The Life of Robert T. Lincoln*. Carbondale: Southern Illinois University Press, 2012. 600 pp., illus., notes, bib., index.

This cradle-to-grave biography of the oldest of the Lincolns' four sons—and the only one to survive into adulthood—focuses on Robert Lincoln's life, but it also contains vast amounts of unknown and previously unpublished information about Mary Lincoln as wife, mother, first lady, and widow. There is also an extensive discussion of Mary's "insanity period" and her commitment to a sanitarium—an action commenced by Robert out of his concern for her health and safety. This book is only the second ever written about Robert Lincoln and the only one currently in print.

112.
———. *Mary Lincoln's Insanity Case: A Documentary History*. Champaign: University of Illinois Press, 2012. 237 pp., appendix, notes, bib., index.

A compilation of the primary documents—nearly two hundred contemporary letters, legal and medical documents, newspaper articles, diary entries, reminiscences, and recollections—relating to Mary Lincoln's mental health and her commitment by her son Robert Lincoln to Bellevue Place sanitarium in 1875. This book tells the story of Mary's insanity case through the writings of the people who participated in and witnessed her deterioration and downfall. This unprecedented work seeks to quiet the arguments over Mary's sanity or insanity by objectively presenting the primary documents in full.

113.
Hamilton, Michelle L. *"I Would Still Be Drowned in Tears": Spiritualism in Abraham Lincoln's White House*. La Mesa, CA: Vanderblumen Publications, 2013. 182 pp., notes, bib.

A look at spiritualism in Abraham Lincoln's White House based on the author's thesis that Mary and Abraham shared a joint belief in the religion. This book, based on primary and secondary sources, mostly restates previous writings on Mary and spiritualism, and leans much too heavily on Nettie Maynard's 1891 book *Was Abraham Lincoln a Spiritualist?* (entry 12). It also suffers from a naive acceptance of biased occultist/spiritualist writings from both the nineteenth and twentieth centuries. The book seeks to prove and defend the Lincolns as spiritualists, rather than examine the historical evidence objectively. While not a great book, it is the best modern book published on the subject, particularly in regard to Mary Lincoln.

114.
Ellison, Betty Boles. *The True Mary Todd Lincoln: A Biography.* Jefferson, N.C.: McFarland, 2014. 288 pp., illus., notes, bib., index.

This biography, one of the most recent about Mary Lincoln, claims to be the "fair appraisal" of the unfairly beleaguered Mary that she has so far been denied. It is not. Rather, this book is a feminist revisionist hagiography, based on shoddy research and mainly secondary sources—many of them unreliable and not respected by established Lincoln scholars—that starts with a predetermined theory of Mary's greatness and infallibility and carries that idea through to the end, to the detriment of the men around Mary, who apparently all were out to get her. Ellison bases entire sections of her book off on previous historians' works (with the note section filled with *ibid.*) and offers no original thinking or research. Instead she offers unfounded suppositions, unproven accusations, a text not only filled with factual errors but also rife with a complete misunderstanding of Mary as a person and historical character. Despite the book's title, it is not a book to be recommended for anyone looking to understand the true Mary Lincoln.

115.
Peet, Tom, and David Keck. *Reading Lincoln: An Annotated Bibliography.* Self-published, CreateSpace, 2014. 340 pp., bib.

This annotated bibliography of over 275 books about Abraham Lincoln ranges from campaign biographies written in 1860 to the latest scholarship in 2014. The two authors take turns writing the detailed bibliographic entries, and sometimes both write an entry on the same book. While *Reading Lincoln* is dedicated to books solely about Abraham Lincoln, many of the entries contain references to how Mary Lincoln and her effect on her husband are portrayed in the respective work. The book also contains one chapter on books about the Lincoln family "and how they affected [Abraham] and his career," within which is thirteen bibliographic references of some of the best-known and most common books on Mary Lincoln, eleven of which date from the twenty-first century. While any such book is subjective in its opinions, this is a good reference for any Lincoln student, and a good starting place for readers interested in books that refer to Mary as part of her husband's story (although not as her own person).

116.
Esty, Mary Lee, and C. M. Shifflett. *Conquering Concussion: Healing TBI Symptoms with Neurofeedback and without Drugs.* Sewickley, Pa.: Round Earth Publishing, 2014. 280 pp., illus., glossary, resources and references, index.

Esty and Shifflett's book about concussions and traumatic brain injury (TBI) and their effects on victims, cites Mary Lincoln and her 1863 carriage accident as one famous historical example. While conceding that Mary was never in perfect emotional or physical health before 1863, the authors believe that Mary's accident, during which she jumped out of a runaway carriage and suffered an injury to her head, resulted in traumatic brain injury that forever altered her personality, abilities, health, and behavior. They cite her worsened migraines, hallucinations, delusions, spending and hoarding, and photophobia all as results of her TBI from 1863. It is an interesting—and unique—hypothesis based on historical facts, medical expertise, and case studies.

117.
McDermott, Stacy Pratt. *Mary Lincoln: Southern Girl, Northern Woman.* N.Y.: Routledge, 2015. 200 pp., illus., notes, bib., index.

McDermott's succinct overview of Mary Lincoln's life aims to show not only the extraordinary aspects and events in her life but also how understanding her life can help broaden the understanding of nineteenth-century women in general, both from the North and from the South. As McDermott states, Mary viewed herself primarily as a wife and mother, not as a public figure, although historically she has become known as a first lady and the wife of Abraham Lincoln. McDermott seeks to "find the human Mary Lincoln" in her work, which is based on Mary's published letters and the secondary works on her life, and she succeeds admirably. While there is nothing new or groundbreaking in this book, it is an excellent short biography of Mary.

118.
Wilson, Douglas L., and Rodney O. Davis, eds. *Herndon on Lincoln: Letters.* Urbana: Knox College Lincoln Studies Center and University of Illinois Press, 2016. 371 pp., notes, index.

This is a comprehensive collection of what William Herndon, Lincoln's former law partner, wrote about Abraham Lincoln in his own letters during a fifty-year period. The majority of the letters come from the time after Lincoln's assassination, when Herndon was researching and writing his biography, *Herndon's Lincoln* (entry 10). Many of the letters included are previously unpublished. Similar to this book's companion volume, *Herndon's Informants* (entry 80), *Herndon on Lincoln: Letters* contains vast amounts of primary materials concerning Mary Lincoln, both in the form of Herndon's own memories, perceptions, and interpretations of her actions and character, and as material obtained from others who knew Mary. Subjects discussed in the letters include the Lincoln-Todd courtship and marriage, Mary's personality and intellect, her temper and bad behavior, and her roles as wife and mother.

119.
Cornelius, James M., and Carla Knorowski. *Under Lincoln's Hat: 100 Objects That Tell the Story of His Life and Legacy.* Guilford, Conn.: Lyons Press, 2016. 226 pp., illus., index.
This is the story of Abraham Lincoln's life as told through one hundred objects (artifacts and documents) from the Abraham Lincoln Presidential Library and Museum collection. Mary Lincoln, being a major part of her husband's life, is also part of the story of twenty-two items included in the book. While a number of the Mary-related items were previously highlighted in the 2007 catalog *Mary Todd Lincoln: First Lady of Controversy* (entry 97)—such as Mary's diamond pendant, her personal seal, and her White House china—this book contains other items pertaining to her life as well, including personal letters and a list of her letters that her son Robert stated he burned. This is an endlessly entertaining and fascinating book in general, but one that also gives a fair amount of space to Mary as wife, mother, and first lady, and is highly recommended.

120.
Emerson, Jason. *Lincoln's Lover: Mary Lincoln in Poetry.* Kent, Ohio: Kent State University Press, 2018. 138 pp., illus., notes, bib., index.
This is a compilation of poetry written by, for, and about Mary Lincoln dating from 1839–40 to 2012. Each poem is prefaced with comments contextualizing the historical events of Mary's life as portrayed in the poem, as well as an explanation of the poem and the poet who wrote it. The chronological order not only arranges the poetic style of the works but also offers a view of the changing perceptions of Mary through the years. The poems show Mary as woman, wife, first lady, and widow, as well as insane woman, complex individual, and

intricate and indispensable part of her husband. The theme of the book is that to experience Mary's words and thoughts, experiences, and legacy as explained and exposed through poetry over the past 179 years advances our understanding and appreciation of an iconic individual.

⊘

Newspaper articles and interviews

121.
"The Next Lady of the White House." *Chicago Tribune*, Nov. 13, 1860, 2.
  This is a glowing description and personality portrait of Mary Lincoln published shortly after the election of her husband to the presidency. The article lavishes praise on Mary as a woman who is dignified and refined, who is familiar with the "courtly drawing rooms" of London and Paris, and who will bring grace and elegance to the White House as first lady. "She is admirably calculated to preside over our republican court," according to the article. This article is a far cry from much of the criticism Mary would endure later during the war in her role as national hostess. Originally printed in the *New York World*, and subsequently reprinted in newspapers across the country.

122.
"The Republican Court; First Levee at the White House." *New York Times*, Mar. 10, 1861.
  A detailed description of the first White House levee hosted by Abraham and Mary Lincoln. In addition to describing the setting, the activities, the guests, and President Lincoln, the writer, whose pen name is "Howard," is voluminous in his praise for Mary as intelligent, beautiful, elegant, poised, tactful, and "eminently qualified for her position." The writer described the event as "a perfect and unmitigated success." Such praise for Mary as White House hostess became less fulsome as the years wore on.

123.
"Movements of Mrs. Lincoln." *New York Herald*, May 16, 1861, 4.
  A report of Mary Lincoln's weeklong shopping trip to New York City, during which she made various purchases for refurbishing the White House, including the famous Lincoln dinner service, the article lists the stores in which Mary shopped, the items she bought, and the other activities in which she engaged. This article is one of many, particularly by the *Herald*, that reports on Mary's

various shopping trips to New York in 1861. Such articles are important to Mary's story in that her love of shopping, her spending habits, her overspending of the 1861 White House decorating appropriation, and her many trips and vacations during the Civil War all had a major impact on her reputation as first lady, both during her life and later.

124.

"A Letter from Mrs. Lincoln." *New York Times,* July 14, 1861.

Publication of a letter from Mary Lincoln to Colonel John Fry in Kentucky, in which Mary acts as the "medium of transmission" of a pair of Navy revolvers and a sabre to the colonel. The letter also declares Mary's devotion to both her native state of Kentucky and the Union, and was published, according to newspapers of the day, to "refute the assertion which has been made that she sympathized with the Secessionists." The letter was originally published in the *Louisville Journal,* and was republished in newspapers across the United States.

125.

"The Entertainment in the White House Last Night." [Washington, D.C.] *Evening Star,* Feb. 6, 1862.

A detailed description of the February 5, 1862, invitation-only presidential ball held at the White House and attended by more than five hundred of the capital's elite citizens. The *Star* report describes the scene, the decorations, the food, the music, and the attendees and their clothing, as well as descriptions of Mary Lincoln's attire. While many people and newspapers lauded Mary for planning such a grand fete, just as many people and journalists around the country pilloried her for having such a frivolous, expensive party while soldiers were suffering and dying on the battlefield. The ball was ultimately more of a detriment to Mary's reputation than it was a help, cementing the idea that she was a heartless aristocrat. Numerous newspapers throughout the country published their own reports of the event, all similar in substance. See also "The Presidential Party," *Frank Leslie's Illustrated Newspaper,* Feb. 22, 1862, 209, 213–214.

126.

"The Social Circle at the White House." [Springfield, Mass.] *Republican,* Feb. 18, 1862, 2.

This article decries a few of the unsavory characters that were frequent guests at the White House—particularly the shady "Chevalier" Henry Wikoff—and the need for the Lincolns to rid their home of such people. It also mentions the arrest of Wikoff for illicitly giving the *New York Herald* a copy of the president's first annual message to Congress before the message was officially transmitted, and states that Wikoff obtained the message "either directly or indirectly" through Mrs. Lincoln. While rumors and innuendo connected Mary to the "stolen" message at the time and after, this is one of the few contemporary articles (perhaps the only one) to actually connect the scheme directly to Mary.

127.
"Mrs. Lincoln." [Montpelier, Vt.] *Daily Freeman*, Feb. 20, 1862, 2.

An editorial criticizing Mary Lincoln as unfit to be first lady due to her "girlish vanity, unbecoming coquetry, [and] passion for display quite out of place in the depressed state of the national finances." The editorial mentions the impropriety of Mary's February 5, 1862, grand ball during a time of war but specifically chastises Mary for the unsavory company she keeps, specifically naming "Chevalier" Henry Wikoff and General Dan Sickles, and the parts they played in publishing President Lincoln's first annual message in the *New York Herald* before the message was officially given to Congress. The editorial states Mary is "not equal to her place" in that she is allowing herself to be made "the weak dupe of lying flattery and cunning intrigue" and "to debase herself to the low level of associations that are offensive and disgusting to all other decent people." The editor suggests that while it may not be possible for Mary to change her character, the president should at least ban men such as Wikoff and Sickles from the White House, as the American people desire. While this editorial was not printed in a major city daily newspaper, its sentiments and criticisms of Mary were indicative of popular opinion at the time, especially during early 1862.

128.
"The Party of Blood." *New York Herald*, Mar. 18, 1862, 4.

This article reprints a collection of articles from newspapers across the North, all of them savaging Mary Lincoln for holding her February 5 grand ball in the White House (see entry 125). While the collected articles give some descriptions of the grand ball itself, generally they traduce Mary as a heartless aristocrat holding a dancing party while soldiers are maimed and dying on the battlefield. One article compares the grand ball to Nero fiddling while Rome burns and dancing on a sinking ship, while the *Jeffersonian Democrat* called the evening "the scene of disgraceful frivolity, hilarity and gluttony" and the *Richmond* [Indiana] *Independent Press* declared Mary should "study humanity instead of French; practice benevolence instead of dancing; visit the sick soldiers . . . instead of gallanting the halls of that mansion on the arm of a European court snob."

129.

"Illness at the White House." [Washington, D.C.] *Evening Star,* Mar. 20, 1862, 3.

This notice, published in both the *Washington Star* and the *National Republican* and republished in papers across the country, states that Mary Lincoln had become so ill in the aftermath of her son Willie's death in February that she was confined to her room and allowed few visitors. While this simple notice was the majority of newspaper coverage of Mary's reaction to Willie's death, in truth she was devastated by the loss and did not stop publicly mourning for more than a year.

130.

"A Good Example." [Washington D.C.] *National Republican,* Aug. 27, 1862, 2.

A brief article describing Mary Lincoln's "devotion and judicious kindness" towards wounded soldiers in Union hospitals, it states a "gentleman in a neighboring city" heard of Mary's good works and gave her $1,000 to be expended on "necessaries" for sick and wounded soldiers. She was reported to be using the money to buy "cooling fruits and other needed comforts" and personally seeing to their distribution. "It is a work worthy of the heart and hands of the most illustrious of the gentler sex," the paper declared, and urged all ladies to follow the first lady's example. Mary's attentions and ministrations to wounded soldiers started in earnest after her son Willie's death in February 1862 and continued throughout the war. While she was occasionally recognized for her work in sympathetic newspapers, her actions were little known both at the time and since. Interestingly, two days later, a letter to the editor of the *National Republican,* signed by "Many Patients," stated that the four hundred of them in Finley Hospital, Camp Sprague, had not seen Mrs. Lincoln for a month or more and would have loved to partake in the comforts she was said to be handing out. Whether this letter was authentic or a false attack on the first lady is unclear.

131.

"Serenade to Mrs. Lincoln." *New York Times,* Oct. 26, 1862.

A brief article that describes a serenade to Mary Lincoln at the Metropolitan Hotel in New York City by federal office holders and naval officers. Colonel A. J. Hamilton, of Texas, thanked the crowd of an estimated three thousand people on behalf of Mrs. Lincoln, although Mary did appear on her balcony and bow to the crowd's enthusiastic applause. This article is one of many examples showing that Mary had just as many supporters and admirers while she was first lady as she did detractors.

132.

"Mrs. Lincoln and the Radicals of Both Parties." *New York Herald*, Feb. 5, 1863, 4.

This is a strong defense of Mary Lincoln against accusations by both political parties who, according to the *Herald*, were assailing the first lady as a way to undermine and attack her husband. The article declares that Mary has character and dignity, as especially evidenced in her kindness and generosity to the wounded soldiers in Washington whom she visits, and that a public man's family should not be targets of political criticism. This is an interesting article that gives not only an insight into the political assaults on Mary during her tenure as first lady—including the duality of the attacks, such as that she was both in favor of and against emancipating slaves—but also brief summaries of some attacks and the multiple newspapers in which they were printed.

133.

"Serious Accident to Mrs. Lincoln." [Washington, D.C.] *Evening Star*, July 2, 1863, 2.

This is an important story in Mary Lincoln's life, in that it is the original report of a carriage accident during which she was injured—and from which, some say, she never fully recovered. The driver's seat detached and the driver fell off, the horses spooked and took off at full speed, and Mary had to jump from the carriage to save herself. She received a serious head injury that became infected and from which it took her weeks to recover. The detached seat was discovered to be a result of sabotage and a possible assassination attempt on the president (who was not in the carriage at the time). Robert Lincoln later said his mother was never the same after the accident. Similar stories were also reported in the Washington, D.C., *Daily National Intelligencer* and the *New York Times*, but the *Evening Star*'s reporting contains the most detail.

134.

"The Assassination of President Lincoln." [Washington, D.C.] *Evening Star*, April 15, 1865, 1.

This report from a writer who was at Ford's Theatre during President Lincoln's assassination describes what he saw and heard, including Mary's screams after assassin John Wilkes Booth fired his bullet. The article also includes a subsection titled "Mrs. Lincoln," which describes Mary's overwhelming grief at her husband's murder and lists a number of officials who visited her at the White House in the hours after the president's death. This article is a typical report of Mary's reaction to the assassination, which was published as part of the overall assassination reporting in newspapers across the country.

135.

"Mrs. Lincoln's Presentiment." *New York Times*, May 1, 1865, 5.

This article covers the statement of a man from New York City who claimed to know Mary Lincoln and had visited with her shortly after her husband's assassination. The man stated that Mary said both she and her husband had a presentiment that something horrible would happen to him. She said she did not believe he would live to see the end of his term of office, and that when she mentioned visiting Europe after his presidency ended, her husband said he believed he would never get to see it.

136.

"From Washington—History of the Selection of the President's Last Resting Place." *Chicago Tribune*, May 9, 1865, 2.

This letter to the editor from Lincoln family friend Anson G. Henry explains the events surrounding the controversy over the burial place of Abraham Lincoln. After the assassination, Mary Lincoln made clear her preference for her husband's burial in Oak Ridge Cemetery in Springfield, Illinois, but the leaders of Springfield chose a site in the heart of the city called the Mather Place. Henry describes the sequence of events in which Mary sent a telegram to Springfield demanding her wishes be complied with or else she would move her husband's body to Chicago. He explained that Mary felt Oak Ridge would be "in better accord with her husband's Republican tastes," and she had no desire to let men who disrespected her husband in life choose his burial place in death. In what has become known as the "battle of the gravesite," Henry's letter to the editor, coming directly from Mrs. Lincoln, is an invaluable piece of primary evidence as to what happened.

137.

"Presentation to Mrs. Lincoln." [Washington, D.C.] *Daily National Intelligencer,* May 23, 1865, 1.

A report that a collection of clerks in both the Treasury Department and Quartermaster General's Bureau presented a cross of wax japonicas, encased in black walnut, to Mary Lincoln as a tribute of their love and esteem for the fallen president. The article also reprints in full a letter to the clerks from Robert Lincoln, on behalf of his mother, thanking them for the gift. This is one of the few tokens of honor and appreciation Mary received after her husband's murder.

138.

"The Lincoln Monument." *Chicago Tribune,* June 14, 1865, 4.

Continuing coverage of Mary Lincoln's battle with Springfield officials over her husband's burial arrangements. The article describes how two officials—one being the governor—visited Mary in Chicago to discuss the burial disagreement. Although they acceded to Mary's burial request, the Springfield officials told Mary they had decided to place the monument to Abraham Lincoln not over his tomb in Oak Ridge Cemetery but in the Mather Place. Mary demanded the monument be placed above her husband's grave and insisted her wishes be complied with or she would bury her husband someplace else. The *Tribune* poses its own opinion at the end of the article, saying that while the citizens of Springfield are divided on the issue, the paper's editors believe Mrs. Lincoln's wishes "should be consulted in the matter."

139.
"The Lincoln National Monument." [Washington, D.C.] *National Republican,* June 15, 1865, 2.
    This article, quoting from coverage in the *Springfield* [Ill.] *Journal,* concerns the disagreement between the Lincoln Monument Association and Mary Lincoln over her husband's burial arrangements. The article refers to, and reprints, a letter to the editor from the association relating Mary's demands and its belief that the state or the federal government should control Lincoln's burial place, not a private individual such as Mary. The letter also states an acceptance of Mary's wishes does not seem likely, despite her threat to have her husband buried in another city if her wishes are ignored.

140.
"From Springfield." *Chicago Tribune,* June 16, 1865, 1.
    A brief notice stating that Mary Lincoln and the Lincoln Monument Association had reached an agreement on the burial place of Abraham Lincoln and the placement of the monument over his grave, and that the association acceded to Mary's wishes.

141.
"The Lincoln Monument Association and Mrs. Lincoln." *New York Herald,* June 17, 1865, 2.
    An article based on a June 10 letter to the editor from Springfield to the *Chicago Republican* describing the state of events of the battle over the Lincoln gravesite between the Lincoln Monument Association and Mary Lincoln. It describes the latest meeting of the monument association and Mary's letter to

the group demanding the gravesite and any monument erected over it be placed in Oak Ridge Cemetery, and that she and her descendants also be buried there. The association members discussed sending emissaries to Chicago to talk with Mary, which they later did. The article also describes the feeling in Springfield about where Abraham Lincoln should be buried. Also published in "The Lincoln Monument—Squabble between Mrs. Lincoln and the Monument Committee" [Washington] *Evening Star,* June 17, 1865.

142.
"Some Curious Statements by Mrs. J. G. Swisshelm—Failure to Poison Mr. Lincoln." *New York Times,* July 18, 1865, 3.

Swisshelm, a noted abolitionist who befriended Mary Lincoln during the Civil War, offers up some statements and experiences which, she believes, shed further light on the assassination plot against Abraham Lincoln. At one point in her narrative, she claims to have spoken with Mary on the day the widow left Washington for Chicago, during which Mary told her she believed her husband had been poisoned. Mary said her husband had been seriously ill for many days after taking a dose of blue pills shortly before his second inauguration—pills she had sent for from the pharmacy where assassination conspirator David Herold was employed. Mary said her husband was overcome for days, and he thought it was strange since the pills had never before affected him so badly. Swisshelm's story is interesting since it is known that Lincoln took blue pills (although he claimed he stopped taking them in 1861 because they made him "cross") and that Swisshelm was a friend of Mary Lincoln.

143.
"Congress—Proceedings of the Senate . . . Brutal Charges against Mrs. Lincoln Refuted." *Chicago Tribune,* Jan. 16, 1866, 1.

This brief notice of recent congressional debates states that according to Congressman John A. Kasson, of Iowa, the rumors that Mary Lincoln pilfered the White House when she left and moved to Chicago in May 1865 were untrue. Kasson said that "not a solitary item belonging to the government was taken away when Mrs. Lincoln left the house," and the dozens of boxes that went with the Lincolns were private possessions. The only item she took that was not hers was a dressing stand the president had admired for which Mary asked and was granted permission to take. Accusations that Mary stole from the White House dogged her for years despite Congress's investigation into it and subsequent dismissal of the charges as false.

144.
"Mrs. Lincoln's Wardrobe for Sale." [N.Y.] *World*, Oct. 3, 1867, 4–5.
This is the original article reporting on what came to be known as the Old Clothes Scandal, in which Mary Lincoln, believing herself in near poverty, sought to sell a large part of her wardrobe in New York City in order to supplement her income. The article reports on Mary's financial history and situation, and prints multiple letters by her which explain how and why she instituted the sale, a list of the items she offered, and her vituperative opinions of Republican politicians she believed owed her their positions and fortunes.

145.
"Mrs. Lincoln's Wardrobe." [N.Y.] *World*, Oct. 5, 1867, 5.
The sequel article to *The World's* original reporting on the Old Clothes Scandal, it offers "further revelations" of the sale, including descriptions and actions of the attending crowds, and amounts of sales realized. The article also reprints an editorial by Thurlow Weed excoriating Mary Lincoln for her previous criticism of Secretary of State William H. Seward and accusing the former first lady of multiple illegal activities while she was in the White House.

146.
"The Widow of Lincoln." *Round Table: A Saturday Review of Politics, Finance, Literature, Society, and Art* 6, no. 142 (Oct. 12, 1867): 240.
This editorial from a weekly magazine defends Mary Lincoln during the Old Clothes Scandal and instead blames the country for ignoring Mary's financial plight. It also contains statements from Thurlow Weed blaming Mary's circumstances as the result of her unbecoming nature as first lady.

147.
Stanton, Elizabeth Cady. "Editorial Correspondence." *Revolution* [New York, N.Y.], Mar. 11, 1869, 1–2.
Stanton, editor of this weekly women's rights newspaper that was owned by Susan B. Anthony, responds to a letter from the previous week's issue in which a man denounces Mary Lincoln for seeking a government pension for which, according to him, she has no need (see entry 217). Stanton fervently defends Mary as one who should be cared for as the widow of the great Lincoln. She also states that Mary's "idiosyncracies [*sic*] of character" should be excused because of her "unhappy organization," her "tendency to insanity," and the deep sadness from her husband's murder. In the same issue, assistant editor Parker Pillsbury responds to Stanton's letter saying not only that Mary Lincoln

is too wealthy to need a pension but also that her desire to receive a pension was simply to "pamper one woman's pride and vanity, who, through the war, was known to sympathize with the rebels" and already has more money than any normal family will ever possess. The article and editorial exchange are an interesting look at the thoughts of early feminists and suffragists on Mary Lincoln's character.

148.
"Mrs. Abraham Lincoln." *San Francisco Bulletin*, Nov. 12, 1869, 2.
  This article is actually a transcript of a letter—or part of a letter—from "the wife of a prominent Philadelphian, writing from Baden-Baden, alluding to Mrs. Lincoln." The writer, Sally Orne, was one of Mary Lincoln's close friends and spent time with her in Europe during Mary's first trip there from 1868 to 1871. The letter talks about Mary's sadness and desolation of spirit. "She is as great a mourner now as she was the day she lost the best of husbands," the letter stated. "Her life is the loneliest I ever saw."

149.
"Mrs. Lincoln and Tad." [N.Y.] *World*, May 13, 1871, 2.
  In this extended interview with both Mary and Tad Lincoln immediately after returning to America from a three-year sojourn in Europe, Mary answers questions about her time in and enjoyment of Europe, where she stayed and how she was treated, and how her husband's memory is regarded across the ocean; Tad answers a few questions about his mother and his German education.

150.
"A Curious Story about Mrs. Lincoln Reiterated." *New York Times*, Feb. 24, 1872, 5.
  This is a reprint of a February 23 article from the *Boston Herald* reporting on Mary Lincoln's ten-day visit to Boston to visit a spiritualist medium. Although Mary was heavily veiled and used a false name, she was recognized by someone who had seen her in Washington. This is the same visit during which Mary visited spirit photographer William Mumler and had her photo taken in which the "spirits" of Abraham and Tad can be seen hovering over her shoulders. It is an important piece of historical reporting concerning Mary's belief in spiritualism.

151.
"Mrs. Abraham Lincoln Sits for a Spirit Picture." *Boston Herald*, Feb. 27, 1872, 2.

A follow-up to a February 23 article that reported Mary Lincoln visited a spiritualist medium and spirit photographer in Boston, this article contains a letter to the *Herald* from spirit photographer William Mumler in which he describes not only Mary's visit to him (under a false name) but also the photograph he took of her containing the supposed ghosts of Abraham and Tad.

152.
Swisshelm, Jane G. "Mrs. Abraham Lincoln." *Chicago Tribune*, July 4, 1872, 2.
In this letter to the editor, Swisshelm, one of Mary Lincoln's wartime friends, defends the former first lady as a good woman and asks that the American people "do her justice." Swisshelm, a noted abolitionist, recounts her first meeting with Mary in 1863, tells of Mary's willingness to visit wounded soldiers in field hospitals and her experiences with them, her loyalty to the Union, and an anecdote about the first lady's shopping habits during the war. The story of the two women's first meeting was later retold in Swisshelm's 1880 memoir, *Half a Century* (entry 6).

153.
C.E.L. "A Kindly Word for Mrs. Lincoln." *Christian Register* 51, no. 36 (Sept. 7, 1872): 1.
In this defense of Mary Lincoln and her actions, the author (who claimed to know Mary when she was first lady) blames many of Mary's embarrassments on "evil counselors" and chastises the scandalmongers. She also recounts Mary's great sympathy and compassion for soldiers and their families, and the great love between Abraham and Mary Lincoln.

154.
"Clouded Reason: Trial of Mrs. Abraham Lincoln for Insanity." *Chicago Tribune*, May 20, 1875, 1.
This contemporary account of Mary Lincoln's Chicago insanity trial includes a list of her symptoms; the names of the judge, jurors, and attorneys; reports of the trial testimony; and the jury's verdict. While the *Tribune*'s coverage is the major—practically the only—newspaper report cited by historians when writing about Mary's insanity trial, it is neither the most thorough nor the most detailed account published by newspapers that day.

155.
"Mrs. Lincoln: The Widow of the Martyred President Adjudged Insane in County Court." *Chicago Inter Ocean*, May 20, 1875, 1.

As with the previous account of Mary Lincoln's Chicago insanity trial, this one also includes a list of her symptoms; the names of the judge, jurors, and attorneys; reports of the trial testimony; and the jury's verdict. This article is the most detailed reporting of the event published by any newspaper at the time, and is the only one to explicitly report rebuttal questions or cross-examination of witnesses by Mary's attorney, Isaac Arnold.

156.
"A Sad Revelation: Mrs. Mary Lincoln, the Widow of the Late President, Adjudged Insane." *Chicago Times*, May 20, 1875, 2.

The third major contemporary account of Mary Lincoln's Chicago insanity trial, this report also includes a list of her symptoms; the names of the judge, jurors, and attorneys; reports of the trial testimony; and the jury's verdict. This is the only contemporary account to state that Mary actually spoke during the proceedings, and to label Mary a spiritualist and directly connect her beliefs to her insanity. It also was the only report to eschew any description of Robert Lincoln's turbulent emotions while testifying.

157.
"Insanity's Freaks—Displayed Yesterday in the Actions of Unhappy Mrs. Lincoln." *Chicago Times*, May 21, 1875, 5.

This is the longest and most detailed newspaper report of Mary Lincoln's attempt at suicide the day after a Chicago jury declared her to be insane. The article, which begins with a narration of the events leading up to and during Mary's court hearing, is so detailed that it may have been given to the newspaper by Leonard Swett, Robert Lincoln's adviser in the matter, whose letter three days later contains the same details that only Swett would have known. The article describes how Mary evaded the guards outside her hotel room, went to three local pharmacies to obtain lethal drugs, and tried to kill herself by ingesting the contents. Only the actions of an astute pharmacist, who recognized Mary and knew about her insanity trial, foiled the widow's plan. This article was reprinted, in whole or in part, by major newspapers across the country.

158.
"Mrs. Lincoln—Attempt at Suicide." *Chicago Tribune*, May 21, 1875, 8.

This brief article about Mary Lincoln's suicide attempt describes her visits to three Chicago pharmacies in an effort to obtain and drink lethal drugs. It also contains the same main facts of the *Chicago Times* article of the same day, with some minor variations.

159.
"Mrs. Lincoln—Another Sad Chapter in the Life of the Demented Widow."
Chicago Inter Ocean, May 21, 1875, 8.

Another detailed report on Mary Lincoln's suicide attempt that also narrates the events that occurred right after her jury trial, leading up to her visits to three pharmacies to obtain and ingest lethal drugs. This article, while containing the same facts as the *Times* and *Tribune* reports, includes some different details of Mary's interactions with the three pharmacists, as well as her interactions with Leonard Swett that morning.

160.
Ingersoll, H. G. "Mrs. Abraham Lincoln: Interesting Revelations Regarding Her Worth and Patriotism." *New York Herald*, June 8, 1875, 4.

This letter to the editor defends Mary Lincoln's reputation against unjust criticism in the wake of her commitment to the insane asylum one month earlier. The author, who had two long interviews with Mary Lincoln in spring 1864, specifically recollects evidence of Mary's patriotism and her explanations on how she endured the vast public criticism as first lady. The author also mentions her belief in abolitionism and comments she made concerning the death of her son Willie in 1862.

161.
"Mrs. Lincoln: A Visit to Her by 'The Post and Mail' Correspondent: How She Passes the Time at Dr. Patterson's Retreat." *Chicago Post and Mail*, July 13, 1875.

This article by a female journalist who visited and interviewed Mary Lincoln at Bellevue Place sanitarium is essential reading for the story of Mary's insanity case. The report offers detailed observations about the sanitarium, Dr. R. J. Patterson's medical opinion of his famous patient, and Mary Lincoln's appearance, mental activity, living accommodations, and medical treatment. The reporter declares that Mary obviously suffers from a "shattered mind" and Dr. Patterson has little hope for her permanent recovery.

162.
"Reason Restored: Mrs. Lincoln Will Soon Return from Her Brief Visit to the Insane Asylum." *Chicago Times*, Aug. 24, 1875, 4.

This article contains interviews with Mary Lincoln and her friend Myra Bradwell concerning Mary's mental health, her stay in Bellevue Place sanitarium, and her prospects for release. The reporter, who was invited to Batavia by the two women specifically to write a laudatory story about Mary, describes both the sanitarium and Mary's mental acuity in great detail, and declares her completely restored to reason.

163.

"Mrs. Abraham Lincoln—Letter from Dr. R. J. Patterson." *Chicago Tribune,* Aug. 29, 1875, 16.

In response to the previous *Chicago Times* story, Mary Lincoln's Bellevue Place physician wrote a letter to the editor to set the factual record straight concerning his patient's mental condition and hospital residence. He declares Mary is not mentally recovered, although she is improved since her commitment in May, and refutes the allegations that she is being held behind locked doors and barred windows in close confinement. He also addresses the rumors that Mary was being released from Bellevue Place, stating that no release was decided although he was willing to consider her being allowed to live with her sister in Springfield. This is an interesting article that gives direct evidence by Mary's doctor about her mental health, her hospital stay, and the procedure in which she was committed and remained incarcerated.

164.

"Mrs. President Lincoln—Her Restoration to Reason and Property." *Chicago Tribune,* June 16, 1876, 8.

A basic report of Mary Lincoln's second insanity trial during which a jury declared her restored to reason and capable of regaining possession of her money and property from her conservator, Robert T. Lincoln. The article prints the petition for Mary's release, the jury's decision, and an account of her estate, and gives a brief report on what happened in the courtroom that day.

165.

"A Happy Denouement—Mrs. Abraham Lincoln Restored to Her Reason and Freedom." *Chicago Times,* June 16, 1876, 3.

This is the most detailed report of Mary Lincoln's second insanity trial. Unlike the *Chicago Tribune* article of the same day, the *Times* article offers a history of Mary's case as well as what led to the 1876 retrial. The *Times* article also prints the petition for Mary's release, the jury's decision, and an account of her estate.

166.

"Mrs. Lincoln's Illness." *New York Times,* Oct. 31, 1880, 5.

A story about Mary Lincoln's current medical condition based on an interview with her physician, Dr. Lewis A. Sayre, whom Mary was consulting in New

York City. The article details Mary's back injury from falling off a chair in France and its medical repercussions, and quotes Sayre as stating that Mary suffers from kidney trouble and "great mental depression." This is an important article in understanding the facts of Mary's later life, travels, and medical conditions.

167.
"Mrs. Lincoln's Health—What Is Claimed to Be an Accurate Statement Respecting It—Her Eccentricities and Whims." *New York Times*, July 22, 1881.

A report of a Chicago journalist in Springfield, Illinois, who purports to offer the "true condition of affairs" of Mary Lincoln's life in her old hometown. The article discusses Mary's habits, her health, her daily routines and preferred topics on conversation, and even records the amount of baggage with which she arrived at her sister's home in Springfield—sixty trunks, weighing about eight thousand pounds. The numerous personal details in this article suggest the reporter got his facts by speaking to Mary's family, friends, neighbors, and other local community members; they also are corroborated by other primary sources on Mary's life. Overall, this article gives a first-hand glimpse into Mary's daily life in the year prior to her death.

168.
"Mrs. Abraham Lincoln—Her Strange Hallucinations." *New York Times*, Aug. 4, 1881, 3.

This reprint of a letter to the editor of the *Cincinnati Commercial* refutes previous press reports that Mary Lincoln was extremely ill. The letter states that Mary's condition is mainly in her head and that her family in Springfield is giving her great care. It also reports on Mary's actions and conversations during the past nine months living at the Edwards home in Springfield, including her physical complaints, her hallucinations, how she spends her days looking through her trunks of possessions, and her fear for her son Robert's safety in his role as secretary of war. The details in this letter, which are corroborated by other primary sources, make clear that either Robert Lincoln or someone close to Mary in Springfield either wrote the letter or gave the writer the information; as such it is an important part of the bibliography.

169.
"Mrs. Lincoln in Want—Sick and Unable to Obtain Much-Needed Attention." *New York Times*, Nov. 23, 1881.

This is an interview with Dr. Lewis A. Sayre, Mary Lincoln's New York physician and lifelong acquaintance, concerning Mary's physical health, the medical treatments she was receiving, and her need for Congress to increase the amount of her government pension. Sayre describes Mary's fall off a stepladder in France in 1879, after which her health was never the same, and describes in detail his diagnosis of her many ailments and the treatments he prescribed for her. This interview is a major source of information on Mary's life and health during this time period.

170.
"Mrs. Lincoln—She Corrects Some Reports Concerning Her Financial Condition." *Illinois State Journal*, Nov. 29, 1881.

In this rare press interview, Mary Lincoln explains the history of her finances since her husband's death, including the two houses she owned and how "frugally" she lived in Europe, and states her belief that she does not have enough money to live on and needs a pension increase by Congress to survive. Mary also offers kind words about her son Robert and explains why she refuses to ask him for financial help. This article, coming straight from Mary herself, offers excellent primary evidence concerning her life.

171.
"The Health of Mrs. Lincoln Not Improving." *Chicago Tribune*, Jan. 15, 1882.

This article, based on separate interviews with Mary Lincoln and her physician, Dr. Lewis A. Sayre, concerns Mary's health and living conditions in what ultimately was the final year of her life. Mary talks specifically about her failing eyesight, while Sayre offers the reporter a copy of the report of four eminent physicians, all of whom examined Mary and gave their diagnoses as to her health in a report to Congress as a way to help increase her pension. The report details all of Mary's physical ailments as determined by these four physicians and, as such, it is one of the most important pieces of primary information published about Mary's health in late life.

172.
"Mary Todd Lincoln—Her Death in This City at 8 O'Clock Sunday Evening." *Illinois State Journal*, July 17, 1882.

The local obituary for Mary Lincoln after her death on July 16. In addition to a review of Mary's entire life, the obituary also details her final few days, her medical condition, and what happened in the hours leading up to her death. It is essential reading for anyone interested in the contemporary facts of Mary's last days and death.

173.
"Awaiting the Burial—The Preparations Made for the Funeral of the Late Mary Todd Lincoln." *Illinois State Journal*, July 18, 1882.

This article reports on the funeral arrangements being made for Mary Lincoln by her son Robert and the local members of her family, as well as the actions and comments of local citizens regarding Mary's death. The historical gem in this article is the statement that Mary's family "found" her wedding ring, which she received from Abraham in 1842 but had stopped wearing recently because her fingers had become so swollen by her illness.

174.
"Laid to Rest—The Last Sad Rites Paid to the Remains of Mary Todd Lincoln." *Illinois State Journal*, July 20, 1882.

This detailed account of Mary Lincoln's funeral in Springfield includes descriptions of the church in which it was held, the floral designs, the funeral procession to the cemetery, names of some attendees, and the complete eulogy delivered by Rev. James A. Reed. A secondary account of the funeral can be found in "Mrs. Lincoln's Funeral," *Lincoln Lore*, March 1965.

175.
Swisshelm, Jane Grey. "Tribute to the Dead from Mrs. Jane Grey Swisshelm." *Chicago Tribune*, July 20, 1882.

Swisshelm's paean to her friend Mary Lincoln recalls their moments together, extolling her virtues as a woman and a first lady, but also states that she believed Mary was "never entirely sane" after the shock of her husband's murder. Swisshelm, an ardent abolitionist, also claims that Mary was a "radical" abolitionist. One interesting piece of history contained in the article is Swisshelm's statement that Mary Lincoln only once after the assassination ever laid aside her widow's weeds and dressed in a plain black silk dress, which was for Tad's birthday and at his request.

176.
"Opening of a Letter Written by Mrs. Lincoln." *Chicago Tribune*, July 21, 1882, 8.

A brief article about a letter received by Cook County Judge Mason B. Loomis from Mary Lincoln, which was posted to him by his insurance company in the event of her death. The article describes Loomis's efforts to find Robert Lincoln and open the letter in front of him. The letter from Mary was dated July 23, 1873, but the article does not describe its contents. (The letter, now part of the Mary Lincoln Insanity File in the Lincoln Financial Foundation Collection at Allen County Public Library, Indiana, concerns Mary's will, which was dated July 23, 1873.)

177.
Glyndon, Howard. "The Truth about Mrs. Lincoln." *Independent* 34, no. 1758 (Aug. 10, 1882): 4.

Personal recollections of Mary Lincoln as first lady by poet and journalist Laura Redden Searing, who published under the pen name Howard Glyndon. The article, written shortly after Mary's death, offers memories of Mary from 1861 to 1862 on topics such as her wardrobe, her social grace, and her grief after the death of her son Willie. The article is a defense of Mary's good nature, a rebuke against the negative gossip and accusations against her during the last twenty years of her life, and a call to sympathetically understand her "extravagance of behavior" and "hallucinations."

178.
"Mrs. Lincoln's Appointee." *New York Times*, Dec. 14, 1886, 9.

This reminiscence by a former Republican U.S. senator recounts efforts to have President Lincoln remove the commissioner of agriculture, only to have Lincoln say he could not do it because "Mrs. Lincoln appointed him." The commissioner, Isaac Newton, was a spiritualist who had befriended Mary Lincoln and introduced her to other spiritualists in Washington.

179.
Wood, William P. Untitled article. *Washington* [D.C] *Sunday Gazette*, Jan. 16, 1887.

This is the recounting of an interview with President Lincoln concerning Mary Lincoln's supposed trading of money for political favors during the war, in which Wood claims the president declared his wife suffered from "partial insanity." While Wood's statement comes twenty-five years after the supposed interview and certainly must be taken with a measure of suspicion, it also is one of only three known recollections regarding Abraham Lincoln's statements declaring his wife to be insane; it therefore must be considered an important item in the Mary Lincoln bibliography.

180.
Badeau, Adam. "Adam Badeau's Letter: A History of the Insanity of Mrs. President Lincoln." *Chicago Tribune*, Jan. 17, 1887, 10.

This is an excerpt from Badeau's book, *Grant in Peace: From Appomattox to Mount McGregor; A Personal Memoir* (entry 9), in which Badeau relates his 1865 experiences at City Point, Virginia, with Mary Lincoln when she had multiple temper tantrums. Badeau expresses his opinion that her insanity explains her bizarre behaviors.

181.
Miner, N. W. "Mrs. Abraham Lincoln: A Letter of Vindication." *New York Tribune*, Apr. 15, 1888, 11.
    A letter to the editor by Noyes W. Miner, a onetime neighbor and longtime friend to Mary Lincoln beginning in 1853, seeking to defend Mary against public and press criticism. Miner refutes the stories that Mary was a secessionist and that she stole items from the White House in 1865; he declares that she was forever unhappy and, at times, mentally deranged after her husband's murder. He also relates Mary's mental and physical conditions in 1881 as he experienced them when he saw her in New York City.

182.
"We Paid Our Honest Debts." *Omaha* [Neb.] *Bee*, July 21, 1889, 13.
    This reminiscence of Hon. John B. Hawley, an Illinois lawyer, state's attorney, and congressman (1869–1875), concerns an attempt by First Lady Mary Lincoln to influence her husband in making a specific political appointment, and how the president responded.

183.
"Personal." [Washington, D.C.] *National Tribune*, April 26, 1894, 4.
    A report that the file clerk of the House of Representatives had recently discovered in some "old papers" a letter from Mary Lincoln to the Speaker of the House presenting her petition to receive a government pension based on her husband's service to the nation and her own financial needs. The article also describes the physical appearance of the letter and the successful result of Mary's petition. Although the article and reprinted letter do not include a date, an exact duplicate letter, sent to the U.S. Senate, was dated December 1868. That letter is printed in *Mary Todd Lincoln: Her Life and Letters* (entry 56), 493.

184.
"A Lincoln Nurse: She Cared for Bob and Willie Lincoln before the War." *Illinois State Journal*, Feb. 12, 1895, 3.
    A reminiscence by "Aunt" Ruth Stanton who supposedly worked in the Lincoln home as a young girl in the late 1840s. Stanton describes Mary Lincoln's personality as wife, mother, and employer, as well as her typical daily duties as a housekeeper.

185.
Hallmark, Harrydele. "Mrs. Abraham Lincoln." *Los Angeles Times*, Feb. 17, 1895, 24.

In this interview with Francis B. Carpenter, a painter who lived in the White House for six months during the war, Carpenter discusses key moments in Mary Lincoln's life, such as her childhood, her first meeting with Abraham Lincoln, her wedding day, and her appearance and actions as first lady, including her visit to Fort Stevens while it was under attack. Some of Carpenter's statements are from firsthand knowledge and observation, while others he quotes as coming from William Herndon.

186.
"Mrs. Dr. Wallace." *Chicago Sunday Times-Herald*, Aug. 25, 1895, 25.

This reminiscence by Mary Lincoln's sister, Frances Wallace, discusses the Lincoln-Todd courtship, wedding, and home life. Wallace portrays the Lincoln marriage as one full of love and understanding, and adamantly refutes the story promulgated by William Herndon that Lincoln left Mary standing at the altar in 1841. Reprinted as "Mrs. Eliza Wallace," *Illinois State Journal*, Sept. 2, 1895, 5, and later as *Lincoln's Marriage: Newspaper Interview with Mrs. Frances Wallace, Springfield, Ill., Sept. 2, 1895* (Privately printed, 1917).

187.
"Another Error Corrected." *Chicago Times-Herald*, Sept. 8, 1895, 40.

An interview with Mrs. General McConnell, a Springfield friend of the Lincolns, who praises Mary Lincoln as a loving mother. McConnell offers examples of Mary's maternal care, such as how she put the children to bed at night, dressed them, and made their clothes.

188.
"How Lincoln and Mary Todd Made Up." *New York Times*, Sept. 13, 1895, 6.

C. C. Bangs, a resident of Springfield, Illinois, offers a brief reminiscence on how Abraham Lincoln and Mary Todd reconciled in 1842 after their broken engagement.

189.
"Abraham Lincoln's True Love Story." *Daily Picayune* [New Orleans, La.], Mar. 14, 1897.

In interview with Emilie Todd Helm, Mary Lincoln's half-sister, Helm defends her sister against the "unkind and uncalled-for" criticism of Mary through the years. Helm describes in detail Mary as a child and young woman, her wedding and marriage to Abraham Lincoln, her life as wife and mother, the difficult times she endured as first lady, the effects of the assassination, and her later years in Europe.

190.
"Friend of the Lincolns." [Syracuse, N.Y.] *Evening Herald*, Aug. 24, 1897.
      This interview with Mrs. Catharine Gibson concerns her interesting firsthand memories and experiences in the White House during the Civil War when her brother, William O. Stoddard, served as President Abraham Lincoln's "third" secretary. Gibson, who was living in Syracuse at the time of the interview, gives her recollections of First Lady Mary Lincoln's appearance, character, love for her family, and treatment by Washington society during her White House years. Gibson also briefly recalls her visits to Mary in Chicago during Mary's widowhood and how changed she was as a person from her time as first lady.

191.
"Abe Lincoln's Joke: How Mrs. Lincoln Was Jealous of Princess Salm-Salm." *New York Tribune*, reprinted in *Los Angeles Times*, July 30, 1899, B7.
      This story, as related "at a recent afternoon reception" by former Civil War general Daniel Sickles, tells of Princess Salm-Salm and other ladies kissing President Lincoln during his visit to an army camp. According to Sickles, Mary Lincoln was furious at the episode and remained frigid toward him during a subsequent dinner, since it was he who orchestrated the kissing.

192.
"His Early Social Life and Marriage." *Chicago Tribune*, Patriotic Supplement no. 4, Abraham Lincoln, Feb. 12, 1900, 14.
      These unique interviews with Mrs. Benjamin S. Edwards (sister-in-law of Ninian Edwards, Mary Lincoln's brother-in-law) and Mrs. John Todd Stuart (Mary's cousin-in-law), recall memories and anecdotes about Mary from various times between 1840 and 1865. This article contains essential facts about Mary from people who knew her intimately, including her character as a young woman, her grief after son Eddie's death in 1850, her immediate postassassination feelings, and the family's plans for life after Abraham Lincoln's second term as president.

193.
"Lincoln's Last Hours." *New York Tribune*, Oct. 14, 1900, 2.

Interview with Dr. Charles Sabin Taft, one of the surgeons in Ford's Theatre on Apr. 15, 1865, regarding Abraham Lincoln's assassination. Taft's account has numerous mentions of Mary Lincoln's words, attitudes, and actions during that night.

194.
Stevens, Walter B. "Recollections of Lincoln." *St. Louis Globe-Democrat*, Mar. 21, 1901, 3.

This installment of a four-month series of articles on Abraham Lincoln—based on original interviews with Lincoln's friends and acquaintances—focuses on the courtship and home life of Abraham and Mary Lincoln as told by their nephew Albert S. Edwards, son of Ninian and Elizabeth (Todd) Edwards. It is an invaluable, and thoroughly believable, account of major issues and scenes of the Lincoln-Todd courtship, wedding, and home life as witnessed by Edwards or told repeatedly to him by family members. His recollections include matters such as Mary Todd's character and education, her role as Springfield belle, the thorough love and compatibility of Mary and Abraham Lincoln, and the true story of the Lincoln-Todd wedding. Reprinted in Stevens, *A Reporter's Lincoln*, edited by Michael Burlingame (Lincoln: University of Nebraska Press, 1998), 110–120.

195.
"Knew Mrs. Lincoln." *Hartford* [Ky.] *Herald*, Oct. 4, 1905, 1.

Interview with Mary Ballenger Jones, a woman who went to boarding school with Mary Lincoln in Lexington, Kentucky, and remained friends with her for many years. Jones recalls Mary's character and personality as a girl and a student, her impressions about male admirers, and also her desire to marry a smart man over a handsome man. Jones also recounts visits she made to Mary in Springfield in the late 1850s.

196.
Tarbell, Ida M. "The Loves of Lincoln." *New York Tribune*, Nov. 29, 1908, 1.

In this story of Abraham Lincoln's courtships with Ann Rutledge, Mary Owens, and Mary Todd, Tarbell specifically refutes William Herndon's tale of the broken engagement with Mary Todd. While Tarbell admits Lincoln loved Ann Rutledge and was devastated by her death, Tarbell does not believe—as Herndon states—that Lincoln thereafter never loved another woman, including Mary Todd. This article is a summary of the argument Tarbell wrote in her 1900 book *The Life of Abraham Lincoln* (entry 15).

197.
"Tells of Insults to Lincoln's Wife" [Philadelphia] *Evening Bulletin*, Feb. 12, 1909, 1–2.

Reminiscence of Dr. Wistar P. Brown, court dentist at Frankfort-on-Main, Germany, about Mary and Tad Lincoln while they lived in that city during 1869 and 1870. Brown recounts the friendship that developed between his family and the Lincolns; how Mary spent her time, behaved, and was treated by people in America and Europe; and Tad's general behavior and character. This is a fascinating glimpse into Mary and Tad's time in Germany by someone who frequented their company.

198.
Rally, Mary Bradley. "Cousin and Childhood Friend of Mary Todd Lincoln Tells of Days When She and Martyr's Wife Were Girls Together." *Lexington* [Ky.] *Herald*, Feb. 14, 1909, 1, and Feb. 17, 1909, 4.

These reminiscences of Margaret Stuart Woodrow, a cousin and devoted childhood friend of Mary Todd, discuss the character, temperament, and intellect of young Mary Todd. Woodrow's statements, especially about Mary's "highly strung" nature and her "love of poetry," have become necessary staples in Mary's story. Woodrow also refutes the notion—as did every friend or relative of young Mary Todd—that Mary was left standing at the altar by Abraham Lincoln. This reminiscence is essential reading for any understanding of Mary's childhood.

199.
"Interesting Stories of Lincoln Related." *Lexington* [Ky.] *Herald*, Feb. 17, 1909, 5.

Todd family friend Mary B. Clay recollects her winter 1864 visit with First Lady Mary Lincoln in this article. Clay interestingly relates the condescending treatment of Mary by Washington society women on her arrival to the capital in 1861, and declares it to have been the "origin of the unpopularity of Mrs. Lincoln."

200.
"Recalls Mrs. Lincoln." *Batavia* [Ill.] *Herald*, Mar. 6, 1909.

This interesting article contains primary statements by two women who knew and stayed with Mary Lincoln while the widowed first lady visited St. Charles, Illinois, to consult a spiritualist medium in the early 1870s. Included in the report are the names of the house in which Mary resided and the medium whom she consulted.

201.

Rockwell, J. H. "Domestic Life of Mr. Lincoln." *Democratic Banner* [Mt. Vernon, Ohio], Feb. 13, 1912, 2.

In this interview with Springfield banker and Lincoln family friend John W. Bunn, he criticizes the many misstatements made about Mary Lincoln and defends her as an exceptional wife, mother, neighbor, and hostess.

202.

"Mrs. Ben Hardin Helm, Sister of Mrs. Abraham Lincoln, Tells of Trials of Widow of Martyred President—Those 'Bitter Letters.'" *Lexington* [Ky.] *Leader*, June 1, 1913.

This interview with Emilie Todd Helm, Mary's last surviving sister at the time, was instigated by a recent auction in New York of a number of Mary Lincoln's letters written to her friend Sally Orne in the late 1860s, mainly concerning Mary's efforts to obtain a government pension. In the interview, Helm discusses Mary's Southern family ties and her loyalty to the Union during the war; she mentions her own visit to the White House during the war; and states that her sister, highly sensitive and burdened with grief in her later years, was a very misunderstood woman. The article also publishes portions of some of the auctioned letters.

203.

"Abraham Lincoln Married 78 Years Ago Today; Mrs. Mary Edwards Brown Tells Story of Hasty Wedding Plans." *Illinois State Journal*, Nov. 4, 1920.

Mary Lincoln's grandniece relates the Todd family tradition concerning the arrangements and service of the Lincoln-Todd wedding in 1842.

204.

Holland, Jane. "Heartache Healed at Waukesha," *Milwaukee Sentinel*, Feb. 12, 1922.

This article includes brief reminiscences by Waukesha, Wisconsin, residents, including H. M. Youmans, former editor of the *Waukesha Freeman* newspaper, about seeing and speaking to Mary Lincoln during her month-long visit to Waukesha in 1872, when she took the water cure and visited with local spiritualists. The article is very short and offers little historical facts, but it does give some apparently firsthand accounts of Mary's appearance at that time ("frail," "worn," and morose), when she still was mourning the 1871 death of her son Tad.

205.
Barton, William E. "The Courting of Mary Todd." *Dearborn [Michigan] Independent,* Oct. 8, 1927, 15–20.

Barton relates the story of Lincoln courting Mary Todd, as well as a brief survey of their married years, their family life, and Mary's own ambitions for her husband's political success. Barton denies William Herndon's claim that Lincoln left Mary standing at the altar for their 1841 broken engagement, but states that it was Lincoln's own self-doubts that caused him to cancel the wedding.

206.
———. "Mrs. Lincoln in the White House." *Dearborn [Michigan] Independent,* Oct. 29, 1927, 16–19.

A general examination of Mary Lincoln's years in the White House and after the assassination, she is characterized as a woman misunderstood and cruelly persecuted who did not have the patience, tact, or self-control necessary to her position as first lady during a time of war. Many of her bizarre actions Barton ascribes to "some element of mental aberration," which led to her commitment in 1875.

207.
"Story of Lincoln's Wedding Is Told by Capital Woman." *Washington Post,* Feb. 13, 1929, 1.

Mrs. H. D. Ames, granddaughter of Mary Lincoln's aunt, recalls the hurry surrounding the Lincoln-Todd wedding arrangements in 1842: the wedding cake was served while still warm, Mary's bangs were scorched by the curling iron, and Mary said to her sister Elizabeth, "Gingerbread is good enough for plebians"—an angry retort to the low opinion the Todd clan held of Abraham Lincoln. Mary's expression on her wedding day was reportedly unknown outside the family at the time of publication and "has been a meaningful expression in the family ever since."

208.
Evans, W. A. "How to Keep Well—Health of Mrs. Lincoln." *Chicago Tribune,* Apr. 18, 1930, 14.

In this brief summary of the supposed cause of Mary Lincoln's death, Evans, a trained physician, outlines her final medical symptoms and declares she died of diabetic coma. This conclusion was later published in Evans's book, *Mrs. Abraham Lincoln: A Study of Her Personality and Her Influence on Lincoln* (entry 34).

209.

"More about Mary Lincoln—Miss Stimson's Story." *Aurora Beacon-News*, Dec. 25, 1932.

Lena Stimson, former superintendent of nurses at Bellevue Place sanitarium, recounts stories about Mary Lincoln during her stay in the sanitarium. While Stimson was not at Bellevue Place when Mary was there in 1875, Stimson recounts stories told her by Mrs. Ruggles, the matron during Mary Lincoln's time, about Mary's hallucinations, temper, passion for clothing, and general life at the sanitarium.

210.

Chenery, William Dodd. "Mary Lincoln Should Be Remembered for Many Kind Acts." *Illinois State Register*, Feb. 27, 1938.

This article by a Springfield native recounts stories of Harriet Waters Dallman, a neighbor of the Lincolns during the 1850s. The author makes the argument that the positive stories about Mary Lincoln's life should be told and published as well as the negative. Chenery recounts Dallman's stories of how she was unable to nurse her baby in 1853 and Mary helped by nursing the baby herself, and also how when Mary added the second story to the Lincoln home in 1856 she called on Dallman's husband, who was an architect, to assist. In his defense of Mary's positive qualities, Chenery concludes that "only domestic tranquility could prevail in a home where such friendship and love was displayed for a sick neighbor."

211.

Gordon, Beulah. "Mrs. Keys Recalls Stories of Her Aunt Mary Lincoln." *Illinois State Journal & Register*, Aug. 23, 1942.

Mrs. Edward D. Keys, daughter of Levi O. Todd and niece to Mary Lincoln, shares her memories and opinions of her aunt, such as the clothing Mary bought her in Europe when Mrs. Keys was a young girl.

212.

Knox, Sanka. "Woman Describes Death of Lincoln." *New York Times*, Feb. 12, 1950, 42.

Knox's article reports the discovery of a previously unknown letter describing the night of April 14–15, 1865, in the Petersen house as President Lincoln lay dying. The letter, written by Elizabeth Dixon, the wife of a U.S. senator and a friend of Mary Lincoln, was dated May 1, 1865, and tells of Dixon's experiences that night after she was called to the Petersen house by Robert Lincoln and spent the night comforting the beleaguered first lady. The article publishes most of the letter's contents and paraphrases the rest.

213.
Mitgang, Herbert. "Has History Wronged Mary Lincoln?" [Louisville, Ky.] *Courier-Journal & Times*, Feb. 11, 1973, G1, G22.
    An impressively discerning consideration of Mary Lincoln's life and historical reputation, which Mitgang labels akin to a Greek tragedy. He declares her "an enigmatic daguerreotype sitting uncomfortably in the shadow of her husband."

214.
Tucker, Sheila. "Who Was the Lady in Black?" *Auburn* [N.Y.] *Citizen*, Dec. 22, 1974, 37.
    This brief story tells of Mary Lincoln's visits to Auburn and Moravia, N.Y., in early 1872 to visit spiritualist mediums.

❦

Government documents

215.
Congressional debate, bill for the relief of Mary Lincoln. *Congressional Globe*, 39th Cong., 1st sess., 1865–66, 1:13–16, 71–72, 77, 80, 88, 99, 101, 104, 107, 114, 172.
    This transcript chronicles the debate over the proposed bill to grant monetary relief to Mary Lincoln based on the amount of presidential salary her husband would have earned had he survived his entire second term in office. While much of the debate is a parliamentary discussion, the major question discussed was whether to give Mary the full $100,000 presidential salary of four years or only one year's worth of salary at $25,000. After looking back on precedent, the Congress passed a bill to pay Mary one year's salary, minus any funds already paid out to President Lincoln before his death. In the end, Mary received $22,000.

216.
Congressional debate, bill for free franking privilege for Mary Lincoln. *Congressional Globe*, 39th Cong., 1st sess., 1866, 1:297, 349, 700, 719, 807.

Mary Lincoln painted in the American folk art style by New Hampshire artist Tim Campbell. COURTESY TIM CAMPBELL, WWW. STURBRIDGEYANKEE.COM.

Woodcut by Charles Turzak depicting Mary and Abraham Lincoln separately grieving, probably for one of their two children, Eddie and Willie, who both died as children. ORIGINALLY PUBLISHED IN TURZAK, *ABRAHAM LINCOLN: BIOGRAPHY IN WOODCUT*, 1933.

Portrait of Mary Lincoln published in Lila Graham Alliger Woolfall, *Presiding Ladies of the White House* (Washington: Bureau of National Literature and Art, 1903). COURTESY LIBRARY OF CONGRESS PRINTS AND PHOTOGRAPHS DIVISION, WASHINGTON, D.C.

Mannequin of Mary Lincoln, clothed in and surrounded by some of Mary's original dresses during her years as first lady. This exhibit at the Abraham Lincoln Presidential Library and Museum in Springfield, Illinois, depicts Mary as the fashionable woman she was during her years as the social leader of Washington, D.C., from 1861 to 1865. COURTESY ABRAHAM LINCOLN PRESIDENTIAL LIBRARY AND MUSEUM.

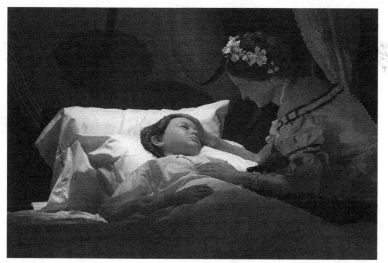

Mannequin exhibit at the Abraham Lincoln Presidential Library and Museum in Springfield depicting Mary Lincoln leaning over her son Willie, who was sick with typhoid fever in February 1862. Willie eventually died from the disease, and the loss nearly destroyed Mary, who had already lost son Eddie in 1850. COURTESY ABRAHAM LINCOLN PRESIDENTIAL LIBRARY AND MUSEUM

This statue of Mary and Abraham Lincoln in Racine, Wisconsin, was the only depiction of Mary in sculpture that existed until the city of Springfield, Illinois, added a Lincoln family group sculpture in the downtown area in 2004. This Associated Press photo of the monument shows the five-ton granite group of Mary and Abraham after it was completed in Chicago on June 26, 1943. The statue was provided for in the will of Lena Rosewall, a student of Lincolniana, as a gift to the city of Racine, where it was officially unveiled on July 4 in East Park. An inscription on the statue reads, "To children, and all people, may this monument inspire devotion and patriotism." AUTHOR'S COLLECTION.

Modern photo of the Mary and Abraham Lincoln statue in East Park, Racine, Wisconsin, as it looked in summer 2017. COURTESY STEVEN ROGSTAD.

Mary Lincoln was depicted in 2010 on her own gold coin by the U.S. Mint as part of the First Spouse Gold Coin series. The series was created to honor the nation's first spouses by issuing one-half-ounce ten-dollar gold coins featuring their images in the order they served as first spouse. The front of the coin shows a portrait of Mary, while the reverse design depicts Mary bringing wounded Union soldiers flowers and books. She also brought them food and wrote letters to relatives on their behalf. COURTESY U.S. MINT. WWW.USMINT.GOV.

The Unhappy Story of Mary Todd,

Illustrations by
DEAN
CORNWELL

This illustration by Dean Cornwell was the cover art for the Honoré Willsie Morrow article "The Unhappy Story of Mary Todd, the Woman Lincoln Loved: Told to Right a Great Wrong," printed in *Cosmopolitan* in May 1927. Morrow's article surveys Mary Lincoln's life from girlhood to death, giving particular attention to the Lincoln courtship and marriage, Mary's role as first lady, and her post–White House pension battle and Old Clothes Scandal.

This illustration depicting Abraham Lincoln and Mary Todd at the dance during which they met, was published in 1956 in *Woman's Home Companion* as part of the article "The Heart of Mary Lincoln," by Mary W. Ballard. The article is a fictionalized account of the "love story of Mary and Abraham Lincoln" that occurs as memories of the aged widow Lincoln as she looks through the trunks full of clothing and mementos of her life. The article was also a basis for a television episode on *NBC Matinee Theater* that same year. COURTESY MARIE SAALBURG.

"Assassination of President A. Lincoln, April 14th, 1865, at Ford's Theater, Washington, D.C.," a hand-colored lithograph published by Gibson & Co. (Cincinnati, Ohio) in 1870. The print shows the president's box at Ford's Theater with John Wilkes Booth, on the right, shooting President Lincoln, who is seated at the front of the box; on the left are Mary Lincoln seated in the front, Major Henry Rathbone rising to stop Booth, and Clara Harris standing behind Mrs. Lincoln. COURTESY LIBRARY OF CONGRESS PRINTS AND PHOTOGRAPHS DIVISION, WASHINGTON, D.C.

"Lincoln and His Family," an engraving by William Sartain based on a painting by S. B. Waugh. This 1866 print shows Abraham Lincoln sitting in a chair at the left end of a table with Thomas seated next to him, Mary sitting on the right, and Robert standing behind the table. A portrait of son Willie, who died in 1862, hangs on the wall behind Robert. COURTESY LIBRARY OF CONGRESS PRINTS AND PHOTOGRAPHS DIVISION, WASHINGTON, D.C.

This still from the 1930 movie *Abraham Lincoln*, directed by film pioneer D. W. Griffith, shows Kay Hammond as Mary Todd and Walter Huston as Abraham Lincoln. This was Griffith's first sound film.
COURTESY THE COLLECTION OF
MARK S. REINHART, AUTHOR OF
ABRAHAM LINCOLN ON SCREEN.

One of the most widely shown and well-known screen dramatizations of Abraham Lincoln's life was the 1940 film *Abe Lincoln in Illinois*, based on the play of the same title by Robert Sherwood. In the film, Mary Lincoln, played by Ruth Gordon, is portrayed as a bitter, scheming woman who ruthlessly pushes her husband (played by Raymond Massey) into greatness. COURTESY THE COLLECTION OF MARK S. REINHART, AUTHOR OF *ABRAHAM LINCOLN ON SCREEN.*

This debate details the proposed bill to grant Mary Lincoln free franking privileges for life, whereby all letters and packages carried by post to and from Mary would be conveyed free of postage. The legislation was approved without significant debate.

217.
Congressional debate, bill for proposed pension for Mary Lincoln. *Congressional Globe*, Senate, 40th Cong., 3rd sess., 1869, 2:1242–46; and 41st Cong., 2nd sess., 1870, 5:4540–43, 6:5390, 5395–400, 5557–60.

This transcription details the Senate debate over a bill to give Mary Lincoln a pension of $3,000 per year as the widow of the president of the United States. These debates, while mainly centered around the type of precedent such a pension would set, also offer insight into Mary's reputation among Washington politicians (which was not flattering), including accusations of her being a rebel sympathizer, being a wealthy and self-centered aristocrat, and just having "bad taste" at publicly soliciting for a pension. Illinois senator Richard Yates, in particular, made a now often-quoted statement denigrating Mary because "a woman should be true to her husband." While Yates was clearly referring to his belief that Mary was a Southern sympathizer during the Civil War, some historians have erroneously taken the statement to mean that Mary was having an adulterous affair while she was first lady. The fact that it took five years for Congress to give Mary a pension, and the sometimes acrimonious debate on the issue in the Senate, is a good indicator of Mary's poor personal relationships and often bad reputation while she was first lady.

❦

Scholarly and popular articles

218.
"Spirit Photographs." *Spiritual Magazine*, May 1872, 210.

Spirit photographer William Mumler describes examples of his spirit photography in this article, including the circumstances of Mary Lincoln's visit to him (under a pseudonym) in Boston only months before and the photo he took of her that contained the spirit likenesses of President Lincoln and her son Tad. Mumler retells this same story in his 1875 memoir (entry 5), although that version is full of embellishment and exaggeration, while this journal article is a simple narration of the facts of the visit.

219.
Perry, Leslie J. "Lincoln's Home Life in Washington." *Harper's New Monthly Magazine* 94, no. 561 (Feb. 1897): 353–359.

Perry's article on the White House life and personal relationships of the Lincoln family—especially Mary Lincoln—draws on numerous family telegrams during the war years. An excerpt of the article that focuses on Mary was published as "Lincoln's Home Life—His Kindly Manner—A Misconception of Mrs. Lincoln," *Los Angeles Times*, Feb. 5, 1897, 2.

220.
Porter, Horace. "Campaigning with Grant: Preparing for the Last Campaign." *Century Magazine* 54, no. 4 (Aug. 1897): 584–602.

An excerpt from Porter's book of the same title, this article mentions Mary Lincoln's 1865 visit to Union Army headquarters at City Point, Virginia, during which she unleashed a vicious verbal harangue on Mrs. General Ord and Julia Grant. Contrary to Adam Badeau's account of the trip (entry 9), Porter says only that Mary was in a bad mood and did not enjoy the day.

221.
Helm, Emily Todd. "Mary Todd Lincoln: Reminiscences and Letters of the Wife of President Lincoln." *McClure's* 11, no. 5 (Sept. 1898): 476–480.

This article by Mary's sister contains a brief history of the Todd family, stories of Mary as a girl in Lexington, recollections of the Lincoln-Todd marriage, and excerpts from Mary's letters. Helm recounts not only her own knowledge and memories of her sister's personality and life, but also quotes from family members and contemporary family friends about their memories of Mary. The article also includes reminiscences from one of Mary's closest childhood friends, Elizabeth L. Norris, who describes Mary's intellect, personality, and typical childhood life. Norris also tells the now-famous story of a ten-year-old Mary using willow branches to make her own hoop skirt. Overall, Helm's article is one of the most important in the bibliography, containing much primary information about Mary Lincoln from family and friends.

222.
Baldwin, Mrs. H. A. "When Lincoln's Wife Pulled His Hair," in "Some Genuine Lincoln Anecdotes." *Frank Leslie's Popular Monthly* 52, no. 4 (Aug. 1901): 25.

This anecdote by Baldwin, a Lincoln family neighbor in Springfield, recalls the story of Lincoln receiving a visitor in his home while reclining across two chairs. Mary Lincoln came in, pulled his hair to turn his head, and "looked at him reprovingly," to which he replied without rising, "Little Mary, allow me to introduce you to Judge so-and-so."

223.
Harris, Gibson William. "My Recollections of Abraham Lincoln." *Woman's Home Companion*, Nov. 1903, 9–11.
These recollections from a law student in the Lincoln-Herndon Law Office from 1845 to 1847 discuss Mary Lincoln's personality as he experienced it, as well as his thoughts on Lincoln's consideration for his wife. Harris found Mary to be an impressive woman full of fun and intelligence but who could also be staid and proper when necessary. He felt Lincoln loved his wife, and stated Lincoln often would take her with him on trips to Chicago and would go home early from the office if there was a thunderstorm approaching because of Mary's fear of storms.

224.
Orr, Lyndon. "The Courtships of Abraham Lincoln." *Munsey's Magazine* 36, no. 4 (Jan. 1907): 445–450.
A story of Lincoln's courtships with Ann Rutledge, Mary Owens, and Mary Todd, Orr's article repeats William Herndon's assertions that Abraham left Mary standing at the altar in 1841 and only "reluctantly" married her in 1842; yet Orr also states that the marriage was happy and aided Lincoln considerably in his political success.

225.
Barnes, John S. "With Lincoln from Washington to Richmond in 1865—Part 1." *Appleton's Magazine* 9, no. 5 (May 1907): 515–524; and Barnes, John S., "With Lincoln from Washington to Richmond in 1865—Part 2." *Appleton's Magazine* 9, no. 6 (June 1907): 742–751.
Reminiscences of President Lincoln during his March 1865 visits to General Grant's military headquarters in City Point, Virginia, as written by a naval commander, these articles also include a description of Mary Lincoln's actions at City Point and Barnes's interpretation of her character. The real historical value of Barnes's writing is that he documents Mary's imperious and outlandish behavior during the trip, including her infamous tirade against Mrs. General Ord, which was also written about by Julia Grant and Adam Badeau. Barnes does not blame Mary for her behavior but excuses it because of her "extreme nervousness approaching hysteria, causing misapprehensions, extreme sensitiveness as to slights or want of politeness or consideration." He also credits Mary's trying behavior as "the cause of the sadness and melancholy" that were

so much a part of Abraham Lincoln's demeanor. Article republished, with the author mistakenly listed as "James" Barnes, in full in the *Magazine of History with Notes and Queries*, Extra Number—no. 161, Rare Lincolniana no. 39; vol. 41, no. 1 (1930): 37–56.

226.
Perrine, William. "The Wife of Abraham Lincoln." *Ladies' Home Journal* 26, no. 2 (Jan. 1909): 9–10, 47.
   A sympathetic defense of Mary Lincoln as a woman whom history barely knows or understands, Perrine's article repeats William Herndon's story of the broken engagement and Abraham leaving Mary standing at the wedding altar, yet depicts the Lincoln marriage as typical and not unhappy. Perrine portrays Mary as a relentlessly criticized first lady and widow who could not win no matter what her actions, including events such as her White House entertainments and purchases, the 1867 Old Clothes Scandal, and her five-year pension battle with Congress from 1865 to 1870.

227.
Steell, Willis. "Mrs. Abraham Lincoln and Her Friends." *Munsey's Magazine* 40, no. 5 (Feb. 1909): 617–623.
   An examination of Mary Lincoln's social aspirations as first lady, especially in regard to the women with whom she surrounded herself, her impulsive friendships and estrangements, and how these affected her reputation as first lady and White House hostess.

228.
Parker, Moses G. "Reminiscences of Personal Interviews with President Lincoln." *Contributions of the Lowell Historical Society* 1 (Apr. 1913): 382–387.
   These reminiscences of a U.S. Army surgeon stationed near Grant's headquarters in City Point, Virginia, in 1865 include the few times Parker met President and Mary Lincoln. Parker describes the first lady visiting hospitals at the front and greeting soldiers, as well as an incident during which president was saluted by a woman (Miss Agnes Joy, later Princess Salm-Salm), which angered Mary.

229.
Burkhardt, M. E. "Lincoln's First Levee." *Journal of the Illinois State Historical Society* 11, no. 3 (Oct. 1918): 386–390.
   This reprint of a February 7, 1861, letter to the editor of the *Missouri Democrat* by a Springfield, Illinois, resident describes the first levee given by the

president-elect and Mrs. Lincoln in their Springfield home. The letter writer, M. E. Burkhardt, attended the event and described the scene, paying particular attention to Mary Lincoln, what she wore, and how well she comported herself. The article also contains a contemporary newspaper account of the Lincolns' February 1862 grand fete in the White House, which was simultaneously a spectacular success and the cause of much criticism by administration opponents.

230.
"A Story of the Early Days in Springfield—And a Poem." *Journal of the Illinois State Historical Society* 16, nos. 1–2 (Apr.–July 1923): 141–146.
This account tells the story of Mary Todd and her friend Mercy Levering going into town after heavy rains in 1839. Mary carried roof shingles, which the young women dropped one at a time and used as steps across the muddy streets, until they ran out on their way home. To avoid walking through the muck, Mary hitched a ride on a dray, which caused a sensation in the aristocratic circles of the town due to its social "inappropriateness." The article includes the text of a letter by Levering's daughter recalling the event, as well as a poem written at the time celebrating Mary's famous ride (entry 401).

231.
Grimsley, Elizabeth Todd. "Six Months in the White House." *Journal of the Illinois State Historical Society* 19, nos. 3-4 (Oct. 1926–Jan. 1927): 43–73.
These recollections of the inaugural journey and beginnings of the war by Mary Lincoln's cousin, who lived in the White House for six months in 1861 and witnessed some of the most trying days of Abraham Lincoln's administration, are some of the seminal writings about Mary as first lady. Grimsley relates the "inner life of the household," such as personal aspects of Mary as wife and mother, and includes anecdotes of Mary as White House hostess, her visits to military hospitals, shopping in New York City, dealing with rebel relatives, and enduring negative press coverage. Grimsley wrote the article in 1894 for serial publication in *McClure's* magazine, but died before it could be completed. The *Journal of the Illinois State Historical Society* published the article only after Robert Lincoln's death in 1926, due to his objections to publishing an "unfinished" article (Elizabeth Todd Grimsley Papers, SC 608, folder 2, Abraham Lincoln Presidential Library).

232.
Foy, Eddie, and Alvin F. Harlow. "Clowning through Life." *Collier's* 78, no. 26 (Dec. 25, 1926): 15–16, 30.

These recollections of famed vaudevillian Eddie Foy Jr. mention his mother, Ellen Fitzgerald, who was Mary Lincoln's personal "nurse, guard, and companion" from 1872 to 1875. Foy recounts his mother's experiences with the former first lady, including examples of Mary's mental illness symptoms.

233.
Miles, Mary Leighton. "'The Fatal First of January, 1841.'" *Journal of the Illinois State Historical Society* 20, no. 1 (Apr. 1927): 13–48.
    This is an in-depth examination of the Lincoln-Todd broken engagement, written to disprove William Herndon's (and concomitantly Ward Lamon's) theory that Lincoln left Mary standing at the altar on January 1, 1841. Miles shows no evidence can be found in contemporary newspapers, in Lincoln's attendance record in the state legislature, or even in the tone of Lincoln's own letters at the time to verify Herndon's statements.

234.
Morrow, Honoré Willsie. "The Unhappy Story of Mary Todd, the Woman Lincoln Loved: Told to Right a Great Wrong." *Cosmopolitan*, May 1927, 22–27, 184–196.
    Printed one year before her Mary Lincoln biography, *Mary Todd Lincoln: An Appreciation of the Wife of Abraham Lincoln* (entry 29) was published, Morrow's extensive article surveys Mary's life from girlhood to death, giving particular attention to the Lincoln courtship and marriage, Mary's role as first lady, and her post–White House pension battle and Old Clothes Scandal. Like Morrow's book, the *Cosmopolitan* article is excellently researched for its time (although it does contain some historical errors) and has a captivating writing style. Morrow's style, however, is more story-driven than fact-driven, as is evidenced by her fictionalized dialogue and assumed character thoughts and motivations. While the article is based on researched facts, Morrow does not let the facts get in the way when an exciting or important scene demands detailed personal interactions.

235.
Tarbell, Ida M. "Mary Todd Lincoln: Wife of Abraham Lincoln—Part 1." *Ladies' Home Journal*, Feb. 1928, 22, 48, 51–52, 54.
    Tarbell tells a largely objective story of Mary Lincoln's life from her childhood in Lexington to the Lincoln family departure for the White House in 1861. Mary is portrayed as vivacious, intelligent, cultured, ambitious, and a great aid and encouragement to her husband's political success, yet also mercurial,

impatient, demanding, and hot-tempered. While the Lincoln marriage was occasionally troubled by disagreements, it was typically a happy one, Tarbell states.

236.
———. "Mary Todd Lincoln: Wife of Abraham Lincoln—Part 2." *Ladies' Home
Journal*, Mar. 1928, 30–31, 218, 221, 223.
The story of Mary Lincoln from her days as first lady to her death in 1882,
this article portrays Mary as an excellent first lady who shopped too much, was
relentlessly criticized by the press, and ultimately was devastated by the deaths
of her son Willie in 1862 and her husband in 1865. After Tad's death in 1871, she
lived a "rambling and unsatisfied life," traveling America and Europe. Her final
years are shown as dreary and depressed in which she received little sympathy
and went briefly insane.

237.
Armstrong, Orland K. "Where Lincoln 'Popped the Question' to Mary Todd."
San Francisco Chronicle Sunday Magazine, Feb. 10, 1929, 2.
The author of this article wonders if Abraham Lincoln proposed to Mary
Todd in the fall of 1840 as he visited her at her uncle's house in Columbia, Missouri. According to the article, which cites Todd family members and one resident of Columbia in 1840 as sources, Lincoln was on a boat bound for a Whig
political convention when the ship ran aground. He missed the meeting and
instead visited Mary in Columbia. While there, it is likely, Armstrong states,
that the two lovers became engaged.

238.
"Sarah Bernhardt and Lincoln's Widow." *Strand Magazine* 78 (1929): 522.
The story of actress Sarah Bernhardt saving Mary Lincoln's life in October 1880
as they both were passengers on the same steamship sailing from Europe to New
York is excerpted from Sarah Bernhardt's memoir *My Double Life: Memoirs of Sarah
Bernhardt* (London: William Heinemann, 1907), 353–354. The title was changed
to *Memories of My Life* for the U.S. printing (N.Y.: D. Appleton & Co., 1907).

239.
Barton, William E. "Mr. and Mrs. Lincoln," *Woman's Home Companion* 57, no.
13 (Feb. 1930).
In this consideration of the Lincolns' relationship and marriage, Barton, a
longtime and well-versed Lincoln scholar, concludes that Mary and Abraham
were together because they both wanted and loved each other even though they

were exact opposites. In Barton's view, the Lincolns made each other unhappy, as they would have made anyone else unhappy, but they also would have been unhappy without the other. "Mr. and Mrs. Lincoln were not always happy together, but they believed in each other and their lives supplemented and enlarged each other," Barton wrote. Overall, this is a viewpoint worth considering by one of the top Lincoln scholars of his time.

240.

Morrow, Honoré Willsie. "Lincoln's Last Day Described in Letters of His Wife." *Cosmopolitan*, Feb. 1930, 30–33, 219–220.

This article offers a reprinting and an interpretation of two letters Mary Lincoln wrote to artist Francis B. Carpenter in 1865 pertaining mainly to her husband, Abraham Lincoln. These letters (while now available in *Mary Todd Lincoln: Her Life and Letters*, entry 56) were relatively unknown and unseen when published in 1930 and represented, in Morrow's opinion, a warm and intelligent side of Mary that had been previously neglected. The letters are incredibly important sources of information not just about Abraham Lincoln but also about Mary and her sons' lives in Chicago in the immediate aftermath of the assassination. One letter describes, as the article title states, the last carriage ride Mary and Abraham took on the day of his murder. In the second letter Mary explains in her own words the infamous Shields duel that Abraham nearly fought for her honor in 1842.

241.

Warren, Louis A. "Mary Todd Lincoln Chronology." *Lincoln Lore*, no. 155 (Mar. 28, 1932).

This article offers a chronology of important moments in Mary Lincoln's life from 1818 to 1882, taken from W. A. Evans's 1932 book *Mrs. Abraham Lincoln: A Study of Her Personality and Influence on Lincoln* (entry 34).

242.

Sandburg, Carl. "Mary Todd Lincoln," parts 1 through 4, *Woman's Home Companion*, Sept.–Dec. 1932.

This four-part series of articles—one a month from September to December—is a slightly condensed version of Sandburg's contribution to his book with Paul M. Angle, *Mary Lincoln: Wife and Widow*, which also came out in 1932 (entry 35). The articles examine Mary Lincoln's life from birth to death. It contains excellent historical facts about Mary (not all of them correct but extremely well done for 1932) and is written in Sandburg's captivating, inimitable prose that helps make him still one of the most popular Lincoln historians.

243.
Warren, Louis A. "The Mother of Lincoln's Children." *Lincoln Lore*, no. 317 (May 6, 1935).
This brief article examines Mary Lincoln as a loving wife and mother, dedicated homemaker and first lady, and bereaved widow.

244.
———. "In Defense of Mrs. Lincoln." *Lincoln Lore*, no. 410 (Feb. 15, 1937).
A defense of Mary Lincoln as a loving wife, and a refutation of numerous myths about her and her marriage to Abraham Lincoln.

245.
Ritze, C. C. "In Defense of Mrs. Lincoln." *Journal of the Illinois State Historical Society* 30, no. 1 (Apr. 1937): 5–69.
Ritze offers a lengthy defense of Mary Lincoln against William Herndon's accusations about her, including her alleged bad character, the terrible state of the Lincoln marriage, the veracity of the Ann Rutledge love story, and numerous other points. The article starts by examining Herndon's own prejudices and motives, then offers evidence of Mary's virtuous qualities. There is also a general discussion of the value of using psychology to interpret history with particular reference to the conclusions of W. A. Evans's 1932 Mary Lincoln book (entry 34).

246.
Kinnaird, Virginia. "Mrs. Lincoln as a White House Hostess," in *Papers in Illinois History and Transactions for the Year 1938*, 65–87. Springfield: Illinois State Historical Society, 1939.
This is an excellent study of Mary Lincoln as White House hostess that both explains her strengths to undertake such a role and the successes she achieved as first lady, while also examining the social, political, and journalistic challenges she faced and the failures that resulted. It is a balanced, well-researched look at Mary that concludes she was an excellent first lady who could not overcome the politics and events of the times to be respected or accepted as a successful grand dame of Washington society.

247.
Stuart, Emily Huntington. "Some Recollections of the Early Days in Springfield and Reminiscences of Abraham Lincoln and Other Celebrities Who Lived in That Little Town in My Youth." *State of Illinois, Daughters of the American Revolution Genealogical Records* 3 (1940–1941): 109–128.

This reminiscence by Emily Huntington, later the wife of John Todd Stuart Jr., who grew up and resided in Springfield, contains numerous firsthand stories and anecdotes about Mary Lincoln, including her personality and social grace as a young belle in Springfield, her behavior as a wife and mother, and the story of the Lincoln-Todd courtship, broken engagement, and marriage.

248.
Brussel, James A. "Mary Todd Lincoln: A Psychiatric Study." *Psychiatric Quarterly* 15, supp. 1 (Jan. 1941): 7–26.
This professional psychiatric case study of Mary Lincoln surveys her life and examines her physical and mental history. Brussel, at the time of his writing the chief psychiatrist at Fort Dix, N.J., declares that while Mary apparently suffered numerous psychiatric symptoms such as hallucinations, terror, depression, suicidal intentions and attempts, and feelings of persecution, his diagnosis was that she was a victim of migraines and possibly epilepsy. This article marks the first time a professional psychiatrist studied Mary's symptoms and made a diagnosis based on the historical facts as he knew them, and as such is an important and fascinating addition to the Mary Lincoln bibliography, especially in regard to her mental health.

249.
Krueger, Lillian. "Mary Todd Lincoln Summers in Wisconsin." *Journal of the Illinois State Historical Society* 34, no. 2 (June 1941): 249–252.
This article offers the previously untold story of Mary Lincoln's two months in Waukesha, Wisconsin, where she went to visit the medicinal spring waters of Bethesda Park during the summer of 1872. Krueger, using contemporary newspaper reporting, reveals that Mary visited the spa daily to help her "dropsical condition," but kept a reclusive life without visitors. Her belief in spiritualism and visits to mediums in the Waukesha area are also mentioned. The story of Mary's visit is also one piece of a larger article by Krueger titled "Waukesha 'The Saratoga of the West,'" *Wisconsin Magazine of History* 24, no. 4 (June 1941): 394–424.

250.
Monaghan, Jay. "Was Abraham Lincoln Really a Spiritualist?" *Journal of the Illinois State Historical Society* 34, no. 2 (June 1941): 209–232.
This detailed examination and judgement of the eleven writings (at the time) about Abraham Lincoln as a believer in spiritualism is the essential reference for those interested in knowing the reliable research on the subject. Monaghan

eliminates all but two of the writings as unreliable—"A political odor is notice-able in some of the source material that treats upon Lincoln as a spiritualist," Monaghan writes. "Other treatises are plainly emotional."—then explains the historical value of the two he deems significant. While focused on Abraham Lin-coln's belief in spiritualism, this article is an essential source for understanding Mary Lincoln's belief in spiritualism and her experiences consulting with spirit mediums during her time in the White House. Monaghan concludes that Mary was the believer in the family and her husband attended séances out of curiosity and the need for diversion from the stress of running the war.

251.
Warren, Louis A. "Mrs. Lincoln and 'Your Soldier Boy.'" *Lincoln Lore*, no. 683 (May 11, 1942).
This brief article relates the story of Mary Lincoln writing a letter for a wound-ed soldier in a Washington hospital, and includes the text of letter.

252.
"The Lincolns at Home." *Abraham Lincoln Quarterly* 2, no. 2 (June 1942): 91–92.
These glimpses of Abraham and Mary Lincoln at home in letters from 1860 by two people who had visited the Lincolns in Springfield say the Lincolns had not changed from the pleasant, friendly people they had been before the pres-idential election.

253.
Hay, Logan. "Lincoln in 1841 and 1842." *Abraham Lincoln Quarterly* 2, no. 3 (Sept. 1942): 114–126.
In this examination of Abraham Lincoln's life during 1841 and 1842 that focuses on his courtship, broken engagement, reconciliation, and marriage to Mary Todd, Hay concludes this to be a seminal period and declares 1841 "per-haps the most critical year in Lincoln's life" in which he was "shaken to his roots by a tremendous emotional crisis" from which he recovered only by regaining a new "mastery of himself."

254.
Pratt, Harry E., and Ernest E. East. "Mrs. Lincoln Refurbishes the White House." *Lincoln Herald* 47, no. 1 (Feb. 1945): 13–22.
This article examines Mary Lincoln's expenditures during the first nine months of her tenure as first lady, particularly in her refurbishing of the White House, which was in a "deplorably shabby condition" when the Lincolns first

moved in. The article explains the social and political conditions that existed in March 1861 when Mary became first lady, discusses her shopping trips, details her many purchases and their costs, and describes the social effect of the newly remade White House. It also includes an appendix with a complete list of Mary's purchases from May to December 1861.

255.
"Letter of Mrs. Abraham Lincoln." *Lincoln Herald* 47, no. 1 (Feb. 1945): 49.
This one-page "From the LMU [Lincoln Memorial University] Archives" section of the journal highlights a January 9, 1867, letter from Mary Lincoln to a Mr. W. about some sort of recommendation for the White House gardeners. As the article states, "The pathos of this letter . . . reveals a tender thought under distressing conditions." While ostensibly a letter about a recommendation, it really focuses on Mary's physical and mental health. The letter, which is not included in *Mary Todd Lincoln: Her Life and Letters* (entry 56), is reproduced in full in the article, both as a photo of the original letter and in transcription.

256.
Hunt, Eugenia Jones. "My Personal Recollections of Abraham Lincoln and Mary Todd Lincoln." *Abraham Lincoln Quarterly* 3, no. 5 (Mar. 1945): 235–252.
These reminiscences by the daughter of John Albert Jones, a legal colleague of Abraham Lincoln from Pekin, Illinois, are more about Abraham than Mary Lincoln, but Hunt recounts the story of the Lincoln-Todd wedding in 1842 as told to her by Mary's sister, Frances Todd Wallace. Hunt also describes her last visit with Mary in the Edwards home just prior to her death in 1882, in which Hunt refutes the notion that Mary lived as a hermit in a dark room.

257.
Lewis, Montgomery S. "Mary Todd Lincoln, Helpmate—Her Springfield Years," and "Mary Todd Lincoln, Helpmate—Her White House Years," in *Legends That Libel Lincoln*. N.Y.: Rinehart & Co., 1946, 101–152, 153–205.
In an examination of Mary Lincoln based on previously published secondary sources, Lewis seeks to exonerate Mary's reputation by proving her to be a loving and loyal wife in a happy marriage, an ambitious woman with a positive influence on her husband's career, and an unfairly and relentlessly criticized first lady.

258.
Warren, Louis A. "The Woman in Lincoln's Life, with Special Emphasis on Her Cultural Attainments." *Filson Club History Quarterly* 20 (July 1946).

This interesting monograph covers the extent to which Mary Lincoln affected her husband, with the conclusion that she improved his social, intellectual, and oratorical achievements through her tutelage and influence as his partner for nearly twenty years before he was elected to the presidency.

259.
Baringer, William E. "'My Tired & Weary Husband': Mary Lincoln on Life in the Executive Mansion." *Abraham Lincoln Quarterly* 4, no. 3 (Sept. 1946): 137–39.
This article offers the text of a previously unpublished November 19, 1864, letter by Mary Lincoln to her friend Mercy Levering Conkling in response to the latter's congratulations on President Lincoln's reelection. It also concerns Washington gossip about Mary's niece Julia Baker. The letter was later published in *Mary Todd Lincoln: Her Life and Letters* (entry 56).

260.
Bullard, F. Lauriston. "Mrs. Lincoln's Pension." *Lincoln Herald* 49 no. 2 (June 1947): 22–27.
Bullard offers the first complete account of the congressional battle from 1869 to 1870 over Mary Lincoln's request to receive a government pension as the result of her husband's death while in office. The article, based on the original Senate testimony for and against Mary from the *Congressional Globe* (entry 217), is an excellent resource not only on the pension issue but also because of the comments made about Mary, both pro and con, by men who knew her in Washington.

261.
Randall, Ruth Painter. "Mary Lincoln: Judgment Appealed." *Abraham Lincoln Quarterly* 5, no. 7 (Sept. 1949): 379–404.
This impassioned defense of Mary Lincoln against her critics, especially William Herndon, portrays Mary as a good person and loving wife and mother, albeit one with a fiery temper and a great ambition for her husband's political success. This is one of the most prominent articles in defense of Mary ever published.

262.
Warren, Louis A. "Mary Lincoln 'Framed.'" *Lincoln Lore*, no. 1067 (Sept. 19, 1949).
This article supports and agrees with Ruth Painter Randall's article "Mary Lincoln: Judgment Appealed," which states that Mary's bad reputation was the fault of William Herndon.

263.
———. "Dr. Henry Lauds Mrs. Lincoln, Chides Sec. Chase." *Lincoln Lore*, no. 1082 (Jan. 2, 1950).
This article includes the context and transcription of an April 1864 letter by Anson G. Henry complimenting Mrs. Lincoln and blaming her negative publicity on Salmon P. Chase and his minions in the Treasury Department.

264.
Stumbough, Virginia. "The Tragic Story of Mrs. Lincoln." *Chicago Sunday Tribune Magazine*, Jan. 15, 1950, 6–7, 12.
A general, brief history of Mary Lincoln's time as first lady, this article focuses mainly on Mary's wardrobe, her shopping, and her role as White House hostess. Stumbough states that although Mary was "basically one of the most socially adept of all the presidents' wives," her tenure as first lady was an utter "failure" because of the social ramifications of geography: North versus South and East versus West.

265.
"Lincoln's Death—Eyewitness Account." *Collector: A Magazine for Autograph and Historical Collectors*, 63, no. 3 (Mar. 1950).
This article offers the full text and explanation of the discovery of a May 1, 1865, letter by Elizabeth Dixon describing the night of April 14–15 that year in the Petersen house as President Lincoln lay dying. Dixon, a friend of Mary Lincoln, was called to the house by Robert Lincoln and spent the night comforting the beleaguered first lady. The complete letter had never been published prior to his article.

266.
Warren, Louis A. "Mrs. Lincoln's Mental Collapse." *Lincoln Lore*, no. 1124 (Oct. 23, 1950).
This examination of Mary Lincoln's mental health, including an interview with Emilie Todd Helm on her sister's personality in the White House, states that Mary's mental deterioration began in Washington after Willie's death in 1862, accelerated after her husband's murder in 1865, and suffered continual blows from negative publicity, William Herndon's Ann Rutledge lecture, and the death of Mary's youngest son Tad in 1871.

267.
———. "The Persecution of Mary Todd Lincoln." *Lincoln Lore*, no. 1146 (Mar. 26, 1951).

In this defense of Mary Lincoln against rumors that she had an affair as first lady with friend Abram Wakeman, Warren concludes that the story is gossipy nonsense. The article includes the text of a March 1865 letter from Mary to Wakeman.

268.
H.E.P. "Mrs. Lincoln Writes to Author Halliday." *Journal of the Illinois State Historical Society* 45, no. 3 (Autumn 1952): 261–262.
   This article gives the full text of a Dec. 31, 1860, letter by Mary Lincoln thanking Rev. Samuel Bryam Halliday for the book he sent her. The article also gives the context of the letter and the background of Halliday, whom Abraham Lincoln met in New York during his trip to give the Cooper Union speech.

269.
Lorant, Stefan. "The Tragic Love Story of Mrs. Lincoln." *McCall's Magazine,* May 1953, 28–29, 104–112, 116–119, 122–125.
   This article is aimed at revising the popular opinion of Mary Lincoln, who Lorant calls "the most maligned woman in American history" and a wife that biographers, needing to "make Lincoln a saint," made "a devil." Lorant's well-researched and well-written article sees in the Lincoln marriage a "passionate love affair" that died only when they died. Using primary sources, he examines the Lincoln's courtship, broken engagement, and eventual marriage, and seeks to show their years together were full of love and happiness, along with the typical arguments and headaches, and was not a veritable hell on Earth, as some biographers have stated. He also examines in detail Mary's tragic life after her husband's murder.

270.
Hatch, Francis Whiting. "Mary Lincoln Writes to Noah Brooks." *Journal of the Illinois State Historical Society* 48, no. 1 (Spring 1955): 45–51.
   This article contains the complete texts of two letters Mary Lincoln wrote to journalist and family friend Noah Brooks in 1865 and 1866 concerning financial issues and personal comments. According to Hatch, who owned the letters, one of the letters was unpublished and the other had been printed previously but "poorly edited." The article briefly describes the friendship of Mary and Brooks and gives the context of the financial issues involved in the letters.

271.
"Took Tea at Mrs. Lincoln's: The Diary of Mrs. William M. Black." *Journal of the Illinois State Historical Society* 48, no. 1 (Spring 1955): 59–64.

This article offers excerpts from the diary of Mrs. William Black, a Springfield friend and neighbor to the Lincolns, which sheds light on Mary Lincoln's social and religious activities in 1852, and includes an early letter by Mary.

272.
Pratt, Harry E. "The Lincolns Go Shopping." *Journal of the Illinois State Historical Society* 48, no. 1 (Spring 1955): 65–81.

This look into the personal finances and shopping of Abraham and Mary Lincoln from 1842 to 1853 is based on newly donated retail business records of Irwin & Co. to the Illinois State Historical Society. The Lincolns' accounts, which are printed in full, show items purchased by the family as lodgers, renters, and homeowners, and offer insight into Mary as a homemaker and mother through the cookbooks, housewares, and clothing material purchased. This article makes a fine addendum to Pratt's 1943 book, *The Personal Finances of Abraham Lincoln* (entry 42).

273.
Randall, Ruth Painter. "When Mary Lincoln Was Adjudged Insane." *American Heritage* 6, no. 5 (Aug. 1955): 10–11, 96–99.

This article offers an examination of Mary Lincoln's insanity trial based on the discovery of new documentary evidence: a detailed letter from Leonard Swett to David Davis explaining Swett's personal experiences with Mary before, during, and after the trial. Randall paints Mary as mentally unbalanced and Robert Lincoln as a heartbroken and conscientious son doing his duty by committing his mother to an asylum. The article is an excerpt from chapter 10 of Randall's book *Lincoln's Sons* (entry 48), published the same year.

274.
"Lincolniana Notes: The Christening of Camp Mary Lincoln." *Journal of the Illinois State Historical Society* 48, no. 3 (Autumn 1955): 328–329.

This reprint of a *New York Times* article from 1861 describes the christening of Camp Mary Lincoln by the 37th New York Volunteers. Mary was present for the dedication, during which "uproarious cheers" were given by the soldiers for the president and "his accomplished lady." The regiment's colonel was presented with a Union cockade in Mrs. Lincoln's name. "Mrs. Lincoln, who looked remarkably well, wore a beautiful silk bonnet sent her as a present from Massachusetts," it was reported.

275.
Donald, David. "Herndon and Mary Lincoln," in *Lincoln Reconsidered* (N.Y.: Alfred A. Knopf, 1956), 37–56.

This selection from Donald's book of essays reviews and rebuts the more damning legends about Mary Lincoln's relationship with her husband. Donald specifically examines the Ann Rutledge–Abraham Lincoln love affair and the story begun by William Herndon that Lincoln never loved his wife, as well as the myth that Lincoln left Mary standing at the altar. Donald proves these myths untrue and declares the Lincolns had a loving marriage with typical ups and downs.

276.
Turner, Justin G. "The Mary Lincoln Letters to Mrs. Felician Slataper." *Journal of the Illinois State Historical Society* 49, no. 1 (Spring 1956): 7–33.

The texts and contexts of eleven previously unpublished letters written by Mary Lincoln between 1868 and 1871 are included in this article. The letters give interesting insight into Mary's travels in the U.S. and Europe during that period, the life and personality of her son and traveling companion Tad, her attendance at her oldest son Robert's 1868 wedding, and her physical and mental health. Turner later included these letters in his book of Mary's life and collected letters (entry 56).

277.
Kunhardt, Dorothy Meserve. "An Old Lady's Lincoln Memories." *Life* 46, no. 6 (Feb. 9, 1959): 57, 59–60.

Kunhardt's interview with Mary Edwards Brown (age eighty-six) shares Brown's recollections of her great aunt Mary Lincoln's last days, during 1881 and 1882, when Brown lived with Mary in the Edwards home in Springfield, Illinois. This is an important part of the bibliography in that it contains much firsthand information about Mary's final years, including her physical health, mental health, and family relations. Reprinted in Philip B. Kunhardt Jr., Philip B. Kunhardt III, and Peter W. Kunhardt, eds., *Lincoln: An Illustrated Biography* (N.Y.: Alfred A. Knopf, 1992), 396–397.

278.
Temple, Wayne C. "Mary Todd Lincoln's Travels." *Journal of the Illinois State Historical Society* 52, no. 1 (Spring 1959): 180–194.

This article surveys all of Mary Lincoln's travels during her lifetime, particularly during her years as first lady. The purpose of the article is to show Mary's interest in boats and water travel, as well as her "penchant for keeping the newspaper reporters guessing about her [travel] plans."

279.
———. "Mary Todd Lincoln as a Sailor." *Lincoln Herald*, 61, no. 3 (Fall 1959): 101–110.

Temple's article relates the known occasions upon which Mrs. Lincoln traveled on water. Most of the content of this article appeared previously in Temple's spring 1959 article, "Mary Todd Lincoln's Travels."

280.
Pratt, Marion D. "Abraham Lincoln Takes a Wife," in *Lincoln for the Ages*, ed. Ralph G. Newman. N.Y.: Doubleday and Co., 1960, pp. 79–84.

This brief look at the courtship and marriage of Mary Todd and Abraham Lincoln uses contemporary newspaper accounts and reminiscences of Todd family members present at the Lincoln wedding. It is a nice general introduction to the Lincolns' early years as a couple.

281.
Temple, Wayne C., and Jeannie H. James. "Mrs. Lincoln's Clothing." *Lincoln Herald* 62, no. 2 (Summer 1960): 54–65.

Temple and James's work describes the dresses worn by Mary Lincoln at various times during her life, with emphasis on the White House years. It declares Mary had a strong interest in clothing from childhood, which was important to her later purchasing mania in maturity.

282.
———. "Mrs. Lincoln's Visit to Springfield in 1866." *Lincoln Herald* 62, no. 4 (Winter 1960): 170–172.

This is the story of Mary Lincoln's visit to Springfield in 1866 to be interviewed by William Herndon for his Lincoln biography project. It includes the text of a previously unpublished letter from September 7, 1866, which further verifies the event.

283.
Sang, Philip D. "Mary Todd Lincoln: A Tragic Portrait." *Journal of the Rutgers University Library*, 24, no. 2 (1961): 46–72.

Sang's tragic portrait is based primarily on eighteen letters by Mary Lincoln written from 1840 to 1876, from a time before her marriage to Abraham Lincoln to her days after the assassination. Three of these letters, according to Sang, were previously unpublished, while numerous others had never before been reproduced in full. The "genesis" of the article, Sang states, was a collection of eight never completely published letters from Mary to Simon Cameron, which Sang acquired in 1960 from Lincoln collector King V. Hostick. Those letters, now available in *Mary Todd Lincoln: Her Life and Letters* (entry 56), show Mary's dire emotional and financial straits after her husband's death, and her efforts to secure a pension from the U.S. Congress.

284.
Temple, Wayne C. "Mrs. Lincoln's Jewelry." *Lincoln Herald*, 64, no. 1 (Spring 1962): 26–27.
This article, along with a photo, briefly examines several pieces of Mary Lincoln's mourning jewelry, including earrings, which prove she had pierced ears.

285.
Bernard, Kenneth A. "Lincoln and the Music of the Civil War—Will the Leader of the Band Please See Mrs. Lincoln?" *Lincoln Herald*, 64, no. 1 (Spring 1962): 3–8.
This articles give a brief overview of the preparations made for the February 5, 1862, White House reception, particularly from the musical aspect. The article describes the event, its food, decorations, and social importance, as well as the fact that Mary Lincoln met with the leader of the Marine Band, Francis Scala, to select the evening's music. The final musical number was "Mrs. Lincoln's Polka," written by Scala especially for the occasion. The article is an excerpt from Bernard's book *Lincoln and the Music of the Civil War* (Boston: Boston University, 1961).

286.
"What Mrs. Lincoln Bought for the White House." *Lincoln Lore*, no. 1492 (June 1962), 4.
This reprint of a May 30, 1861, newspaper article is highly condemnatory of Mary Lincoln's purchases of "extravagances" for herself and for the White House while on a shopping tour of New York City.

287.
Coleman, J. Winston, Jr. "Mary Todd's Birthplace." *Lincoln Herald* 65, no. 1 (Spring 1963): 3–5.
Coleman's brief article offers a history of the house in which Mary Todd was born, including an artist's sketch and a historic photograph taken right before the structure was razed in the 1880s. The original Robert S. Todd residence was sold to the Catholic Church, used as a parish residence for a time, and demolished, but the bricks and most of the building materials were salvaged and used to erect a cemetery gatehouse.

288.
Hickey, James T. "The Lincolns' Globe Tavern: A Study in Tracing the History of a Nineteenth-Century Building." *Journal of the Illinois State Historical Society* 56, no. 4 (Winter 1963): 629–654.

This work is a history of the Globe Tavern in Springfield, Illinois, where Abraham and Mary Lincoln lived for about one year after their marriage in 1842. Hickey concludes the Globe was not a fourth-rate hotel as has been characterized but a well-respected boardinghouse that other Todd family members had previously lived in and, therefore, for Mary to live there for one year was not the humiliation it has been portrayed as. Reprinted in Hickey's *Collected Writings*, 49–73 (entry 68).

289.
Suarez, John M. "Mary Todd Lincoln: A Case Study." *American Journal of Psychiatry* 122, no. 7 (Jan. 1966): 816–819.

Suarez's article is a professional psychiatric case study of Mary Lincoln that examines her symptoms based on the handful of books written about Mary up to that time. Suarez, who was with the University of California Medical Center's Department of Psychiatry at the time of the writing, offers little direct evidence of Mary's mental state, just general impressions based on secondary sources. He declares her to have suffered from a violent temper, emotional instability, depression, auditory and visual hallucinations, and delusions of poverty and grandeur. Ultimately, Suarez concludes that Mary's lifelong personality disorder erupted in 1875 into full-blown paranoid psychosis that made her a danger to herself and others. While not as impressive an article as that by Dr. James Brussel in 1941 (entry 248), Suarez's expert psychiatric conclusions are an important addition to the Mary Lincoln canon.

290.
Ostendorf, Lloyd. "White House Words Overheard: A True Lincoln Anecdote." *Lincoln Herald* 68 no. 2 (Summer 1966): 59–60.

This reconstruction of an argument between Abraham and Mary Lincoln is based on a previously unpublished recollection of artist Francis B. Carpenter, who lived in the White House for six months in 1864. Supposedly, Mary was extracting some sort of promise from her husband, and withheld his pants until he acquiesced.

291.
Wefer, Marion. "Another Assassination, Another Widow, Another Embattled Book." *American Heritage* 18, no. 5 (Aug. 1967).

In the aftermath of the John F. Kennedy assassination, Wefer's article seeks to draw a connection between that event and the Lincoln assassination in examining the book *Behind the Scenes* by Elizabeth Keckley, Mary Lincoln's dressmaker (entry 1). The article gives a brief summary of the relationship between Keckley and Mary and how Keckley came to write her 1868 memoir that has since become an indispensable book for Lincoln scholars. The majority of the article is simply excerpts from Keckley's book concerning events in the White House, Mary's life in Chicago after the assassination, and the Old Clothes Scandal of 1867. This article is no substitute for reading Keckley's book but does distill a few of the more interesting scenes in the book into one article.

292.
Bell, Patricia. "Mary Todd Lincoln: A Personality Profile." *Civil War Times Illustrated* 7, no. 7 (Nov. 1968): 4–11.

A basic personality profile of Mary Lincoln from childhood to death, based primarily on biographies of Mary written by Ruth Painter Randall and by Carl Sandburg and Paul Angle, and the biography of Abraham Lincoln written by William Herndon. Mary is presented as a "troubled and troublesome woman" who was attractive, smart, outspoken, and strong-willed, but also sharp-tongued, irrational, overemotional, and undisciplined. She is shown as a woman with both virtues and vices; and Bell sees part of Mary's poor historical reputation stemming from Herndon's "uncomplimentary picture" he painted of her in his writings, while part of her more unsavory actions were caused by "a mental illness not understood in her own day." It is an interesting article in a popular history magazine for a popular history audience.

293.
Ross, Rodney A. "Mary Todd Lincoln: Patient at Bellevue Place, Batavia." *Journal of the Illinois State Historical Society* 63, no. 1 (Spring 1970): 5–34.

In an excellent article about Mary Lincoln's four months in Bellevue Place sanitarium after being declared insane in 1875, Ross gives a brief history of Mary's mental issues and insanity trial, a description of the Bellevue Place grounds and accommodations, its doctors, and Mary's medical treatment while a patient, as well as the facts behind her ultimate release. Most important, the article contains transcriptions of the Bellevue Place sanitarium daily reports about Mary during her commitment from May to September 1875, which offer readers a look at Mary's life, actions, treatment, and progress. This article is an invaluable addition to the literature on Mary's insanity period.

294.
Hackensmith, C. W. "The Much Maligned Mary Todd Lincoln." *Filson Club History Quarterly* 44 no. 3 (July 1970): 282–292.
This sympathetic defense portrays Mary Lincoln as a woman who suffered enough tragedies in life to drive any woman insane. Hackensmith characterizes Mary as a good woman, full of ambition and family pride, and recounts the numerous traumas she endured as the reason for her ultimate insanity: the deaths of her children and the murder of her husband, her money troubles and purchasing mania—including a synopsis of the Old Clothes Scandal of 1867—and the unfriendly lectures of William Herndon.

295.
———. "Family Background and Education of Mary Todd." *Register of the Kentucky Historical Society* 69 no. 3 (July 1971): 187–196.
This is an excellent overview of the Todd family history and Mary Todd's girlhood life and education, written using primary source materials. It is one of the few works in the bibliography to examine Mary's education in Lexington since William Townsend's 1929 book, *Lincoln and His Wife's Home Town* (entry 30).

296.
Hickey, James T. "Lincolniana (Mary Lincoln and Edward Kirk letters)." *Journal of the Illinois State Historical Society* 65, no. 2 (Summer 1972): 206–209.
This article includes descriptions and transcriptions of two letters acquired by the Illinois State Historical Society: one written by Mary Lincoln and one in which she is mentioned. The letter written by Mary, dated June 4, 1860, reveals previously unknown facts, including that the Lincolns entertained the Republican State Committee for dinner at their house on June 1. It also illustrates "the busy life Mrs. Lincoln led as wife of a presidential candidate." The second letter includes observations of Mary in church in January 1861 by a visitor to Springfield. The article also includes a photo of some of Mary Lincoln's possessions donated to the historical society by a Todd family descendant. The June 4 letter by Mary is not included in *Mary Todd Lincoln: Her Life and Letters* (entry 56). Reprinted in Hickey's *Collected Writings*, 95–98 (entry 68).

297.
Neely, Mark E., Jr. "Abraham Lincoln Did NOT Defend His Wife before the Committee on the Conduct of the War." *Lincoln Lore*, no. 1643 (Jan. 1975).

Neely's work is a detailed examination of the myth that Abraham Lincoln visited a secret session of a congressional committee investigating rumors that Mary Lincoln was leaking military secrets to the Confederacy. Neely traces the origins of the story and its subsequent retellings by other historians and writers, and examines the question of why the story even matters to history. He concludes the story to be not only a false rumor but also a form of "Mary Lincoln apologetics" to improve her historical reputation.

298.

Massey, Mary Elizabeth. "Mary Todd Lincoln." *American History Illustrated* 10, no. 2 (May 1975): 4–9, 44–48.

This is an impressively astute examination of Mary Lincoln's life and character, with a focus mostly on the Washington years. Massey, a noted southern historian, delves not just into what Mary did but who she was, and examines the various emotional and psychological trials Mary suffered: family deaths, vicious Washington society gossip, a critical press, overspending and debt, and her own sensitivity to real and imagined slights. This is an excellent attempt at understanding Mary Lincoln.

299.

Robbins, Peggy. "The Lincolns and Spiritualism." *Civil War Times Illustrated.* 15, no. 5 (Aug. 1976), 4–6, 8–10, 46–47.

A review of Mary and Abraham Lincoln's beliefs and interactions regarding spiritualism during their years in Washington, this article recounts the well-known stories about the Lincolns attending séances in and around the capital held by mediums Lord Colchester, Nettie Colburn, and Mrs. Cranston Laurie. Robbins states that while Mary clearly believed in spiritualism, her husband did not, but he participated in séances because he believed it gave his wife some emotional relief from her grief. This is an interesting general history article that also tells about the various capital citizens and government officials who shared Mary's belief in spiritualism.

300.

Neely, Mark E., Jr. "Thurlow Weed, the New York Custom House, and Mrs. Lincoln's 'Treason.'" *Lincoln Lore*, no. 1679 (Jan. 1978).

This sequel to "Abraham Lincoln did NOT Defend His Wife before the Committee on the Conduct of the War" (entry 297) determines Thurlow Weed started the rumor that Mary Lincoln was leaking military secrets to the Confederacy due to a "wrangle over patronage" between Weed and the first lady.

301.
Sklar, Kathryn Kish. "Victorian Women and Domestic Life: Mary Todd Lincoln, Elizabeth Cady Stanton, and Harriet Beecher Stowe," in *The Public and Private Lincoln: Contemporary Perspectives*, ed. Cullom Davis, Charles B. Strozier, Rebecca Monroe Veach, and Geoffrey C. Ward. Carbondale: Southern Illinois University Press, 1979: 20–37.
    This examination of nineteenth-century family life from a female perspective, and the strategies women adopted in response to change in the domestic arena, is a fascinating and rather unique look at Mary Lincoln. She is analyzed as a woman with "total commitment to husband and children," yet also someone more akin to a twentieth-century woman in that she practiced family planning to limit the number of children as a way to decrease distraction to her husband's career, and she satisfied her own personal ambitions by helping her husband achieve political success.

302.
Sprague, Ver Lynn. "Mary Lincoln—Accessory to Murder." *Lincoln Herald* 81, no. 4 (Winter 1979): 238–242.
    Sprague states that Mary Lincoln inadvertently caused her husband's death because her bad personal conduct at City Point, Virginia, in March 1865 prevented Gen. and Mrs. Grant from attending Ford's Theatre with the Lincolns on April 14, 1865, thus depriving the president of an excellent bodyguard. Sprague also blames Mary for securing John Parker the position of presidential bodyguard—the post he abandoned at Ford's Theatre that night—stating it was "stupid if not criminally negligent" and therefore part of the cause of the assassination.

303.
Hickey, James T. "Robert Todd Lincoln and the 'Purely Private' Letters of the Lincoln Family." *Journal of the Illinois State Historical Society* 74, no. 1 (Spring 1981): 58–79.
    This is a fascinating look into the disposition and fate of the Lincoln family papers, as revealed by then newly discovered documents at Robert T. Lincoln's summer home in Vermont. Hickey, given access to the papers by the Lincoln descendants, explains the preservation and loss of private family correspondence through the years, including letters between Mary Lincoln and her husband and oldest son. Given the large absence of personal Lincoln family correspondence in existence today, this article puts the dearth into perspective. Reprinted in Hickey's *Collected Writings*, 159–179 (entry 68).

304.
Gallardo, Florence. "'Til Death Do Us Part: The Marriage of Abraham Lincoln and Mary Todd." *Lincoln Herald* 84, no. 1 (Spring 1982): 3–10.

In this general examination of the Lincoln marriage taken almost exclusively from Ruth Painter Randall's sympathetic biography of Mary Lincoln, Gallardo decries William Herndon's negative characterizations of the Lincoln marriage as false and concludes the Lincolns were a loving couple with typical ups and downs. The article was the first-prize winner in a Lincoln essay competition sponsored by Miami University, Oxford, Ohio.

305.
Cowden, Gerald Steffens, ed. "'My Dear Mr. W': Mary Lincoln Writes to Alexander Williamson." *Journal of the Illinois State Historical Society* 76, no. 1 (Spring 1983): 71–74.

This works includes a transcript and an explanation of a previously unpublished Mary Lincoln letter to Alexander Williamson, dated August 20, 1866. The letter is part of Mary's longtime correspondence with Williamson while he acted as her agent to help her repay debts accrued as first lady. The new letter specifically tells Williamson to retrieve a letter addressed to Mary's seamstress Elizabeth Keckley.

306.
Hickey, James T. "Lincolniana: The Lincoln Account at the Corneau & Diller Drug Store, 1849–1861, a Springfield Tradition." *Journal of the Illinois State Historical Society* 77, no. 1 (Spring 1984): 60–66.

This article offers a consolidated list of all purchases made by the Lincoln family at the Corneau & Diller Drug Store from 1849 to 1861. The ledgers, along with Hickey's narrative, offer insight into the daily life of Mary Lincoln as woman, wife, and mother through the items she purchased. As Hickey points out, purchases included items used for face cosmetics and beauty preparations, patent medicines for physical complaints, typical mixtures for cough and cold treatment, remedies for stomach complaints, and purchases used to battle flea and mosquito bites. Portions of the ledgers containing the Lincoln drugstore accounts were published in Harry Pratt's *Personal Finances of Abraham Lincoln* (entry 42). Reprinted in Hickey's *Collected Writings*, 220–226 (entry 68).

307.
Strozier, Charles B. "The Psychology of Mary Todd Lincoln." *Psychohistory Review* 17, no. 1 (1988): 11–24.

This review by a psychobiographer is an interesting compare-and-contrast of Jean Baker's *Mary Todd Lincoln: A Biography* (entry 64) and Mark E. Neely Jr. and R. Gerald McMurtry's *The Insanity File: The Case of Mary Todd Lincoln* (entry 63), both of which examine Mary's psychology. As Strozier states, there was, at the time, a dichotomy in interpretations of Mary between the "Gothic novel" version of her life (in which she adored Lincoln and he her) and the "chauvinist pig" version of her life (in which she is the relentless shrew). The fact that the two books under review came to such radically different conclusions about who Mary was makes one wonder, Strozier stated, "whether evidence matters in matters of historical importance."

308.
Porter, Doris Replogle. "The Mysterious Browning Letter." *Lincoln Herald* 90, no. 1 (Spring 1988): 20–23.
    This article examines a long-ignored May 26, 1865, letter by former U.S. senator Orville Hickman Browning, which states that Mary Lincoln was responsible for the dismissal of her brother-in-law Ninian W. Edwards from government service. Porter contends that the letter, which is printed in the article, raises new questions about Mary's actual influence in governmental affairs.

309.
Baker, Jean H. "Mary Todd Lincoln: Biography as Social History." *Register of the Kentucky Historical Society* 86, no. 3 (Summer 1988): 203–215.
    This article is a look at how Mary Lincoln's life was "a prism" through which one can observe important social aspects of nineteenth-century American female life. Baker sees Mary as a woman simultaneously conventional and ahead of her time, struggling to be both feminine and independent in areas such as her education, romantic female relationships, courtship and marriage, and political inclinations and activities.

310.
Braden, Waldo W. "A Todd Legend about the Lincolns' Romance." *Lincoln Herald* 91, no. 1 (Spring 1989): 9–11.
    Braden examines the origins of a Todd family legend that Abraham Lincoln once visited Columbia, Missouri, in 1840 while he was courting Mary Todd, who was there visiting family. Braden traces the story to William Barton and Katherine Helm, and concludes it may have originated from Mary Lincoln's sister Emilie Todd Helm.

311.
Schwartz, Thomas F., and Anne V. Shaughnessy. "Unpublished Mary Lincoln Letters." *Journal of the Abraham Lincoln Association* 11, no. 1 (Spring 1990): 34–50.
This work includes the context and transcriptions of previously unpublished Mary Lincoln letters, dating from 1860 to 1877 (with some undated), concerning her family, friends, health, pension battle, and influence on political patronage. As Schwartz and Shaughnessy state, the letters "do not reveal startling new information, but they do reinforce known views" about Mary.

312.
Baker, Jean H. "Mary Todd Lincoln: Managing Home, Husband, and Children." *Journal of the Abraham Lincoln Association* 11, no. 1 (Spring 1990): 1–12.
This is an examination of Mary Lincoln's domestic duties as wife and mother as typified in the nineteenth century. Baker states that Mary—who was basically a "single mother" at hard labor—personifies the "conventional notions of domesticity" at the time, and this provides insight into her life. Mary cooked, cleaned, sewed, raised the children, and, as such, was "completely enmeshed in the domesticity established for middle-class women."

313.
Ostendorf, Lloyd. "A New Mary Todd Lincoln Photograph: A Tour of the White Mountains in Summer, 1863." *Illinois Historical Journal* 83, no. 2 (Summer 1990): 109–111.
This is the first publication and explanation of a previously unknown photograph of Mary Lincoln (along with sons Robert and Tad) on vacation in the White Mountains of New Hampshire in 1863. The photo was not included in Ostendorf's previous book, *The Photographs of Mary Todd Lincoln* (entry 54).

314.
Temple, Wayne C. "Ruth Stanton Recalls the Lincolns." *Lincoln Herald* 92, no. 3 (Fall 1990): 88–92.
This is the examination and reprinting of reminiscences by "Aunt" Ruth Stanton, who supposedly worked in the Lincoln home as a young girl in the late 1840s. Stanton describes Mary Lincoln's personality as wife, mother, and employer, as well as her typical daily duties as a housekeeper. Temple studies Stanton's assertions and concludes the story seems plausible and should be used by historians "with caution." Originally printed in *Illinois State Journal*, Feb. 12, 1895 (entry 184).

315.
Neely, Mark E., Jr. "Mary Todd Lincoln's Spirit Photograph," *Lincoln Lore*, no. 1825 (Mar. 1991): 3–4.
This is a brief discussion of the existence and impact of Mary Lincoln's spirit photograph, taken by William Mumler in 1872, which shows a seated Mary, dressed in her widow's weeds, with the spirits of her dead husband and son Tad hovering behind her. Neely declares that Mary's long-obscured belief in spiritualism would probably be even less known had it not been for the existence of the spirit photo. He calls the photograph—which is reproduced with the article—a "silly portrait" that "testifies to the desperate widow's gullibility and potential as a victim of the more serious spiritualist fraud."

316.
Boas, Norman F. "Unpublished Manuscripts: Recollections of Mary Todd Lincoln by Her Sister Emilie Todd Helm; An Invitation to a Lincoln Party." *Manuscripts* 43, no. 1 (Winter 1991): 23–34.
Boas's article concerns the relationship between Mary and Abraham Lincoln based on an unpublished fifteen-page recollection written by Mary's sister Emilie Todd Helm, as well as a portion of one unpublished letter by Mary. Helm has long been an important historical source for the Lincoln story because of the diary she kept, articles she wrote and published, and the biography of Mary written by her daughter, Katherine Helm, based on Emilie's diary, letters, and recollections. The unpublished manuscript contains Helm's recollections about the Lincolns' wedding (which is incorrectly dated as 1840 in the manuscript) and happiness as a couple, Lincoln's final words to his wife, Mary's travels in Europe after her husband's death, and her death and funeral. The portion of the unpublished letter included contains only two sentences from 1856 about Washington, D.C., politics, which is nothing interesting. Boas also includes some facts about Helm's relationship with the Lincolns during the Civil War. This is an interesting article overall, but Helm's unpublished recollections are general and repeated in other sources, while four of the five letters in the article are previously published.

317.
Wendt, Kristine Adams. "Mary Todd Lincoln: 'Great Sorrows' and the Healing Waters of Waukesha." *Wisconsin Academy Review* 38, no. 2 (Spring 1992): 14–19.
Wendt tells the story of Mary Lincoln's visit to the resort town of Waukesha, Wisconsin, during the summer of 1872 to utilize the health spas. The article contains various newspaper coverage of Mary's travels, her health, and her visits

to spiritualist mediums in the area. Reprinted in two parts in the *Lincoln Ledger: A Publication of the Lincoln Fellowship of Wisconsin*, 1, no. 2 (Feb. 1993): 1, 3–5; and 1, no. 3 (May 1993): 1, 3–4.

318.
Wilson, Douglas L. "Abraham Lincoln and 'That Fatal First of January.'" *Civil War History* 38, no. 2 (June 1992): 101–130.
This is an exhaustive examination of the courtship and broken engagement between Abraham Lincoln and Mary Todd: how it came to be broken, by whom, and under what circumstances. Wilson uses overlooked statements by Joshua Speed and reevaluates statements about Lincoln's "love" for Matilda Edwards to offer a new timeline for the Lincoln-Todd romance and breakup as well as a new explanation for the "fatal first of January" quotation of Lincoln. Republished in Douglas L. Wilson, *Lincoln before Washington: New Perspectives on the Illinois Years* (Urbana: University of Illinois Press, 1997), 99–132.

319.
Burlingame, Michael. "The Lincolns' Marriage: 'A Fountain of Misery, of a Quality Absolutely Infernal,'" in *The Inner World of Abraham Lincoln*, 268–355. Urbana: University of Illinois Press, 1994.
This groundbreaking examination of the Lincoln marriage declares it to have been an unhappy match between two irreconcilably different people. Burlingame portrays Mary as an emotional and physical abuser of her husband, a jealous woman with an uncontrollable temper, an influence peddler as first lady, and possibly even an unfaithful wife. While Burlingame's condemnation of Mary is similar to the castigations of William Herndon, his essay is far superior and just as influential because of the sheer volume of primary source materials on which his conclusions are based.

320.
———, ed. "Martinette Hardin McKee Recalls Lincoln and Mary Todd." *Lincoln Herald* 97, no. 2 (Summer 1995): 71–74.
This reminiscence of McKee, the sister of Abraham Lincoln's friend John J. Hardin, tells of the Lincoln-Todd courtship, broken engagement, and marriage, but, as Burlingame correctly points out, some of the "recollections" are clearly the result of later readings about Lincoln's life. There are also multiple errors and unverifiable assertions by McKee that make the entire reminiscence suspect. The reminiscence is reprinted from an 1896 newspaper clipping found in the Lincoln Museum collections.

321.
Schwartz, Thomas F., and Kim M. Bauer. "Unpublished Mary Todd Lincoln."
Journal of the Abraham Lincoln Association 17, no. 2 (Summer 1996): 1–21.
This article includes the context and transcriptions of previously unpublished
Mary Lincoln letters, dating 1857 to 1873 (and some undated), concerning family
affairs, White House patronage, and Mary's pension battle. "Many sad and poi-
gnant moments are revealed in this correspondence," Schwartz and Bauer state.

322.
Laderman, Gary. "The Body Politic and the Politics of Two Bodies: Abraham
and Mary Todd Lincoln in Death." *Prospects* 22 (1997): 109–132.
Laderman's work offers a unique and fascinating look at Mary Lincoln in
relation to the apotheosis of her husband after the assassination, particularly
in the battle between the public's insistence to make Lincoln a national icon
and "father," and Mary's insistence to keep him the head of her private, nuclear
family. This battle was waged between Mary's family-centered handling of her
husband's funeral and burial and her actions during her widowhood, and the
public's need to sever her from her husband's life and legacy in order to nation-
alize him in the collective memory.

323.
Stronks, Jim. "Mary Todd Lincoln's Sad Summer in Hyde Park." *Hyde Park
Historical Society Newsletter* 20, no. 1 (Spring 1998).
Quoting liberally from Mary Lincoln's letters, the article describes the Hyde
Park, Illinois, hotel and seaside resort community in which the Lincolns lived
in summer 1865. It describes the basic lives of Mary and her sons Robert and
Tad as they moved to a new city and tried to resume living in the aftermath of
their patriarch's assassination only a few months before.

324.
Rietveld, Ronald D. "The Lincoln White House Community." *Journal of the
Abraham Lincoln Association* 20, no. 2 (Summer 1999): 17–48.
This is a well-researched look into the White House community, mainly the
lives of Abraham and Mary Lincoln, but also certain staff members, servants, and
visitors. Based on both primary and secondary sources, the article is broken into
various aspects of White House living, including moving in, redecorating, daily
routines, receptions, and security. Mary figures prominently in all these sections,
and the reader sees her as a wife, housekeeper, hostess, and first lady—or more than
just a one-dimensional historical figure moving around in her husband's shadow.

325.
Emerson, Jason. "'Of Such Is the Kingdom of Heaven': The Mystery of Little Eddie." *Journal of the Illinois State Historical Society* 92, no. 3 (Autumn 1999): 201–221.

This is an examination of the authorship of the poem "Little Eddie," which was published shortly after the death of three-year-old Edward Baker Lincoln in 1850. Part of the discussion is whether or not Mary Lincoln could have written the poem, based on her educational background, her love of literature, her character as a mother, and her emotional reaction to death.

326.
Hirschhorn, Norbert, and Robert G. Feldman. "Mary Lincoln's Final Illness: A Medical and Historical Reappraisal." *Journal of the History of Medicine and Allied Sciences* 54, no. 4 (Oct. 1999): 511–542.

This is an excellent medical study of Mary Lincoln's physical health during her final years, with the authors declaring that Mary died from untreated diabetes. The authors also suggest Mary suffered from post-traumatic stress syndrome and the spinal disease tabes dorsalis, and that many of her physical ailments were "misinterpreted as madness" during her commitment in 1875. This article is not only excellent in general but is important in the bibliography by being one of the few examinations of Mary's health actually written by physicians.

327.
Smyer, Ingrid. "Mary Todd Lincoln: Troubled First Lady," in *Best Little Ironies, Oddities & Mysteries of the Civil War*, ed. C. Brian Kelly, 359–392. Nashville, Tenn.: Cumberland House, 2000.

Smyer's article is a brief survey of Mary Lincoln's early life and an examination of how her dreams and ambitions for glory as first lady were thwarted by troubles and tragedies—some of her own making, some not—such as the cruel Washington gossip, the negative publicity due to her temper and jealousy, her loneliness and personal insecurities, her son Willie's death in 1862, and her husband's murder in 1865.

328.
Burlingame, Michael. "Mary Todd Lincoln's Unethical Conduct as First Lady," in *At Lincoln's Side: John Hay's Civil War Correspondence and Selected Writings*, 185–203. Carbondale: Southern Illinois University Press, 2000.

This is a groundbreaking study of Mary Lincoln's bad behavior in the White House, including her taking of bribes and gifts, padding of White House accounts, conspiring to defraud the government, leaking of government documents to the press, influence peddling, theft of government property, and possible sexual affairs. Burlingame's work, while seemingly unsavory, is based on exhaustive research and bolstered by myriad citations. It is an essential contribution to the Mary bibliography and while it can be disagreed with, it cannot be ignored. This is a revision of Burlingame's 1994 talk at the Lincoln Fellowship of Wisconsin, *Honest Abe, Dishonest Mary* (entry 70).

329.
Ricker, Ann. "Mary Lincoln and the Swings." *For the People: A Newsletter of the Abraham Lincoln Association* 2, no. 1 (Spring 2000): 1–2, 6, 8.
This article, written by the great-great-granddaughter of Mary Lincoln's friend and spiritual adviser, Rev. David Swing, details Ricker family stories and knowledge about their association with the former first lady. It also shares the contents of a previously unknown letter from Mary to Elizabeth Swing and photos of gifts given to the Swings. This article offers important insights into Mary's behavior, character, and mental state in the years prior to her 1875 insanity trial. More information about Mary's relationship with the Swings, as well as the full text of Mary's 1874 letter to Elizabeth Swing, was later published by Thomas Schwartz in a 2003 article in the *Journal of Illinois History*.

330.
Spangler, Michael. "Benjamin Brown French in the Lincoln Period." *White House History* 8 (Fall 2000): 4–17.
This is a look at French's life when he served as commissioner of public buildings during the Lincoln administration—a position that put him into daily contact with First Lady Mary Lincoln. The article, based on French's detailed journal and personal letters, offers numerous observations about Mary. French was highly impressed by Mary when they first met, but through the years he criticized what he called her social fakery, inordinate spending, and need to always have her way. He also pitied her misery after the deaths of her son Willie and her husband, and the poor way she was treated by the press and Washington society. French's writings about life in the Lincoln White House offer a treasure trove of commentaries and observations about Mary, and the many distilled in this article are well worth reading.

331.
Williams, Frank J. "Mary Todd Lincoln 'On the Wing of Expectation': Wife, Mother, and Political Partner." *Lincoln Herald* 102, no. 4 (Winter 2000): 168–176.

In this article, Mary Lincoln is portrayed as a true political partner to her husband and as the woman who "began the institutionalization of the partnership presidency" and the establishment of the activist first lady. Williams also credits Mary with creating an aristocratic prig of a son in Robert, whom Williams characterizes as all Todd and no Lincoln.

332.
Baker, Jean H. "Mary and Abraham: A Marriage," in *The Lincoln Enigma: The Changing Faces of an American Icon*, ed. Gabor Boritt. Oxford: Oxford University Press, 2001.
This vehement defense of Mary Lincoln (pp. 36–55) portrays her as the only woman Abraham Lincoln ever loved and the Lincoln union as a "typical middle-class marriage." Baker attacks head-on and discards the notions of multiple historians that Abraham loved any other woman; she declares the Lincolns' broken engagement, wedding, and marriage years as generally misunderstood because they have been excised from their historical contexts, and that the Lincoln marriage was more modern (twentieth-century) and genial than is credited. Reprinted in Sean Wilentz, ed., *The Best American History Essays on Lincoln* (N.Y.: Palgrave Macmillan, 2009), 107–128.

333.
Wilson, Douglas L. "William H. Herndon and Mary Todd Lincoln." *Journal of the Abraham Lincoln Association* 22, no. 2 (Summer 2001): 1–26.
This is a revolutionary reexamination of the William Herndon and Mary Lincoln relationship before, during, and after Abraham Lincoln's death. Wilson offers the unique argument that the two were on friendly terms until 1866, thereby refuting the long-held and one-dimensional notion of a perpetual and mutual animosity between them. While Wilson provides vast evidence to show that Mary did in fact begin to hate Herndon after his infamous 1866 lecture on Lincoln's love for Ann Rutledge, he also shows that there is, in fact, no evidence to support the claims that Herndon, in turn, hated Mary and that his writings about her and the Lincoln marriage therefore were tainted by that supposed hatred. This is an insightful and important article, especially given the fact that Herndon's writings about Mary are typically believed to have been written out of hatred. The Herndon-Mary relationship, however, is far more complicated and nuanced than that, Wilson proves.

334.
Baker, Jean H. "Mary Todd Lincoln: Civil War First Lady." *White House Studies* 2, no. 1 (2002): 73–82.

Baker's article is an interpretation of Mary Lincoln as an active, highly political spouse who understood the importance of image and social events in
the making of the presidency. Baker argues that Mary—through actions such
as redecorating the run-down White House, purchasing expensive personal
fashions, holding lavish public parties and events, and even seeking to influence political appointments—sought to support her husband and "testify to
the power of a besieged government" but unfairly received only ridicule and
criticism for her efforts. This is an interesting look at the gender politics of the
Civil War presidency. Reprinted in Robert W. Watson, ed., *White House Studies
Compendium*, vol. 2 (N.Y.: Nova Science Publishers, 2007), 335–343.

335.
———. "Mary Lincoln: Symbol, Historical Target, and Human Being," in *The
Lincoln Forum: Rediscovering Abraham Lincoln*, ed. by John Y. Simon and Frank
Williams, 122–34. N.Y.: Fordham University Press, 2002.
    This article, the printing of a speech at the Lincoln Forum, is a defense of
Mary Lincoln and an inquiry into why she is, in Baker's words, "among the most
detested women in American history." In reviewing the Lincolns' relationship
and Mary's actions as mother, wife, and first lady, as well as Mary's commitment to a sanitarium in 1875, Baker sees Mary's bad reputation as the result
of her being an untraditional woman in nineteenth-century America and, for
historians, someone to criticize and condemn as a selfish, heartless termagant,
which thereby ennobles Abraham and his saintly qualities for living with such
a despicable woman. This article is an impressive and perspicacious look into
Mary's life and historical reputation.

336.
Schroeter, Joan G. "Julia Butler Newberry and Mary Todd Lincoln: Two 'Merry'
Widows." *Journal of the Illinois State Historical Society* 95, no. 3 (Autumn 2002):
264–274.
    This article is a look into the widowhoods of Mary Lincoln and Julia New-
berry, the wives of two famous and successful men in the mid-nineteenth century, and how these two women "were forced to secure their futures by bold actions going beyond the limits of behavior society considered proper to women."
Among the many similarities between their lives, Schroeter (who gives greater
attention to Newberry) focuses on the issue of money, and how the women
sought to secure their financial futures after their husbands' deaths. It is an interesting article from an original angle of inquiry, although it suffers from a lack of

understanding of Mary Lincoln's imperial personal character and generally poor interpersonal relationships when she was first lady. Instead of understanding who Mary was, Schroeter simply blames her difficult widowhood on what she was—a woman in a patriarchal society.

337.
Burkhimer, Michael. "Mary Todd Lincoln: Political Partner?" *Lincoln Herald* 105, no. 2 (Summer 2003): 67–72.

This is a well-argued refutation of the revisionist notion of Mary Lincoln as an active political partner of Abraham Lincoln. Burkhimer characterizes Mary as a supportive wife with large political ambitions for her husband, but nothing more.

338.
Schwartz, Thomas F. "'My Stay on Earth, Is Growing Very Short': Mary Todd Lincoln's Letters to Willis Danforth and Elizabeth Swing." *Journal of Illinois History* 6 (Summer 2003): 125–136.

This work includes the context and transcriptions of previously unpublished Mary Lincoln letters from 1874 to 1875, with many to her physician, Dr. Willis Danforth. The letters are an important addition to the bibliography, not only because so few letters from these years were previously known to exist but also because the new letters deal specifically with Mary's physical and mental health in the year leading up to her insanity trial. The letters include one rare mention of her taking prescription medications and her detailed funeral plans.

339.
Hirschhorn, Norbert. "Mary Lincoln's 'Suicide Attempt': A Physician Reconsiders the Evidence." *Lincoln Herald* 104, no. 3 (Fall 2003): 94–98.

This is a definitive examination of Mary Lincoln's attempted suicide on May 20, 1875, the day after she was declared insane by a Chicago jury. Utilizing multiple contemporary newspaper reports published the day after the incident, as well as a lengthy letter from Leonard Swett to David Davis recounting Mary's actions, Hirschhorn proves that Mary made a serious and calculated attempt to take her own life in a fit of despair after being declared insane. Hirschhorn also rebuts the argument from one writer that there was no suicide attempt but that it was a fake story planted in the newspapers by Mary's son Robert in order to vindicate his own actions of calling the jury inquest. This is the only article in the entire bibliography that deals solely and specifically with Mary's suicide attempt and, as such, is an important contribution to the literature.

340.
Bach, Jennifer L. "Acts of Remembrance: Mary Todd Lincoln and Her Husband's Memory." *Journal of the Abraham Lincoln Association* 25, no. 2 (Summer 2004): 25–49.

This is an examination of Mary Lincoln as guardian of her husband's legacy, particularly how she used her widowhood as a social identifier and a way to obtain power and influence for herself.

341.
Plummer, Mark A. "A Tomb for All Time: Governor Richard J. Oglesby and the Battle over the Lincoln Gravesite." *Illinois Heritage* 8, no. 3 (May-June 2005): 10–14.

Plummer recounts the story of the building of the Abraham Lincoln tomb in Springfield, Illinois, and particularly tells of Mary Lincoln's fight to have her husband buried and the tomb built in Oak Ridge Cemetery rather than in downtown Springfield, as the city council attempted.

342.
Bach, Jennifer L. "Was Mary Todd Lincoln Bipolar?" *Journal of Illinois History* 8, no. 4 (Winter 2005): 281–294.

This is a well-argued investigation of Mary Lincoln's personality and symptoms to determine if she suffered bipolar disorder, which Bach concludes was likely. The article describes symptoms of bipolar disorder, looks at Mary's family history for other instances of the disease, and examines many of Mary's actions and characteristics that seem to show she suffered from this illness.

343.
Schwartz, Thomas F. "Mary Todd's 1835 Visit to Springfield, Illinois." *Journal of the Abraham Lincoln Association* 26, no. 1 (Winter 2005): 42–45.

This short article cites evidence in the form of a legal document Mary Todd signed that appears to show her first visit to Springfield, Illinois, was in 1835, not 1837 as typically believed.

344.
Rogstad, Steven K. "A Look Back: Two Receipts Disprove Local Legend That Tad Lincoln Attended Racine College." *The Outlook: A Publication of the Racine* [Wis.] *Heritage Museum*, Mar. 2006, 3–8.

This is a new look at Mary Lincoln's summer 1867 visit to Racine, Wisconsin, based on overlooked manuscripts. It explains her visit was intended to examine

Racine College for Tad's possible enrollment, but proves that despite the myths to the contrary, Tad was never a student there.

345.
Emerson, Jason. "The Madness of Mary Lincoln." *American Heritage* 57, no. 3 (June-July 2006): 56–65.

Emerson's article reveals the discovery of a cache of Mary Lincoln's letters to her friend Myra Bradwell, most of which were written from Bellevue Place sanitarium in 1875, and which have been missing for over eighty years. The article briefly explains the story of the discovery, the contents of the letters, and their historical importance to the story of Mary's insanity trial and subsequent commitment.

346.
Ricker, Jewett E., Jr. "The Other Side of Mary Lincoln: Part 1." *For the People: A Newsletter of the Abraham Lincoln Association* 8, no. 4 (Winter 2006): 1, 3–8.

This is the first installment of a two-part article on the tragic history—and the often overlooked positive attributes—of Mary Lincoln, written in 1937 by the grandson of Mary's friend and spiritual adviser Rev. David Swing. The thesis is that Mary, while not faultless, was not the monster that her detractors have depicted her to be. This first installment focuses on Mary's family history and surveys her childhood, early years, and relationship with Abraham Lincoln up to their 1842 wedding. The article contains no primary evidence or Swing family stories about Mary. It is a transcription of a presentation Ricker gave to the Joliet, Illinois, Women of Rotary in 1937.

347.
———. "The Other Side of Mary Lincoln: Part 2." *For the People: A Newsletter of the Abraham Lincoln Association* 9, no. 1 (Spring 2007): 1–2, 7–9.

This second installment of Ricker's two-part article continues his story of Mary Lincoln from when she was first lady of the United States to her death in 1882. Unlike part 1, part 2 offers descriptions of Mary's characteristics and actions from the firsthand perspective of the Swing family, mainly from the years 1865 to 1875. To the Swings, Mary was "undoubtedly mentally disturbed" as the result of the deaths of her son Willie and her husband, and suffered mood swings, depression, and hallucinations, but at most times was completely normal. Ricker describes Mary's visits to his family in Chicago and her close relationship with his sister Mary Swing; he also discusses Mary Lincoln's insanity trial and the impact it had on Robert Lincoln.

348.
Clinton, Catherine. "Wife versus Widow: Clashing Perspectives on Mary Lincoln's Legacy." *Journal of the Abraham Lincoln Association* 28, no. 1 (Winter 2007): 1–19.
    Clinton's piece is a revisionist reevaluation of Mary Lincoln's legacy as wife, political partner, criticized first lady, and historians' whipping girl.

349.
Steers, Edward, Jr. "The Mole in the White House: Mary Todd Lincoln," in *Lincoln Legends: Myths, Hoaxes, and Confabulations Associated with our Greatest President*, 80–88. Lexington: University of Kentucky Press, 2007.
    This is an examination of the myth that Abraham Lincoln visited a secret session of a congressional committee investigating rumors that Mary Lincoln was leaking military secrets to the Confederacy. Unfortunately, this is simply a rehash—but not nearly so well done—of Mark E. Neely Jr.'s 1975 article, "Abraham Lincoln did NOT Defend His Wife before the Committee on the Conduct of the War" (entry 297). Readers interested in this topic will be better served to read Neely's article.

350.
Baker, Jean. "Varieties of Religious Experience: Abraham and Mary Lincoln," in *Lincoln Revisited: New Insights from the Lincoln Forum*, ed. John Y. Simon, Harold Holzer, and Dawn Vogel, 105–116. N.Y.: Fordham University Press, 2007.
    Using the religious theories of William James as a starting point, Baker examines how Abraham and Mary Lincoln demonstrated the validity of James's theory of "subjective religion." Baker reviews Mary's religious experiences from Presbyterianism to Episcopalianism, back to Presbyterianism and then to Spiritualism, and shows how she was "unorthodox" in her religious views. This article is an interesting perspective on Mary Lincoln's religious beliefs.

351.
Watson, Robert P., Dale Berger, and Richard M. Yon. "The Real Mrs. Lincoln: The Nature and Extent of Scholarship on Mary Todd Lincoln." *Lincoln Herald* 110, no. 1 (Spring 2008): 6–38.
    In this examination of the scholarly treatment of Mary Lincoln in works written about her husband, the authors conclude that Mary's life, while looked at overall objectively in their sampling of major books about Abraham Lincoln, is generally glossed over or ignored and must be better integrated into

SCHOLARLY AND POPULAR ARTICLES

the mainstream of Lincoln studies. The article contains references to various first lady studies that are not explained well and therefore add nothing to the argument the authors seek to make. The article also suffers from a major lack of credibility in that the works consulted for this study were written not solely about Mary but only about her husband, and that the authors chose only twenty works as a sampling of thousands of books written about Abraham Lincoln. To call this an accurate or reliable study of scholarship on Mary Lincoln in any way strains credulity. The article includes a selected bibliography.

352.
Emerson, Jason. "New Mary Lincoln Letter Found." *Journal of the Illinois State Historical Society* 101, no. 3-4 (Fall-Winter 2008): 315–328.
    Emerson's article includes a transcription and historical examination of a newly discovered Mary Lincoln letter to Myra Bradwell dating from August 1867, which places the letter within the context of Mary's life and of the previously discovered cache of letters to Bradwell. The article—which also contains a synopsis of the only four articles about Mary's mental health written by physicians—shows that while the new letter contains no "smoking gun," it does contain numerous previously unknown facts about Mary that, taken together, add new depth to the story of her life.

353.
Wildemuth, Susan. "Elizabeth Keckley and the Mary Todd Lincoln Quilt." *Quilter's World*, 31, no. 1 (Feb. 2009).
    This is a brief biography of Elizabeth Keckley, seamstress to First Lady Mary Lincoln, and the story of their friendship, with a specific emphasis on the history of the quilt Keckley supposedly made from leftover fabric pieces of Mary's White House gowns. The quilt currently resides in the Kent State University Museum, which the author describes as "a work of art and a tribute to an excellent needlewoman."

354.
Clinton, Catherine. "Mrs. Lincoln Goes Shopping." *New York Archives* 8, no. 3 (Winter 2009): 27–30.
    This is an examination of Mary Lincoln's connection and travels to New York City, beginning with her wartime clothing and furniture shopping. The article focuses mostly on the story of the 1867 Old Clothes Scandal in which Mary sought to sell her wardrobe to help pay her debts, only to be criticized and ridiculed for her unseemly conduct.

355.
Dick, Carina, Susan L. Renes, and Anthony T. Strange. "Mary Lincoln's Madness: Understanding the Factors That Influence the Diagnosis and Treatment of Bipolar Disorder." *Journal of Creativity in Mental Health* 5, no. 1 (2010): 99–104.
This article is a survey of Mary Lincoln's mental health and the factors influencing it throughout her life, based on a reading of a half-dozen historical and psychiatric texts, mainly *The Madness of Mary Lincoln*, by Jason Emerson (entry 96).

356.
Emerson, Jason. "Mary Lincoln: An Annotated Bibliography." *Journal of the Illinois State Historical Society* 103, no. 2 (Summer 2010): 180–235.
This extensive annotated bibliography includes 243 writings about Mary Lincoln in nonfiction (books and pamphlets), juvenilia, selected nonfiction articles, fiction, poetry, and drama.

357.
Temple, Wayne C. "The Mathers and Lincoln's Unused Tomb." *Journal of the Illinois State Historical Society* 103, no. 3-4 (Fall-Winter 2010): 362–376.
This article covers the story of Abraham Lincoln's burial place in Springfield, Illinois, and how it was originally intended to be in the middle of the city rather than in the bucolic cemetery outside of town. Central to the narrative is how Mary Lincoln waged an indefatigable fight against her former neighbors to have her husband interred in Oak Ridge Cemetery, where she wanted, and not in the "Mather Plot" in the city, as the city fathers wanted. This "battle of the gravesite" is an important part of Mary's story that shows not only her steely resolve in the wake of her husband's assassination but also the utter contempt with which many of her former neighbors held her opinion.

358.
Emerson, Jason. "A Medal for Mrs. Lincoln." *Register of the Kentucky Historical Society* 109, no. 2 (Spring 2011): 187–206.
This article tells the story of the engraved gold medal given to Mary Lincoln in 1867 as the tribute of forty thousand French citizens to the memory of President Lincoln. This story of the medal—its creation, its transmittal, its subsequent history, and its effect on Mary—has never previously been examined or written about, and yet it was the only tangible public tribute Mary ever received after her husband's assassination.

359.
————. "Mary Lincoln: An Annotated Bibliography Supplement." *Journal of the Illinois State Historical Society* 104, no. 3 (Fall 2011): 238–249.

This supplemental article to Emerson's summer 2010 annotated bibliography on Mary Lincoln (entry 356) includes thirty-four additional entries of nonfiction books, nonfiction articles, and poetry.

360.
Kaikobad, Vera. "An Acupuncture 'Diagnosis' of Mary Todd Lincoln's Health Issues." *Medical Acupuncture* 23, no. 3 (Sept. 2011): 159–163.

This article attempts to create a clinical profile of Mary Lincoln, to look at her health problems using an acupuncture system, and to put together a protocol that could have aided her in managing her health troubles. Unfortunately, the article is based on slim and outdated secondary sources and shows no real understanding of Mary's health issues. It also suffers from such bad writing, obscene medical jargon, and esoteric medical principles that no one but an acupuncture specialist can even hope to understand what the author is saying. The author's conclusions offer no real "conclusions" at all.

361.
Wheeler, Samuel P. "Solving a Lincoln Literary Mystery: 'Little Eddie.'" *Journal of the Abraham Lincoln Association,* 33, no. 2 (Summer 2012): 34–46.

For decades, Lincoln scholars have argued over whether Mary Lincoln did or did not write the poem "Little Eddie" published in the February 7, 1850, issue of the *Illinois Daily Journal* in memory of her recently deceased son, Edward Baker Lincoln (entry 402). In this article, Wheeler has proven without a doubt that Mary did not write the poem—nor did Abraham—but that it was written in 1849 by a St. Louis woman "who most likely had no knowledge of the Lincoln family." In addition to solving the mystery, the article offers the full text of the poem and reviews the previous arguments over authorship by other writers.

362.
Irvine, Cyndy. "Mary Lincoln and Her Visit to Wisconsin's Wild Region." *Wisconsin Magazine of History,* 95, no. 4 (summer 2012): 2–11.

Using newly discovered source material, Irvine uncovers and explains a practically unknown steamboat excursion Mary Lincoln took with youngest son Tad to the Lake Superior region in August 1867. The fifteen-day, seventeen-hundred-mile trip from Chicago to Bayfield, Wisconsin, and back was typically taken by tourists as a reprieve from the summer heat and an opportunity to see the wild country of the north. For the Lincolns, the trip came immediately after Tad (and Robert) had been to Washington, D.C., to testify at the trial of assassination conspirator John Surratt and just before Mary went to New York City on her ill-fated attempt to sell her old White House clothing. Based on newspaper articles and newly uncovered letters and diary entries, this enticing article reveals a never-before-examined moment in Mary's life after the White House.

363.
Holst, Erika. "A Puzzling Lincoln Purchase at Corneau & Diller's Drug Store: What Is Pennyroyal?" *For the People: A Newsletter of the Abraham Lincoln Association* 16, no. 2 (Summer 2014): 9–10.
This exciting article set Lincoln scholars and enthusiasts abuzz in 2014 by its contention that Mary Lincoln may have tried to abort her fourth pregnancy in 1852 by taking the medicinal herb pennyroyal, and, if so, that Tad Lincoln's health may have been permanently harmed as a result. Holst's thesis was the result of a single known purchase by the Lincolns of pennyroyal in August 1852 and the fact that the herb, while used for numerous purposes, was mainly used at the time as an abortifacient. The 1852 pennyroyal purchase "invites us to reexamine what we think we know about the Lincolns and their desire for children," Holst concludes.

364.
"What Is Pennyroyal? Comments and Responses." *For the People: A Newsletter of the Abraham Lincoln Association* 16, no. 3 (Fall 2014): 8–9.
This article offers responses from two writers who have penned books about Mary Lincoln—Jean Baker and Daniel Mark Epstein—to Erika Holst's contention that someone in the Lincoln family purchased the medicinal herb pennyroyal in 1852 and Mary may have taken it to abort her fourth pregnancy. Epstein calls Holst's article well done and her conclusion plausible, given what is known about Mary's state of mind in 1852. Baker accuses Holst of writing assumptions and speculations that are irresponsible and no better than gossip, and that Holst did not take into account possible alternatives as to who else could have taken the pennyroyal.

365.
Emerson, Jason. "As Willie Lay Dying, Mary Lincoln Gets Pilloried in a Poem." *For the People: A Newsletter of the Abraham Lincoln Association* 17, no. 2 (Summer 2015): 7–9.

This article includes the context behind and story of George Boker's poem "The Queen Must Dance," published in February 1862 as a scathing satire against Mary Lincoln and her decision to hold a lavish, invitation-only White House ball while Union soldiers were suffering and dying on the battlefields (entry 400). Boker's poem, published anonymously at the time, was widely reprinted across the U.S. and much discussed. Until this publication, the poem had not been reprinted since 1862. The poem and its context are also published in Emerson's book *Lincoln's Lover: Mary Lincoln in Poetry* (entry 120).

366.
Solomon, Burt. "When Lincoln's State of the Union Leaked." *Atlantic*, www. theatlantic.com, Jan. 19, 2015.

Solomon's article describes the leak to the press of President Abraham Lincoln's first State of the Union message to Congress in December 1861 before it was officially delivered, and the likely role Mary Lincoln played in the scandal. The event led to the arrest of the "Chevalier" Henry Wikoff, an infamous rogue who insinuated himself into Mary's social circle in 1861, and his naming of White House gardener John Watt as the leaker. As the article states, it was generally known around Washington that Mary was deeply involved in the scandal, and Congress, at the president's behest, agreed to blame the gardener and leave the first lady alone as a favor to the president. While this story was top news in early 1862, and is mentioned in many books about the Lincolns, Solomon's is the only article solely on the event to be found. The leak, and Mary's association with men such as Wikoff and Watt, is one of many examples of Mary's poor conduct while first lady.

367.
Etulain, Richard W. "Mary Lincoln and the Lincoln Assassination: Grief Unbounded," in *The Lincoln Assassination Riddle: Revisiting the Crime of the Nineteenth Century*, ed. by Frank J. Williams and Michael Burkhimer, 125–136. Kent, Ohio: Kent State University Press, 2016.

This chapter is a survey of Mary Lincoln's life after her husband's assassination and its effect on her. Etulain, using all the major primary and secondary sources relating to this period, looks at Mary's struggles with her unstable emotions in the years after 1865, including how she dealt with the burial of her husband, the Old Clothes Scandal in 1867, and the death of her son Tad. Etulain believes that the assassination "unhinged" Mary and "dealt a near deathblow" to such an "emotionally challenged" person.

368.
Sotos, John G. "'What an Affliction': Mary Todd Lincoln's Fatal Pernicious Anemia." *Perspectives in Biology and Medicine* 58 no. 4 (Autumn 2016): 419–443.

This new medical theory about Mary Lincoln claims to explain and unify all of her physical and mental illnesses into a single diagnosis of pernicious anemia, a syndrome of vitamin B_{12} deficiency. Sotos, a medical doctor who previously published an exhaustive medical study on Abraham Lincoln (entry 99), offers a medical narrative of Mary's life and a historical explanation of pernicious anemia. He claims that Mary's litany of physical ailments during her lifetime, combined with her proven mental issues, contain all the earmarks of a disease that is now "extinct" and no longer familiar to or diagnosed by modern physicians. While Sotos admits that a medical diagnosis of any historical person is subjective, he also is convinced that his diagnosis is the true explanation for Mary's behavior, and that a historical reinterpretation is now in order. This is an interesting article offering a new and unique theory about Mary's life and medical health, although one that fails to convince considering that every ailment Mary ever complained of is apparently a part of pernicious anemia, and the disease is, as Sotos admits, now extinct, unknown to modern doctors and, therefore, impossible to prove.

Fiction books and stories

369.
Babcock, Bernie. *Lincoln's Mary and the Babies*. Philadelphia: J. B. Lippincott, 1929. 316 pp., sel. bib.

A novel in third-person narrative depicting the Lincoln family between the years 1856 and 1865, the book focuses on Mary, Willie, and Tad, and characterizes Abraham Lincoln as the overall father figure and lynchpin that holds the family together. This is a well-written and at times heartwarming book that strives for realism and depicts Mary and the two younger children in all their respective positive and negative personal qualities.

370.
Colver, Anne. *Mr. Lincoln's Wife*. N.Y.: Farrar & Rinehart, 1943. 406 pp.

This novel in third-person narrative begins during Mary Todd's courtship in Springfield and ends shortly after Abraham Lincoln's assassination. Mary is portrayed as a woman of many contradictions, a loving wife and mother, and a politically astute spouse with great ambitions for her husband.

371.

Stone, Irving. *Love Is Eternal: A Novel of Mary Todd and Abraham Lincoln*. N.Y.: Doubleday & Co., 1954. 438 pp., bib.

Stone's novel in third-person narrative begins in Mary Todd's girlhood and ends at Abraham Lincoln's assassination. It is overall a great love story between two compatible people who complement and need each other—a direct confrontation in prose of the accusation that the Lincolns never were in love. Stone's book is certainly the most famous, and arguably the best written, novel about Mary Lincoln.

372.

Ballard, Mary W. "The Heart of Mary Lincoln." *Woman's Home Companion* 83, no. 2 (Feb. 1956): 40–41, 85, 87, 99, 102–103, 117.

This fictionalized account of the "love story of Mary and Abraham Lincoln" is presented in the form of memories of the aged widow Lincoln as she looks through trunks full of clothing and mementos of her life. The memories begin with Mary and Abraham meeting at a dance in Springfield in 1840 and go through their broken engagement, their twenty-two-year marriage, and the climax that is the assassination. This is a well-written, engaging, historically accurate fictional depiction of Mary's love for her husband and the years they spent together. The article was the basis for an NBC television *Matinee Theater* episode in February 1956 (entry 425). According to the magazine, the scenes from the article were taken from a novel Ballard wrote about Mary Lincoln. That novel, if it ever was published, has proven impossible to find.

373.

Rhodes, James, and Dean Jauchius. *The Trial of Mary Todd Lincoln*. Indianapolis: Bobbs-Merrill, 1959. 200 pp., bib.

This is a fictional account of Mary Lincoln's insanity trial as it "should have happened," i.e., with cross-examination of witnesses and Mary Lincoln on the stand. It advances the theory that Robert Lincoln's political enemies tricked him into committing his mother as a way to destroy his presidential aspirations. The book originally was released as nonfiction but was relabeled as fiction after Robert's Chicago law firm of Isham, Lincoln, and Beale threatened to sue the publisher and authors for libel (Harry J. Dunbaugh to Hughes Miller, president, the Bobbs-Merrill Company, Chicago, May 19, 1959, John Goff Papers, Friends of Hildene, Inc., Manchester, Vt.).

374.
Rogers, Gayle. *My Name Was Mary: The Woman Lincoln Loved.* Wake Forest, N.C.: Sojourner Publishing, 2003. 400 pp.
This first-person narrative of Mary Lincoln's life, labeled as historical romance, focuses on her love for and by Abraham Lincoln. This is an emphatic—even obsessive—defense of Mary against her critics and poor historical reputation.

375.
duPont, M. Kay. *Loving Mr. Lincoln: The Personal Diaries of Mary Todd Lincoln.* Atlanta: Jedco Press, 2003. 362 pp., bib.
This story of Mary Lincoln's life, love, and daily struggles with Abraham in their twenty-six years together is written as a journal in Mary's "own words." Winner of the 2003 Georgia Writers Association Fiction Award.

376.
Hambly, Barbara. *The Emancipator's Wife: A Novel of Mary Todd Lincoln.* N.Y.: Bantam, 2005. 608 pp.
This novel through Mary Lincoln's eyes as she struggles to endure life inside Bellevue Place sanitarium, the sane victim of a heartless son, remembering her past years, is one of the better-written historical novels about Mary that accurately depicts her mercurial personality.

377.
Newman, Janis Cooke. *Mary: A Novel.* San Francisco: MacAdam/Cage, 2006. 707 pp.
This first-person narrative is presented as notes written by Mary Lincoln remembering her life while unjustly imprisoned inside Bellevue Place sanitarium by a heartless son. This book, based on Jean Baker's 1987 biography, portrays Mary as a misunderstood feminist ahead of her time who guides her lackluster backwoods husband into political greatness. While dubbed "historical fiction," this poorly written book, which reads at times like a bodice-ripping romance novel, is light on actual history and heavy on fiction.

378.
Holleran, Andrew. *Grief.* N.Y.: Hyperion, 2006. 150 pp.

This literary novel centers on a lonely, exhausted professor dealing with his grief after the death of his invalid mother. He finds in the "strange and impassioned" letters of Mary Lincoln a realization about the nature of grief and the power of mourning. While not a novel specifically about Mary, her presence pervades the book; and the protagonist's thoughts about Mary's life and the deep grief she endured after the assassination of her husband—which Holleran handles deftly with masterful prose—offer a unique interpretation about her life and suffering not found elsewhere in the bibliography.

379.
Schleifer, Nancy. *A Warrant for Mrs. Lincoln: A Novel.* Xlibris, 2007. 276 pp., bib.
Schleifer's first-person narrative, in a voice that continually shifts between Mary Lincoln and a fictional protagonist, focuses on Mary's insanity trial and her stay in Bellevue Place sanitarium. Mary is portrayed as a perfectly sane woman ruthlessly railroaded into the unbearable asylum by a heartless son. Though supposedly a historical novel, the majority of the historical "facts" in the book are incorrect.

380.
Hunter, Frederic. *Abe and Molly: The Lincoln Courtship.* Santa Barbara, Calif.: Nebbadoon Press, 2010. 401 pp., bib.
This is an exquisite—and unique—work of historical fiction focused solely on the courtship of Abraham Lincoln and Mary Todd, a time when he called her "Molly" and she called him "Mr. Lincoln." As the author states, it is the story of two young people attracted across barriers of class and background who break those barriers to find their own happiness. The book is meticulously researched and uses educated interpretations of the facts when necessary (with a bibliography and more than forty pages of historic notes in the back), but it is the writing and characterization that impress. It is a wonderful read, difficult to put down, and one in which the reader feels that he knows and understands both Abraham and Mary, how they acted, and why they acted the way they did in the name of love. This is a must-read for anyone who loves historical fiction and the story of the Lincolns.

381.
Chiaverini, Jennifer. *Mrs. Lincoln's Dressmaker: A Novel.* N.Y.: Plume, 2013. 356 pp.
This is a story of the friendship between Mary Lincoln and her modiste Elizabeth Keckley during and after Mary's White House years, with Keckley as

the protagonist. The book is meticulously researched and reads like history with dialogue—which is both positive and negative. Much of the dialogue is taken verbatim from the letters, interviews, and reminiscences of both Mary and Keckley, and so anyone with a thorough knowledge of the story's history may get bored. It could be said this work of historical fiction is so historical that it lacks imagination. On the other hand, Chiaverini is a skilled writer who brings the time period, the characters, and the scenes in the book completely to life. This is definitely one of the better pieces of historical fiction ever written about Mary Lincoln, and a must-read for devotees of the genre and the subject. Chiaverini's subsequent book, *Mrs. Lincoln's Rival* (N.Y.: Plume, 2014) is not about Mary, despite the title's reference, but is about Kate Chase's life during the Civil War.

@

Juvenile books and articles

382.
"Mary Todd's Hoop-Skirt." *Youth's Companion* 72, no. 48 (Dec. 1, 1898): 608.
    This account by a schoolmate of Mary Todd describes the girls' attempt to make hoop skirts for Sunday church out of willow branches, and the subsequent trouble they got into for it. It is taken from Emilie Todd Helm's article in *McClure's* magazine (entry 221).

383.
Corneau, Octavia Roberts. "Childhood in Lincoln's Town." *Youth's Companion* 99, no. 6 (Feb. 5, 1925): 86.
    A Springfield girl's memories of stories about Abraham and Mary Lincoln from elderly neighbors who knew the Lincolns, this article includes brief anecdotes about the Lincoln wedding, the children, and the family's farewell reception to Springfield in 1861.

384.
Wilkie, Katharine E. *Mary Todd Lincoln: Girl of the Bluegrass*. Indianapolis: Bobbs-Merrill, 1954. 192 pp., illus., reading level: ages 9–12.
    This story of Mary Todd portrays her as an intelligent, strong-willed girl and young woman who engages in numerous adventures as she grows up. The final chapter tells of her marriage to Abraham Lincoln and ends with his election to the presidency.

385.
Miller, Helen Topping. *Christmas for Tad: A Story of Mary and Abraham Lincoln.* N.Y.: Longmans, Green, & Company, 1956. 92 pp.

This is a fictional tale of the Lincoln family during Christmas 1862, in which all Tad wants as a gift is the return of his lost nanny goat. It is a well-written narrative but grossly inaccurate in its characterizations of Mary, Abraham, and Robert Lincoln.

386.
Randall, Ruth Painter. *I Mary: A Biography of the Girl Who Married Abraham Lincoln.* Boston: Little, Brown & Co., 1959. 242 pp., illus., index.

This is a version of Randall's previous nonfiction book *Mary Lincoln: Biography of a Marriage* (entry 47) revised for young readers. It is a sympathetic narrative of Mary Lincoln's life from childhood to death with a focus on her married years.

387.
Anderson, LaVere. *Mary Todd Lincoln: President's Wife.* Champaign, Ill.: Garrard Publishing Company, 1975. 80 pp., illus., reading level: grades 2–4.

This basic retelling of Mary Lincoln's life from her childhood to her death includes the most well-known events of her life, such as making a hoop skirt of willow branches, riding her new pony to Henry Clay's house, adding a second story to the Lincoln home without her husband's knowledge, and experiencing her husband's assassination.

388.
Collins, David R. *Shattered Dreams: The Story of Mary Todd Lincoln.* N.Y.: Morgan Reynolds, 1994. 128 pp., illus., chronol., bib., index.

Reading level: ages 9–12. This is a well-crafted biography of Mary Lincoln that is written with more of a narrative flare than most history books for young readers. It tells Mary's story from childhood through death, with special emphasis on the insanity period of 1875 to 1876. While the characterization of Robert Lincoln is misguided, and the description of his relationship with his mother after the assassination is flawed, these errors corrupt only a small part of the story.

389.
Santow, Dan. *Mary Todd Lincoln: 1818–1882.* Encyclopedia of First Ladies series. New York: Children's Press, 1999. 111 pp., illus., timeline, fast facts, websites, further reading, index.

This biography of Mary Lincoln discusses her upbringing, marriage, years as first lady, and the many tragedies that marred her life. This very readable book is filled with illustrations, sidebars, and explanations about not only Mary's life but also the people, places, and events around her. This is an excellent starting place for young readers interested in Mary Lincoln.

390.
Hull, Mary E. *Mary Todd Lincoln: Tragic First Lady of the Civil War.* Berkeley Heights, N.J.: Enslow Publishers, 2000. 128 pp., illus., notes, glossary, index, reading level: ages 9–12.

Hull's biography of Mary Lincoln portrays her as a vivacious and intelligent girl, a supportive and loving wife, a harshly criticized first lady, and a tragic widow.

391.
Larkin, Tanya. *What Was Cooking in Mary Todd Lincoln's White House?* Cooking throughout American History series. N.Y.: Rosen Publishing Group, 2001. 24 pp., glossary, index, websites.

This short biography of Mary Lincoln offers some of her favorite recipes as appropriate to periods and places of her life, such as her childhood in Kentucky, her years in Springfield, and her time as first lady.

392.
Rinaldi, Ann. *An Unlikely Friendship: A Novel of Mary Todd Lincoln and Elizabeth Keckley.* N.Y.: Harcourt, 2007. 256 pp., reading level: young adult.

This is a strangely written book, portraying the contrasting lives and ultimate friendship of Mary Lincoln and her black White House seamstress Elizabeth Keckley, that jumps around from first- to third-person narrative and between fiction and nonfiction. While the introduction and conclusion of the book do discuss (one fictively, one nonfictively) the relationship between these two women, the majority of the "novel" is two separate first-person accounts of Mary's and Elizabeth's childhoods. There are also multiple historical inaccuracies in the book.

393.
Mattern, Joanne. *Mary Todd Lincoln.* First Ladies Abdo series. Checkerboard Books, 2007. 32 pp., illus., timeline, glossary, websites, index, reading level: ages 8 and up.

This is a very basic story of Mary Lincoln's life from childhood to death, filled with excellent illustrations. The book is a valuable learning tool for young readers, having vocabulary words in bold throughout the text and then defined in the back, a timeline of Mary's life, and a "Did You Know?" section with highlights of her life and legacy. This is a great primer for young readers and history lovers.

394.
Fleming, Candace. *The Lincolns: A Scrapbook Look at Abraham and Mary.* N.Y.: Schwartz & Wade, 2008. 181 pp., illus., notes, bib., index, reading level: young adult.

The story of the everyday lives of Abraham and Mary Lincoln from their childhoods to their respective deaths, the book is visual as well as narrative history, with a plethora of photographs and images, and an overall layout like a nineteenth-century newspaper (with large headings and subheadings and each topic its own text box).

395.
Suits, Linda Norbut. "Meet Mrs. Lincoln." *Cobblestone* 29, no. 8 (Oct. 2008): 26–27.

This is a basic introduction to Mary Lincoln, including the primary facts about her life.

396.
Jones, Lynda. *Mrs. Lincoln's Dressmaker: The Unlikely Friendship of Elizabeth Keckley and Mary Todd Lincoln.* Washington, D.C.: National Geographic, 2009. 80 pp., illus., bib., index, reading level: grades 5–8.

This book tells the story of the friendship between First Lady Mary Lincoln and her free black modiste Elizabeth Keckley. Starting when both were children, Jones explains who these women were, how they came together during the years of the U.S. Civil War, and what their relationship was like after the war ended. Among the score of books about the Lincoln-Keckley relationship, this one offers nothing new or special, just the basic information, some nice illustrations, and a short bibliography.

397.
Kerr, Mary C., and Catherine M. Kerr. *Mary Lincoln's Journey.* Miami Beach, Fla.: C. R. Crabb Publications, 2013. 91 pp., illus., notes, bib., web sources, reading level: young adult.

This book, written by a retired teacher and her teenage granddaughter, is about as education-friendly a book as one can get. This is more than just the story of Mary Lincoln's life told in prose; it is an educational experience with the main text supplemented by numerous photos, illustrations, maps, timelines, factual sidebars, informational breakout boxes, word definitions, and quotations from primary source materials. The story is detailed without being either simplistic or pedantic, and presents the facts of Mary's life empirically and without seeking to forward any specific agenda. The endnotes, bibliography, and web sources offer excellent suggestions for further research and reading. This is definitely one of the best books on Mary Lincoln for young adult readers.

398.
Krull, Kathleen. *Women Who Broke the Rules: Mary Todd Lincoln.* N.Y.: Blooms-bury USA Children's, 2015. 48 pp., illus., sources and further reading, index, reading level: ages 6–9.
This lively little book with great illustrations is well written for the intended age of the reader. Unfortunately, the book suffers from multiple factual errors and, in seeking to inspire young female readers, the author (with a twenty-first-century feminist viewpoint) grossly inflates Mary Lincoln's power, influence, and role throughout her husband's entire political career to present her as Abraham's top adviser and political partner, which she was not.

✏

Poetry and music

399.
Scala, Francis. "The Mary Lincoln Polka."
The song was first performed by the U.S. Marine Band at the Feb. 5, 1862, White House ball. The original score is now part of the Lincoln Financial Foundation Collection, whose management is shared by the Indiana State Museum and the Allen County Public Library. A 2013 performance of "The Mary Lincoln Polka" by the Chicago Bar Association Symphony Orchestra can be heard on the Lincoln Financial Foundation Collection website at www.lincolncollection.org.

400.
Boker, George H. "The Queen Must Dance." Philadelphia *Sunday Dispatch*, Feb. 9, 1862.
This stinging satire criticizes Mary Lincoln's decision to hold an invitation-only presidential ball on February 5, 1862, while the country was in the midst of

a Civil War and soldiers were suffering on the battlefields and in field hospitals. The ball was considered a great success socially, but Mary was excoriated in newspapers and editorials across the country as being aristocratic and heartless for holding such a lavish and exclusive event.

401.
Merryman, E. H. "Riding on a Dray." *Journal of the Illinois State Historical Society* 16, nos. 1–2 (April–July 1923): 146.

This poem, written in 1839 by an acquaintance of a young Mary Todd, is based on Merryman's personal observation of an event in Mary's life. Mary and her friend walked into downtown Springfield through the muddy streets by dropping shingles in the mud and hopping onto each one. When the shingles were gone, Mary hailed the driver of a two-wheeled wagon called a dray and asked for a ride back home. Drays were used for hauling goods, not people, and Mary's ride caused quite a sensation in the upper social circles of Springfield.

402.
"Little Eddie." *Illinois Daily Journal*, Feb. 7, 1850.

This poem, written about the death of three-year-old Edward Baker Lincoln, the second Lincoln son, was published anonymously in a local Springfield newspaper just days after the boy's passing from tuberculosis. For decades, it was hotly debated whether or not Mary Lincoln could have, or did, write this poem. It was recently discovered by Lincoln scholar Samuel Wheeler that Mary did not write it (entry 361).

403.
Emissus. "To Mrs. Lincoln," in *Poetical Tributes to the Memory of Abraham Lincoln*, ed. J. N. Plotts, 81–83. Philadelphia: J. B. Lippincott & Co., 1865.

This poem, written in the aftermath of Abraham Lincoln's assassination, offers comfort and commiseration for his widow.

404.
Dennison, Mary A. "To Mrs. Lincoln," in *Poetical Tributes to the Memory of Abraham Lincoln*, ed. by J. N. Plotts, 222–223. Philadelphia: J. B. Lippincott & Co., 1865.

Another poem written in the aftermath of Abraham Lincoln's assassination offering comfort and commiseration for his widow. Dennison was a prolific nineteenth-century writer and volunteered as a nurse during the Civil War.

405.
Horton, George Moses. "Mrs. Lincoln's Lamentation," in *Naked Genius*, 155–157. Raleigh, N.C.: Wm. B. Smith & Co., 1865.

This poem laments the murder of President Lincoln and sympathizes with his widow's loss. The author, known as the "Black Bard of North Carolina," was illiterate until age thirty-one and was the only black person to publish a book while still in bondage.

406.
Miller, Marion Mills. "Lady of Lincoln," in *Contemporary American Men Poets: An Anthology of Verse by 459 Living Poets*, ed. Thomas Del Vecchio, 164. N.Y.: Henry Harrison, 1937.

This is the first known poem about Mary Lincoln that sought to understand who she was, how she contributed to her husband's success, and how her memory had been maligned. Written by a classical scholar, the poem's final stanza has been quoted in at least two books about Mary Lincoln.

407.
Fite, Courtenay Fraser. "The Spirit of Mary Todd Speaks." *Jackson* [Miss.] *Daily News*, Feb. 18, 1940.

Fite's poem, written in the voice of Mary Lincoln from the spirit world, explains that although Mary was destined for criticism and hate during her time as Abraham Lincoln's wife and widow, she was happy to suffer "negation" to have been his love and allow him to be "transcendent world light," admired by mankind.

408.
Perkins, Reed Miles. "Mary Todd Lincoln," in *Prairie Poems*, 16. Springfield, Ill.: Frye Printing, 1946.

In this sonnet for Mary Lincoln, Perkins admires her as a loving wife and a helpful mate. Perkins grew up in Springfield while Mary was still alive, and his father actually knew Abraham Lincoln. The book contains numerous poems about Abraham as well.

409.
Merchant, Jane. "Valentine for Mary Lincoln." *Washington Star*, Feb. 14, 1955.

A panegyric written for a woman whom the poet saw as admirable yet misunderstood, it was published in the *Washington Star* newspaper on Valentine's Day, 1955. Merchant told historian Ruth Painter Randall that her inspiration came after reading Randall's 1953 book *Mary Lincoln: Biography of a Marriage* (entry 47). Randall, who believed and often wrote that Mary Lincoln's reputation had been wrongly maligned, later reprinted Merchant's poem in her children's book about Mary, stating, "The very fact that such a poem has been written is a heartwarming sign that at last justice to Mary has been done." Reprinted in Randall, *I Mary*, 219–220 (entry 386).

410.
Lynskey, Edward C. "Mrs. Lincoln Enters Bellevue Place." *College English* 49, no. 8 (Dec. 1987): 891.
    Lynskey's poem, written from Mary Lincoln's perspective, concerns her mental health and stay at Bellevue Place sanitarium in 1875.

411.
Lynskey, Edward C. "Mrs. Lincoln's Epistle from Bellevue Place." *Commonweal* 124, no. 11 (June 6, 1997): 12.
    This poem, written from Mary Lincoln's perspective, deals with her time at Bellevue Place sanitarium in 1875.

412.
Baggott, Julianna. "Mary Todd on Her Deathbed." *Quarterly West* 48 (Spring-Summer 1999): 34–35.
    This poem is a representation of Mary Lincoln's thoughts while in Bellevue Place Sanitarium in 1875 during which she reflects on her life, the loss of her husband and three children, and the situation she found herself in due to the actions of her oldest child. Included in *Best American Poetry 2000*, ed. Robert Bly and David Lehman (N.Y.: Scribner, 2000), 32–33. Reprinted in Julianna Baggott, *Lizzie Borden in Love: Poems in Women's Voices* (Carbondale: Southern Illinois University Press, 2006), 17–18.

413.
Lynskey, Edward C. "Mrs. Lincoln's Terror of Moths." *Strange Horizons*, www.strangehorizons.com, May 6, 2002.
    Lynskey's poem, written from Mary Lincoln's perspective, tells of her stay at Bellevue Place sanitarium in 1875.

414.
Overmire, Laurence. "Willie at the Foot of the Bed (An Ode to Mary Todd Lincoln)." Ancestry.com, 2003.

Overmire, popularly known as "the Genealogist-Poet," sympathetically explores Mary Lincoln's feelings in the aftermath of her beloved son Willie's death in 1862.

415.
Flenniken, Kathleen. "To Ease My Mind." *Iowa Review* 34, no. 2 (Fall 2004): 69–70.
   In this poem, Flenniken considers the juxtaposition of war and suffering as seen through the perspective of Mary Lincoln. Reprinted in Flenniken, *Famous* (Lincoln: University of Nebraska Press, 2006).

416.
Baggott, Julianna. "An Open Letter to Mrs. Lincoln." *Compulsions of Silk Worms and Bees: Poems.* Baton Rouge: Louisiana State University Press, 2007.
   This is a poem written as a response to Abraham Lincoln's famous story of seeing the omen of his death in a mirror shortly before assuming the presidency.

417.
Guillory, Dan. "Litany for Mary T.," in *The Lincoln Poems*, 52–53. Mahomet, Ill.: Mayhaven Publishing, 2008.
   This passionate poem is written from Abraham Lincoln's perspective of Mary as an attractive, sexual woman of whom he cannot get enough.

418.
Guillory, Dan. "Love Is Eternal," in *The Lincoln Poems*, 48–49. Mahomet, Ill.: Mayhaven Publishing, 2008.
   This is another poem in Abraham Lincoln's voice expressing his love for Mary Todd.

419.
Smith, R. T. "Mary Lincoln Triptych." *Missouri Review* (Winter 2012): 119–133.
   In this series of three poems about Mary Lincoln, each one is focused on different aspects of her life, including her love of shopping but simultaneous parsimonious nature, her personal grief and belief in spiritualism, and her institutionalization for insanity by her son Robert and subsequent relationship with him. Smith received the 2013 Gerald T. Perkoff Literary Prize in Poetry for the triptych.

420.
Guillory, Dan. "Those Irish Girls," in *House Poems*, 18–21. Mahomet, Ill.: Mayhaven Publishing, 2013.

Guillory offers this poem composed in Mary Lincoln's voice lamenting the difficulty in finding good housemaids and dealing with the ones—the majority being Irish immigrants—that she has.

421.
Guillory, Dan. "Mary Todd Lincoln Expropriates the Garden Fund, 1862," in *House Poems*, 137. Mahomet, Ill.: Mayhaven Publishing, 2013.

This is a poem on Mary Lincoln's efforts to refurnish the White House upon her arrival as first lady and "restore this presidential seat of power to its rightful glory."

Drama

422.
Mirick, Edith. *Storm: A Biographical Drama of the Life of Mary Todd Lincoln*. 1940.

A nine-scene play composed in separate yet connected vignettes, the story begins with Mary as a girl in school, tells of her love and marriage to Abraham Lincoln, and ends at her widowhood. Copyright of the drama is under the title *Molly Lincoln*. It received second honors from the Dramatists' Alliance of Stanford University in 1943.

423.
Sergel, Ruth. *Irving Stone's Love Is Eternal*. 1955.

This play in three acts is based on Stone's novel of the same title (entry 371).

424.
Breckinridge, Frank P. *Mary the Wife (of Abraham Lincoln): A Drama Adapted for Television*. Chicago Literary Club, 1955. 31 pp.

This story in three acts depicts Mary in 1840, 1862, and 1865, first as an ambitious woman who insists the man she marries will be president one day and then a grieving mother and widow trying to endure the deaths of her son Willie and her husband. The story's subtext is not only Mary's lifelong presentiments that she could be forewarned of approaching death and tragedy in her life but also that her fear of such loss indelibly shaped her high-strung, nervous temperament.

425.
Ballard, Mary. "The Heart of Mary Lincoln." *NBC Matinee Theater*, Feb. 10, 1956, season 1, episode 73, adapted for television by Kathleen and Robert Howard Lindsay, broadcast live.

After the death of her husband and having never overcome the death of their eleven-year-old son Willie, Mary Lincoln is so filled with grief and sadness that her mental state declines. The show was adapted by Ballard's story "The Heart of Mary Lincoln," published in the Feb. 1956 issue of *Woman's Home Companion* (entry 372).

426.
Sylvia, Kenneth. *The Shadow Years*. 1957.

This drama in three acts recounts Mary Lincoln's life starting in the White House in 1862 and ending in Springfield in 1881. The play shows Mary as an anxious, high-strung wife and mother who is lovable and sensitive, but who ultimately becomes mentally undone by family deaths, suffers from melancholy hallucinations, and gradually falls to pieces.

427.
Cullinan, Thomas. *Mrs. Lincoln*. 1969.

This is a play in three acts during which Mary Lincoln recalls the incidents of her married life as she resides in the confines of her room at Bellevue Place Sanitarium. Her deranged mind sees everyone a villain and herself always a victim. In the second act, Mary's doctor has another patient impersonate Abraham Lincoln in an effort to relieve her troubled mind.

428.
Wright, Kenneth. *Wing of Expectation*. 1970.

The libretto of this opera in three acts based on the life of Mary Lincoln centers around the bitter antagonism between Mary and William Herndon, Abraham Lincoln's law partner, with Lincoln himself as the third main character in the production. The show premiered at Ford's Theatre in Washington, D.C., with proceeds used to restore the Petersen House, in which Abraham Lincoln died, across the street from Ford's.

429.

Samples, M. David. *Mrs. President: A Play about Mary Todd Lincoln.* 1970.

This four-act play (introduction, acts 1 and 2, and epilogue) begins with the Lincoln-Todd courtship and ends with Mary's death. It seeks to vindicate Mary Lincoln from her bad reputation as described by William Herndon and shows her to be a strong woman ultimately crushed by tragedy and posthumously covered with lies.

430.

Kilty, Jerome. *Look Away.* 1972.

This play in two acts takes place in Bellevue Place sanitarium in Batavia, Illinois, during the last night of Mary Lincoln's stay there. Later adapted by Cynthia Whitcomb and aired as a made-for-television movie on November 18, 1987, it starred Ellen Burstyn as Mary.

431.

Pasatieri, Thomas. *The Trial of Mary Lincoln.* 1972.

This opera in three acts opens during Mary Lincoln's 1875 insanity trial. By means of Mary's hallucinations and memories, back and forth through time, the opera shows the events of her life unfold, from uncertain fiancée of Abraham Lincoln to widow of the president. It was adapted by Anne Howard Bailey for television and aired on Feb. 14, 1972. Bailey won an Emmy award for Outstanding Writing Achievement in Comedy, Variety, or Music; the show also was nominated for an Emmy for Outstanding Single Program—Variety or Musical—Classical Music.

432.

Prideaux, James. *The Last of Mrs. Lincoln.* 1973.

This play in two acts depicts the final seventeen years of Mary Lincoln's life following her husband's assassination. It ran on Broadway from December 12, 1972, to February 4, 1973, featuring Julie Harris as Mrs. Lincoln, for which she won a Tony Award. Harris reprised her role in a 1976 film adaptation.

433.

Wenzel, Doris Replogle Porter. *"Without Discretion": A Play in Three Acts Based on the Life of Mary Todd Lincoln.* 1981.

This play depicts Mary Lincoln's life before and after her White House years: in Springfield, in Chicago, and at Bellevue Place sanitarium in Batavia, Illinois. It was the winner of the Lincoln Academy Award.

434.
McBride, Vaughn. *Pass My Imperfections Lightly By.* 1991.
This is a one-woman play that takes place in 1876 after Mary Lincoln's release from Bellevue Place sanitarium. It depicts Mary as a strong and emancipated yet also irrational and mercurial woman reminiscing on her life and dealing with her husband's murder and her own commitment.

435.
Nilsson, Nancy M. *Very Truly Yours, M.L.: A Visit with Mary Todd Lincoln.* 1992.
This is a theatrical conversation in two acts that depicts Mary Lincoln's entire life.

436.
Sexton, Nancy Niles. *Eternal Love: Mary Todd Lincoln, the Early Years.* 1992.
This one-woman show follows Mary Lincoln's life from her childhood in Lexington to Abraham Lincoln's election as president. The play ends before the Civil War. It is intended for young adult audiences.

437.
Barnes, Jane. *Final Payments.* 2000.
This two-act play covers Mary Lincoln's life from April 14, 1865, to November 9, 1871, and takes place in Washington, D.C.; Chicago; Bloomington, Illinois; New York City; England; and Germany. It is based in equal parts on Elizabeth Keckley's book *Behind the Scenes* and Mary's correspondence.

438.
Filloux, Catherine. *Mary and Myra.* 2000.
This is a two-woman play depicting the relationship between Mary Lincoln and Myra Bradwell as the latter arrives at Bellevue Place sanitarium in 1875 to help the former first lady gain her release. Myra's motives and Mary's sanity are both up for debate as they grapple with their pasts and their perceptions of freedom and womanhood.

439.
Wallnau, Carl N. *Mary Todd Lincoln: A Woman Apart.* 2003.
This is a one-woman show of Mary Lincoln looking back on her life, set on the day of her release from Bellevue Place sanitarium. It presents her as a complicated, well-intentioned, and persecuted public figure, although with a distraught and disturbed mental state.

440.

Bingham, June; music and lyrics by Carmel Owen. *Asylum: The Strange Case of Mary Todd Lincoln*. 2006.

This musical in two acts takes place ten years after President Lincoln's assassination. Mary Lincoln faces off against her late husband's former political allies and her only remaining son as they attempt to have her committed to an insane asylum for her erratic behavior.

441.

Thompson, Tazewell. *Mary T and Lizzie K*. 2013.

This is an "insider's look" at the unlikely friendship between First Lady Mary Lincoln and her seamstress Elizabeth Keckley, looking at their relationship both inside and outside of the White House, based on Keckley's 1868 book *Behind the Scenes* (entry 1).

442.

Dugan, Tom. *The Ghosts of Mary Lincoln*. 2013.

Offering a private visit with history's most haunted first lady, this one-person play includes tales of White House séances, presidential grave robbers, warnings from the undead, and the fateful night at Ford's Theatre. Set on a dark and stormy night, *The Ghosts of Mary Lincoln* is an evening of "blood, madness and murder."

443.

Latham, Donna. *The Haunted Widow Lincoln*. 2014.

This is a story of Mary Lincoln in Bellevue Place sanitarium after being declared insane by a Chicago jury. There, Mary hoards trunks of her possessions and vials of poison, waging a great battle with John Wilkes Booth and other ghosts of the past while endlessly mourning the death of her husband and sons.

444.

Still, James. *The Widow Lincoln*. 2015.

Set in the White House during the weeks following Lincoln's assassination, *The Widow Lincoln* portrays a very human Mary in the aftermath of her husband's death as she mourns the postwar life they will never share. The play was commissioned by Ford's Theatre as part of Ford's 150: Remembering the Lincoln Assassination, a series of events marking the 150 years since Abraham Lincoln's assassination at Ford's Theatre.

Websites

445.
National First Ladies Library: Firstladies.org.
A search for "Mary Todd Lincoln" will bring up adult and juvenile/educational biographies, book and manuscript bibliographies, teacher lesson plans, and numerous articles about Mary Lincoln specifically and first ladies in general. This is the most informative website to be found about Mary.

446.
Mary Todd Lincoln Research site: Rogerjnorton.com/Lincoln15.html.
Roger Norton's website on Mary Lincoln contains a trove of interesting and useful information, including articles on the Lincoln-Todd marriage, the Lincoln assassination, Mary's insanity case, and Mary's séances in the White House. There is also a Mary Lincoln chronology, photo gallery, list of quotes, and bibliography.

447.
"Mary Todd Lincoln." *New York Times—Times Topics*, online only at http://www.nytimes.com/info/mary-todd-lincoln, posted 2010.
This site offers an overview of Mary Lincoln's life from birth to death. It includes a list of Mary's personal letters and historical resources available online, and a list of the major books and articles about her life. It was compiled and written by Lincoln scholar Jason Emerson.

448.
Mary Todd Lincoln House: Mtlhouse.org.
While this website offers a brief history of Mary Lincoln and her family house in Lexington, Kentucky, it is mainly a resource for the Todd home as a historic site.

449.
Lincoln Home National Historic Site: Nps.gov/liho.
This website gives information about the Lincoln Home as a national historic site. Viewers can take a virtual tour of the house and find a few basic facts about the Lincoln family in general.

450.
Biography.com: biography.com/people/mary-todd-lincoln-248868.

This website offers a general overview of Mary Lincoln's entire life, a list of "quick facts" about her, and short videos on aspects of her life such as her early married life, her time as first lady, and her role as "influence peddler" in the White House.

451.
The History Channel: history.com/topics/first-ladies/mary-todd-lincoln.

There is very little information on Mary Lincoln on this site: just a general biography and a brief video.

452.
The White House: whitehouse.gov/about-the-white-house/first-ladies/mary-todd-lincoln.

This site offers a five-hundred-word biography of Mary Lincoln but nothing else.

❧

NOTES
INDEX OF ESSAY "COMMON CANON"
INDEX OF AUTHORS AND EDITORS
INDEX OF TITLES
INDEX OF SUBJECTS

NOTES

INTRODUCTION

1. Robert P. Watson, Dale Berger, and Richard M. Yon, "The Real Mrs. Lincoln: The Nature and Extent of Scholarship on Mary Todd Lincoln," *Lincoln Herald* 110, no. 1 (Spring 2008), 26.

2. William O. Stoddard, *Inside the White House in War Times*, ed. Michael Burlingame (1890; repr. Lincoln: University of Nebraska Press, 2000), 33.

3. These works include Tom Peet and David Keck, *Reading Lincoln: An Annotated Bibliography* (self-published, CreateSpace, 2014); Watson, Berger, and Yon, "The Real Mrs. Lincoln," 6–38; Jason Emerson, "Mary Lincoln: An Annotated Bibliography," *Journal of the Illinois State Historical Society* 103, no. 2 (Summer 2010): 180–235; Jason Emerson, "Mary Lincoln: An Annotated Bibliography Supplement," *Journal of the Illinois State Historical Society* 104, no. 3 (Fall 2011): 238–249; Mary Todd Lincoln Research site, rogerjnorton. com/Lincoln15.html; "Mary Todd Lincoln," *New York Times—Times Topics*, online at www.nytimes.com/info/mary-todd-lincoln; National First Ladies Library, www.firstladies.org.

4. Myra Helmer Pritchard, *The Dark Days of Abraham Lincoln's Widow, as Revealed by Her Own Letters*, ed. and annot. Jason Emerson (Carbondale: Southern Illinois University Press, 2011).

5. Barbara W. Tuchman, "In Search of History," in *Practicing History: Selected Essays* (N.Y.: Alfred A. Knopf, 1981), 21.

6. Octavia Roberts, *Lincoln in Illinois* (N.Y.: Houghton Mifflin, 1918); Mrs. John Todd Stuart interview, in "His Early Social Life and Marriage," *Chicago Tribune*, Patriotic Supplement No. 4, Abraham Lincoln, Feb. 12, 1900, 14.

7. Reminiscences of Margaret Stuart Woodrow, in Mary Bradley Rally, "Cousin and Childhood Friend of Mary Todd Lincoln Tells of Days When She and Martyr's Wife Were Girls Together," *Lexington* (Ky.) *Herald*, Feb. 14, 1909, 1, and Feb. 17, 1909, 4; Katherine Helm, *The True Story of Mary, Wife of*

Lincoln: Containing the Recollections of Mary Lincoln's Sister Emilie (Mrs. Ben Hardin Helm), Extracts from Her War-Time Diary, Numerous Letters and Other Documents Now First Published (N.Y.: Harper & Brothers, 1928), 31–32.

8. Mary Lee Esty and C. M. Shifflett, *Conquering Concussion: Healing TBI Symptoms with Neurofeedback and without Drugs* (Sewickley, Pa.: Round Earth Publishing, 2014); Vera Kaikobad, "An Acupuncture 'Diagnosis' of Mary Todd Lincoln's Health Issues," *Medical Acupuncture* 23, no. 3 (Sept. 2011): 159–163.

9. Daniel J. Boorstin, "The Age of Negative Discovery," in *Cleopatra's Nose: Essays on the Unexpected* (N.Y.: Random House, 1994), 3–17.

THE COMMON CANON OF MARY LINCOLN

1. This essay is concerned with published sources on Mary Lincoln, not primary archival materials. It should be understood that all historical research must be grounded in primary sources in archives and museums. While documents on Mary exist in numerous places, the main archival sources on her life are the Abraham Lincoln Presidential Library in Springfield, Ill.; the Library of Congress in Washington, D.C.; the Lincoln Financial Foundation Collection, shared between the Indiana State Museum in Indianapolis and the Allen County Public Library in Fort Wayne, Ind.; and the University of Kentucky Library Special Collections Research Center in Lexington.

2. Herbert Mitgang, "Has History Wronged Mary Lincoln?" *Courier-Journal and Times* [Louisville, Ky.], Feb. 11, 1973, G1, G22.

3. Mary Lincoln, interviews by William Herndon, Sept. 1866, in Douglas L. Wilson and Rodney O. Davis, eds., *Herndon's Informants: Letters, Interviews, and Statements about Abraham Lincoln* (Urbana: University of Illinois Press, 1998), 357–361. The original interviews are in the Herndon-Weik Collection in the Library of Congress.

4. Robert Lincoln to David Davis, Nov. 19, 1866, folder A-109, box 7, David Davis Family Papers, Abraham Lincoln Presidential Library.

5. Walter B. Stevens, "Recollections of Lincoln," *St. Louis Globe-Democrat*, Mar. 21, 1901, 3. Also published in Walter B. Stevens, *A Reporter's Lincoln*, edited by Michael Burlingame (Lincoln: University of Nebraska Press, 1998), 118.

6. William Herndon to Jesse Weik, Jan. 8, 1886, in Emanuel Hertz, *The Hidden Lincoln: From the Letters and Papers of William H. Herndon* (N.Y.: Viking Press, 1938), 130.

7. Elizabeth Keckley, *Behind the Scenes; or, Thirty Years a Slave, and Four Years in the White House* (1868; repr., N.Y.: Arno Press and New York Times, 1968), 182.

8. Jennifer Fleischner, *Mrs. Lincoln and Mrs. Keckly: The Remarkable Story of the Friendship between a First Lady and a Former Slave* (N.Y.: Broadway Books, 2003), 317. Fleischner spells her subject's name "Keckly" rather than the commonly used "Keckley" after discovering this was the way Elizabeth actually spelled her name. While I believe Fleischner's spelling to be the correct one, I have decided throughout this book to spell the name "Keckley," as has been done for more than 150 years, to avoid confusion since every other writing about Keckley was spelled this way.

9. Mary Lincoln to Rhoda White, May 2, 1868, in Justin G. Turner and Linda Levitt Turner, *Mary Todd Lincoln: Her Life and Letters* (N.Y.: Alfred A. Knopf, 1972), 476; John E. Washington, *They Knew Lincoln* (N.Y.: E. P. Dutton & Co., 1942), 241. Washington's book contains nearly forty pages concerning Keckley, her relationship with Mary Lincoln, and the creation of and reaction to Keckley's 1868 book.

10. Two other sources on Mary during this time, one of which is sometimes referenced by modern writers, are Mary Clemmer Ames's 1873 memoir, *Ten Years in Washington: Life and Scenes in the National Capital as a Woman Sees Them*, and William Mumler's 1875 memoir, *The Personal Experiences of William H. Mumler in Spirit-Photography*. Ames's work was highly critical of Mary as first lady, saying that during a time of civil war and self-sacrifice, Mary Lincoln "was incapable of lofty, impersonal impulse. She was self-centered, and never in any experience rose above herself." Mumler's memoir, on the other hand, was not critical, but by exposing Mary's visit to his shop in 1872 during which he took a spirit photo of her that developed with images of Abraham and Tad Lincoln standing over her shoulders, it solidified people's perceptions that Mary was suffering from some sort of insanity.

11. William Herndon to Jesse Weik, Jan. 8, 1886, in Hertz, *Hidden Lincoln*, 130. By "after 1862," Herndon meant after the death of eleven-year-old Willie Lincoln.

12. Emily Todd Helm, "Mary Todd Lincoln: Reminiscences and Letters of the Wife of President Lincoln," *McClure's* 11, no. 5 (Sept. 1898): 478–479.

13. Apparently, multiple writers in the 1920s had the same idea to write the first biography of Mary Lincoln. In 1923 Emilie Helm wrote her nephew Robert T. Lincoln, "Everybody just now wants to write a life of your mother. I have had a number of letters asking for information." Emilie Helm to Robert Lincoln, Apr. 25, 1923, file 32, container 2, part 2, Robert Todd Lincoln Family Papers, Manuscripts Division, Library of Congress, Washington, D.C. Three years later, Robert's attorney and secretary, Frederic Towers, told Katherine

Helm that, "from time to time this past winter requests, both oral and written, have come to Mr. and Mrs. Lincoln almost imploring them to go to work on a biography of Mrs. Abraham Lincoln." Frederic Towers to Katherine Helm, May 7, 1926, Lincoln Family Papers, Friends of Hildene, Inc., Manchester, Vt. In 1927 there was also a book written about Mary Lincoln's insanity period by Myra Pritchard, granddaughter of Mary's friend Myra Bradwell. The book, based on letters Mary sent to Bradwell, was not published at the time, however, after Mary Harlan Lincoln, Robert's widow, found out about it and suppressed it. It ultimately was published in 2011. See Myra Helmer Pritchard, *The Dark Days of Abraham Lincoln's Widow, As Revealed by Her Own Letters*, ed. and annot. by Jason Emerson (Carbondale: Southern Illinois University Press, 2011).

14. Elizabeth Todd Grimsley, "Six Months in the White House," *Journal of the Illinois State Historical Society* 19, nos. 3–4 (Oct. 1926–Jan. 1927), 67.

15. W. A. Evans, *Mrs. Abraham Lincoln: A Study of Her Personality and Her Influence on Lincoln* (N.Y.: Alfred A. Knopf, 1932), 4–5.

16. Carl Sandburg and Paul M. Angle, *Mary Lincoln: Wife and Widow* (N.Y.: Harcourt, Brace, and Company, 1932), 7.

17. Ibid., viii.

18. Randall's subsequent book two years later, *Lincoln's Sons*, also delves into Mary Lincoln as mother and wife, but it is heavily based on *Mary Lincoln: Biography of a Marriage* and offers little new information on Mary in that sense.

19. Avery Craven, review of *Mary Lincoln: Biography of a Marriage*, by Ruth Painter Randall, *Mississippi Valley Historical Review* 40, no. 3 (December 1953): 537–538. Lincoln scholar Paul M. Angle agreed with Craven that Randall's work was a bit more sympathetic than necessary, although ultimately well done. Paul M. Angle, "The Woman in His Life," *New York Times*, Feb. 8, 1953, BR4.

20. While today Mary is always called "Mary Todd Lincoln," Mary never identified herself with her maiden name after her marriage to Abraham Lincoln. She signed her name as either "Mary Lincoln" or "Mrs. Abraham Lincoln," while her personal letterhead typically had "ML" at the top. While Jean Baker was not the first to add the "Todd" surname to Mary's identity, the popularity and endurance of Baker's book can certainly be said to have had some influence on the cultural permanence of that change.

21. Women's studies, feminism, and feminist revisionism are not only beneficial to historical inquiry but necessary: to bring to light people, events, and issues (women and women's issues) that have been ignored for centuries by historians, and to incorporate that discarded information into history and show what, how, and why this female perspective, influence, and impact must

be considered if one wants to tell an honest and holistic story. Unfortunately, through the years feminist writers and historians began to go beyond incorporating the ignored or forgotten past, tipped the scales too far in the opposite direction, and made women and their issues of far greater import than the facts allowed. In the case of Mary Lincoln, the feminist revisionists ignore or excuse all of Mary's faults and bad behaviors, calling her simply a victim of male chauvinism, or they make her into some sort of superhero at the expense of her husband, i.e., she was the real president, the brains behind the bumpkin Lincoln, the person who actually won the Civil War, etc., and turn her into someone she never was, and someone she would never recognize.

22. The idea of what constitutes the "common sources" referenced by writers about Mary Lincoln is certainly subjective, and there are some sources that my colleagues in the Lincoln field may believe should be included with my list of seven. But even being generous, I would go no higher than fifteen works (5 percent of the total nonfiction bibliography) being the common sources used today for learning about Mary Lincoln's life.

23. While Neely and McMurtry's book is a well-done work, more updated information, based on never-before-published sources in two recent books, offers a greater understanding of Mary's mental health and her insanity period. See Jason Emerson, *The Madness of Mary Lincoln* (Carbondale: Southern Illinois University Press, 2007), and Jason Emerson, *Mary Lincoln's Insanity Case: A Documentary History* (Champaign: University of Illinois Press, 2012). To understand Mary's insanity case, it is also essential to understand the character and motivations of Robert T. Lincoln, Mary's oldest son and the one who had her committed. See Jason Emerson, *Giant in the Shadows: The Life of Robert T. Lincoln* (Carbondale: Southern Illinois University Press, 2012).

24. The usual John Hay quote comes from his diary in which he calls Mary a "Hellcat"; one quote in particular is representative: "The Hellcat is getting more Hellcattical day by day." John Hay to John Nicolay, Apr. 9, 1862, in Michael Burlingame, ed., *At Lincoln's Side: John Hay's Civil War Correspondence and Selected Writings* (Carbondale: Southern Illinois University Press, 2000), 20. Stoddard's typical quote is more of a defense of Mary Lincoln: "It was not easy, at first, to understand why a lady who could be one day so kindly, so considerate, so generous, so thoughtful and so hopeful, could, upon another day, appear so unreasonable, so irritable, so despondent, so even niggardly, and so prone to see the dark, the wrong side of men and women and events." William O. Stoddard, *Inside the White House in War Times* (1890; repr. ed. Michael Burlingame; Lincoln: University of Nebraska Press, 2000), 33.

25. Paul M. Angle, "Editor's Preface," in *Herndon's Life of Lincoln*, by William H. Herndon and Jesse W. Weik, ed. Paul M. Angle (Cleveland: World Publishing, 1942), xxxviii.

26. David Herbert Donald, "Herndon and Mary Lincoln," in *Lincoln Reconsidered* (1956; repr. N.Y.: Vintage Books, 2001), 77.

27. See for example, William Herndon to Isaac Arnold, Nov. 20, 1866, in Hertz, *Hidden Lincoln*, 37, and William Herndon to Charles H. Hart, Nov. 26 and Dec. 12, 1866, in Douglas L. Wilson and Rodney O. Davis, eds., *Herndon on Lincoln: Letters* (Urbana: Knox College Lincoln Studies Center and University of Illinois Press, 2016), 41, 55.

28. To be fair, it should also be said that many of Lincoln's friends, neighbors, and colleagues shared Herndon's view that Mary was not an easy person to live with and that the Lincoln household was not always a happy one. As Lincoln scholar Paul M. Angle once wrote, "As to Lincoln's domestic difficulties, no fair-minded student can disregard what Herndon wrote. The supporting testimony of other contemporaries is just too overwhelming." Angle, "Editor's Preface," in *Herndon's Life of Lincoln*, xliv.

29. William Herndon to Joseph Fowler, Nov. 3, 1888, in Wilson and Davis, *Herndon on Lincoln*, 287.

30. Jean H. Baker, *Mary Todd Lincoln: A Biography* (N.Y.: W. W. Norton & Company, 1987), 185–187. Baker reiterated this convoluted excuse for Mary's overspending in a later essay, "Getting Right with Mary Lincoln," when she again said it was the commissioner's fault for approving the purchases, but, if it was Mary's fault, does that not simply show what a strong and feminist character she was? "Was Mary Lincoln, to whom all criticisms stick like barnacles, so persuasive and powerful that she could suggest purchases beyond the budget and get the commissioner to sign for them?" Baker asks. "I wondered because, if so, it suggested another side of Mary Lincoln—her authoritative ability to transcend the limitations of female influence." Jean H. Baker, "Getting Right with Mary Lincoln; or, How a First Lady Taught Me to Be a Feminist," in *Lincoln Lessons: Reflections on America's Greatest Leader*, ed. Frank J. Williams and William D. Pederson (Carbondale: Southern Illinois University Press, 2009), 12.

31. For Baker's description of the insanity trial and suicide attempt, see Baker, *Mary Todd Lincoln*, 315–326. For a thorough debunking of Baker's false suicide story, see Norbert Hirschhorn, "Mary Lincoln's 'Suicide Attempt': A Physician Reconsiders the Evidence," *Lincoln Herald* 104, no. 3 (Fall 2003): 94–98, and Emerson, *The Madness of Mary Lincoln*, 67–70.

NOTES TO PAGES 25-28

NOTES TO PAGES 25-28   189

32. For thorough rebuttals of Baker's interpretations of this event, see Emerson, *The Madness of Mary Lincoln*; Emerson, *Mary Lincoln's Insanity Case*; Emerson, *Giant in the Shadows*, 162–183; Evans, *Mrs. Abraham Lincoln*, 214–223; Randall, *Mary Lincoln*, 41–433; and Neely and McMurtry, *Insanity File*, 17.

33. Leopold von Ranke, "The Historian's Task," in *Leopold von Ranke: The Secret of World History; Selected Writings on the Art and Science of History*, ed. and trans. Roger Wines (N.Y.: Fordham University Press, 1981), 258.

34. Evans's book, out of print for decades and difficult to find, was reprinted in 2010 by Southern Illinois University Press.

35. As Evans wrote, understanding Mary's financial worries is essential to understanding her personality because "when Mrs. Lincoln later became unbalanced, money was the thread through which ran the fabric of her aberrations." Evans, *Mrs. Abraham Lincoln*, 148.

36. Harold Holzer, ed., *Lincoln's White House Secretary: The Adventurous Life of William O. Stoddard* (Carbondale: Southern Illinois University Press, 2007), 242.

37. Ruth Painter Randall, "Mary Lincoln: Judgment Appealed," *Abraham Lincoln Quarterly* 5, no. 7 (Sept. 1949), 392.

38. Stoddard, *Inside the White House in War Times*, 33. Lincoln biographer and family friend Isaac Arnold (who also served as Mary's lawyer during her 1875 insanity trial) made a similar statement in 1884 that bears repeating:

Mrs. Lincoln has been treated harshly—nay, most cruelly abused and misrepresented by a portion of the press. That love of scandal and of personality, unfortunately too general, induced reporters to hang around her doors, to dog her steps, to chronicle and exaggerate her impulsive words, her indiscretions, and her eccentricities. There is nothing in American history so unmanly, so devoid of every chivalric impulse, as the treatment of this poor, broken-hearted woman, whose reason was shattered by the great tragedy of her life. . . . The abuse which a portion of the American press so pitilessly poured upon the head of Mary Lincoln, recalls that splendid outburst of eloquence on the part of Burke, when, speaking of the Queen of France, he said: "Little did I dream that I should live to see such disasters fall upon her in a nation of gallant men. . . . I thought ten thousand swords must have leaped from their scabbards to avenge even a look that threatened her with insult. But the age of chivalry is gone."

Isaac N. Arnold, *The Life of Abraham Lincoln* (1884; repr. Lincoln: University of Nebraska Press, 1994), 439–440.

39. James A. Brussel, "Mary Todd Lincoln: A Psychiatric Study," *Psychiatric Quarterly* 15, supp. 1 (Jan. 1941): 7–26; John M. Suarez, "Mary Todd Lincoln: A Case Study," *American Journal of Psychiatry* 122, no. 7 (Jan. 1966): 816–819; Norbert Hirschhorn and Robert G. Feldman, "Mary Lincoln's Final Illness: A Medical and Historical Reappraisal," *Journal of the History of Medicine and Allied Sciences* 54, no. 4 (Oct. 1999): 511–542.

40. Stephen Berry, "There's Something about Mary: Mary Lincoln and Her Siblings," in *The Mary Lincoln Enigma: Historians on America's Most Controversial First Lady*, ed. Frank J. Williams and Michael Burkhimer (Carbondale: Southern Illinois University Press, 2012), 32.

41. Elodie Todd to Nathaniel Dawson, May 23, 1861, quoted in ibid, 28.

42. Michael Burlingame, *The Inner World of Abraham Lincoln* (Urbana: University of Illinois Press, 1994), xv.

43. Burlingame's essay "The Lincolns' Marriage" is printed in his book *The Inner World of Abraham Lincoln*, 268–355, while his article on Mary Lincoln's unethical conduct as first lady is printed in his book *At Lincoln's Side: John Hay's Civil War Correspondence and Selected Writings* (Carbondale: Southern Illinois University Press, 2000), 185–203. Burlingame's findings and thoughts on the Lincoln marriage are also examined in great detail in his two-volume biography, *Abraham Lincoln: A Life* (Baltimore: Johns Hopkins University Press, 2008).

44. Burlingame, "The Lincolns' Marriage," in *The Inner World of Abraham Lincoln*, 325.

45. Margarita Spalding Gerry, ed., *Through Five Administrations: Reminiscences of Colonel William H. Crook* (N.Y.: Harper & Brothers Publishers, 1907), 16.

46. Mary Lincoln to A. D. Worthington, Mar. 7, 1868, Gilder Lehrman Collection, The Gilder Lehrman Institute of American History, New York, N.Y.

47. Mary Elizabeth Massey, "Mary Todd Lincoln," *American History Illustrated* 10, no. 2 (May 1975): 48.

48. Randall, "Mary Lincoln: Judgment Appealed," 379.

INDEX OF ESSAY "COMMON CANON"

INDEX OF AUTHORS AND EDITORS

Locators in index entries are bibliographic entry numbers, not page numbers.

INDEX OF TITLES

Locators in index entries are bibliographic entry numbers, not page numbers.

INDEX OF SUBJECTS

Locators in index entries are bibliographic entry numbers, not page numbers.

Jason Emerson is an independent historian and journalist living near Syracuse, New York. He is the author or editor of multiple books about Abraham Lincoln and his family, including *The Madness of Mary Lincoln, Giant in the Shadows: The Life of Robert T. Lincoln,* and *Lincoln the Inventor.* He has published numerous articles and book reviews in both scholarly and popular publications, and has appeared on the History Channel, H2, Book TV, and American History TV.

He has worked as a National Park Service park ranger at the Lincoln Home National Historic Site, Gettysburg National Military Park, and the Jefferson National Expansion Memorial (the Arch) in St. Louis. He is currently the editor of the *Cazenovia Republican* and *Eagle Bulletin* newspapers.

For more information, visit Jason's website at www.jasonemerson .com.